CROSSING COLOR

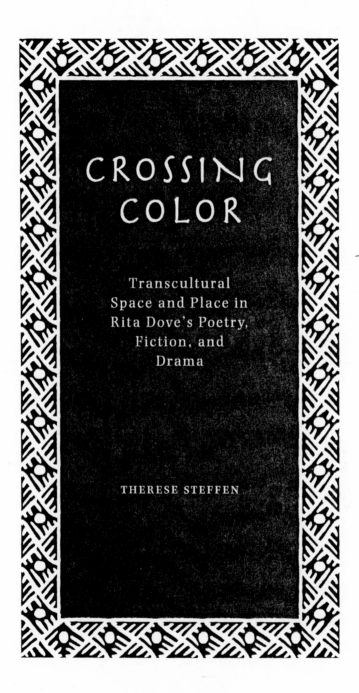

CROSSING COLOR

Transcultural
Space and Place in
Rita Dove's Poetry,
Fiction, and
Drama

THERESE STEFFEN

OXFORD
UNIVERSITY PRESS

2001

OXFORD
UNIVERSITY PRESS

Oxford   New York
Athens   Auckland   Bangkok   Bogotá   Buenos Aires   Calcutta
Cape Town   Chennai   Dar es Salaam   Delhi   Florence   Hong Kong   Istanbul
Karachi   Kuala Lumpur   Madrid   Melbourne   Mexico City   Mumbai
Nairobi   Paris   São Paulo   Shanghai   Singapore   Taipei   Tokyo   Toronto   Warsaw

and associated companies in
Berlin   Ibadan

Published by Oxford University Press, Inc.
198 Madison Avenue, New York, New York 10016

Oxford is a registered trademark of Oxford University Press.

Published with the support of the National Foundation for the Arts and Sciences.

Library of Congress Cataloging-in-Publication Data
Steffen, Therese
Crossing color : transcultural space and place in Rita Dove's poetry,
fiction, and drama / Therese Steffen.
p.   cm.
Includes bibliographical references and index.
ISBN 0-19-513440-0
1. Dove, Rita—Criticism and interpretation.   2. Place (Philosophy) in literature.
3. Culture in literature.   4. Ethnicity in literature.   5. Race in literature.
6. Afro-Americans in literature.   I. Title.
PS3554.O884 Z87   2001
811'.54—dc21   00-024573

1 3 5 7 9 8 6 4 2

Printed in the United States of America
on acid-free paper

Thinking is a dialogue between me and myself that can take place only in solitude.

Hannah Arendt, "Life of the Mind"

Die Grenze ist nicht das, wobei etwas aufhört, sondern . . . die Grenze ist jenes von woher etwas sein Wesen beginnt.

Martin Heidegger, "Bauen Wohnen Denken"

Broken color, this kind of wanting, its tawdriness, its awkward uncertainties.

Rita Dove, "Dedication"

PREFACE

"Ah, on *The Wings of the Dove*," was the dry reply of the eminent Henry James scholar when he perceived the content of my shopping bag. We flew back to Switzerland after an invigorating encounter with the master during two "Sesquicentennial Conferences" at New York University's Washington Square venue in June 1993, and I was supposed and ready to write a postdoctoral thesis on "Female Artists in Henry James." Only later did I come to realize the long-term effects and consequences of the enchanted hour I spent at Barnes & Noble's poetry section lost in the dense and surprising imagery of Rita Dove's *Grace Notes*. I did not know the author was black, nor did I notice the fact in my first and frantic reading. Certainly, there was "the colored-only-shore" in poems like "Crab Boil" and "Summit Beach, 1921" heading the collection. Yet a "Fifth Grade Autobiography" would reveal no other pigment than "lemon." The scene of action included Auburn, Alabama; Manhattan; Paris; even a mysterious "Neutral City." And the penultimate poem "On the Road to Damascus" eventually led to a final "Old Folk's Home, Jerusalem." This was the sweep and scope of a linguistic and thematic diversity with which I was familiar through Henry James. Here was the international theme revisited and revived in an exquisitely crafted language whose poignant visual vigor created landmarks of its own. Here was a multiperspective view of the world and its people, full of psychologic acumen but without the drawbacks of a reluctant "I can't" whenever Life called to duty. Dove's tightly wrought verse bore no resemblance to the "loose baggy monsters," the rambling writing the master dreaded and notoriously despised. Here was an artist who certainly could "do portraits," not "merely backs," as Henry James, in the judgmental footsteps of Nathaniel Hawthorne, would concede the "damned mob of scribbling [and painting] women." I was hooked.

In an epiphany, not unlike mine, Dove discovered Toni Morrison's work in graduate school. When she pulled *The Bluest Eye* from the library shelf in what Dove praises as "one of those flukes" (Kirkpatrick 1995: 56), it did not reveal a black author. She "just knew" in the process of trying to figure out where the author came from. It was an immense feeling of relief for her to find: "This is my country she's talking about," an Ohio apart from the Harlem or South so far ubiquitous in African-American literature, regions to which Dove could not relate her experience of growing up as a midwesterner. The sense "of not being all alone out there, feeling like a freak, was incredible" (Kirkpatrick 1995: 56). Dove found her voice and eventually developed a poetic landscape and an architecture in which even a Middle-European like myself could feel at home. How did she mold her space, how did she cross those boundaries to reach out for the world to join her? I was ready to explore her art in a systematic way.

The *Boston Globe*'s 25 May 1993 Living/Arts section, sent by Elsa Gontrum, announced: "Poetry in Motion. Rita Dove, the nation's new laureate, wants to bring verse to life." Thank you, Elsa. I read: "Dove, a 40-year-old English professor at the University of Virginia, writes poetry that pulses with the real world. She has a toehold in academia, but academia has no stranglehold on her." It was fate, I decided.

One important issue remained: "The problem of the Twentieth Century," as W. E. B. Du Bois avowed in his now famous prophecy in "The Forethought" to *The Souls of Black Folk*: "the problem of the color-line." Like a geological fault, in Henry Louis Gates, Jr.'s words, it is "a line along which tensions build and find at times violent release. But it is also a place where the larger contradictions and conflicts of a society are played out" ("Introduction" 1993: vii). What does color mean to Dove and to a potential reader from a different cultural background? In her official function within a larger culture—"a kind of representative national stipend for distinguished older poets," as she described the honor bestowed on Stanley Kunitz in 1981 (*Frankurter Rundschau* 29 Apr.: 11)—the first poet laureate of African-American and Cherokee descent no longer needed to adhere to the definition of a specifically black literature, as it was reflected in the aesthetic and ethic ideal of the Black Arts Movement since the late 1960s. In Gwendolyn Brooks's words: "Black literature BY blacks, ABOUT blacks, directed TO blacks. ESSENTIAL black literature is the distillation of black life."[1] Moreover, Dove also was raised on the European tradition and studied German early on. I was eventually privileged to partake in this heritage beyond the color-line.

Dove's color system extends from her multicolored fingertips to a filing scheme she has used since her days in Berlin: plastic folders in yellow, blue, crimson, purple, green, pink, peach, or clear with a particular purpose and feeling attached. She writes in the Berliner *Tageszeitung* (*TAZ* 13 Nov. 1981: 11):

> Ich erinnere mich daran, wie ich beim Schreiben meinen eigenen Rhythmus entdeckte. Jahrelang war ich überzeugt, es sei der richtige Weg, ein Gedicht anzufangen und dann intensiv daran zu arbeiten, bis es fertig war. . . . Doch eines Tages, es war im Frühsommer 1980, in einem Schreibwarengeschäft hier in Berlin . . . fielen mir diese farbigen, doppelseitigen Plastikschuber auf. Es gab sie in klarem Rot und purpurn und gelb und blau. . . . Und plötzlich änderte sich alles.

> [I remember how I discovered my own rhythm in writing. All these years I was convinced that beginning a poem and then working on it extensively, until it

was finished would be the right way. . . . But one day, it was spring 1980, in a stationer's shop here in Berlin, these colorful double sided folders attracted my attention. They came in crimson and purple and yellow and blue. . . . And suddenly everything changed.]

This is still the case today, the poet disclosed to Walt Harrington, who explored "The Shape of Her Dreaming":

"She doesn't file her nascent poems by subject or title, as a scientist or historian might file documents. She files poems by the way they *feel* to her. Red attracts poems about war and violence. Purple, Rita's favorite color, accumulates introspective poems. Yellow likes sunshine. Blue likes the sky. Green likes nature. Pink—after a line she wrote about her daughter: "We're in the pink / and the pink's in us"—is a magnet for poems about mothers and daughters. But the categories aren't fixed: Blue is the color of sky, but blue is also the color of the Virgin Mary's robe. (1995: 15)

A clear folder, which holds very little, is reserved for pure thought, the perfect, clear lyrical poem. Very few poems ever reach that stage.

W. E. B. Du Bois's 1903 declaration about the color-line being decisive to our century has found, despite the temporal, racial, and cultural differences separating it from our days, remarkably similar treatment in the visions of Dove and the scholar of Palestinian descent Edward W. Said:

No one today is purely one thing. Labels like Indian, or woman, or Muslim, or American are not more than starting-points, which if followed into actual experience for only a moment are quickly left behind. Imperialism consolidated the mixture of cultures and identities on a global scale. But its worst and most paradoxical gift was to allow people to believe that they were only, mainly, exclusively, white, or Black, or Western, or Oriental. (*Culture and Imperialism* 1993: 336)

My task was to enter as best I could, all the shades and hues of Dove's literary realm, a body of texts embedded in its specific historical context. Race, as I came to realize, was less an essence than a text or pretext, according to Henry Louis Gates, Jr. ("Introduction" 1993: xvi), one that is written and rewritten, singly and collectively. All I had to do was "read fully," which meant "to restore all that one can of the immediacies of value and intent in which speech actually occurs" (Gates, *Figures in Black* 1987: 191). I was confident enough and ready to dismiss concerns that were decisive in earlier struggles of the black community and dominant in poems such as these:

A critic advises
not to write on controversial subjects
like freedom or murder,
but to treat universal themes
and timeless symbols
like the white unicorn.
A white unicorn?

(Dudley Randall,
Black Poet, White Critic)[2]

Black feminists speak
as women and do
not need others to
speak for us.
(Audre Lorde,
The Black Unicorn)[3]

Personal and institutional help, without responsibility for my shortcomings, encouraged this project. Elisabeth Bronfen (University of Zürich) was the first to listen and to support my work in every conceivable way: as a demanding teacher, experienced author, inspiring scholar, and emphatic partner in research. I am greatly indebted to her for opening up new vistas. An "Athena"-grant of the Swiss National Science Foundation enabled me to study what VèVè Clark terms "diaspora literacy"[4] at Harvard University. The W. E. B. Du Bois Institute for Afro-American Research and its director, Henry Louis Gates, Jr., with his energy, comforting competence, and enthusiastic ability to connect literature with culture at large, made all the difference. Richard Newman's relaxed, sophisticated familiarity with African-American history was a revelation. I also learned from Kwame Anthony Appiah, Barbara Johnson, Orlando Patterson, Werner Sollors, Cornel West (Harvard University), Isobel Armstrong (Harvard; Birkbeck College, London), Wlad Godzich (University of California, Santa Cruz), and earlier from Irit Rogoff (University of California, Davies) and Diane Wood Middlebrook (Stanford University). Anthony Glenn Miller proved instrumental as research assistant; Katharina Ernst and Catherine Schelbert gave unceasing help in reading various stages of the manuscript.

Fred Viebahn, Leslie Williams, and above all Rita Dove at the University of Virginia at Charlottesville offered their support in the most gracious and generous manner.

Cambridge, Massachusetts   T. S.
Basel, Switzerland
August 2000

CONTENTS

ABBREVIATIONS AND DOCUMENTATION

DF	*The Darker Face of the Earth*
FS	*Fifth Sunday*
GN	*Grace Notes*
IG	*Through the Ivory Gate*
M	*Museum*
ML	*Mother Love*
PW	*The Poet's World*
RP	*On the Bus with Rosa Parks*
SP	*Selected Poems*
SV	*The Siberian Village*
TB	*Thomas and Beulah*
YH	*The Yellow House on the Corner*

I have followed, or rather expanded, some formal guidelines that need to be explained. In MLA documentation style, sources are acknowledged by keying brief parenthetical citations in the text to an alphabetical list of works cited at the end of the paper or book. A citation in MLA style contains only needed information to enable readers to find the source in the list of works cited. In the sciences, however, where timeliness of research is crucial, the date of publication is given prominence. In order to combine maximum information with brevity (so far reserved to the natural sciences), I have included author, year, page, and, if necessary, a short title in parenthetical citations. Thus the text will be kept as readable and free of disruptions as possible. For the reader's convenience full references can be found in notes or in the list of works cited.

CROSSING COLOR

BIO-CRITICAL INTRODUCTION, STATE OF THE ART, AND OUTLOOK

The Aim of *Crossing Color*

"A Great Day" after "The Long Night," in Ann DuCille's words (1995: 23), refers to Fall 1993 when, after a long period of dearth and endurance, the novelist Toni Morrison won the Nobel Prize in Literature and her Ohio compatriot, Rita Dove, was installed as poet laureate of the United States. Both authors had previously won Pulitzer Prizes: Dove in 1987 for *Thomas and Beulah* (1986) and Morrison in 1988 for *Beloved* (1987). These prestigious awards and posts marked momentous events of empowerment in American letters, for the two recipients were not only female but African American as well. It was a time of great communal significance, of personal and public, national, racial, and engendered honor. "Rooms of Their Own: Toni Morrison, Rita Dove" was the title of Paul Gray and Jack E. White's accolade in *Time* 18 (Oct. 1993: 86–89).

Crossing Color is meant as a critical inquiry into the transcultural spacings and spatiotemporal relations of Dove's oeuvre from the beginning of her career in the late 1970s into the late 1990s. This first book-length study on her work addresses academics as well as the wide audience she was able to reach during her successful two years as the Library of Congress Consultant in Poetry (1993–1995). Analyzing Dove's oeuvre and collecting and evaluating critical responses available since the early 1980s, *Crossing Color* offers an extensive dialogue between primary and secondary sources. A reading of Dove must be broadened and deepened by her articles on Lucille Clifton, Ralph Ellison, Langston Hughes, Melvin Tolson, Derek Walcott, among others, and by numerous interviews, essays, media performances, and public speeches given in the list of works cited. I have used these equally informative metatexts not only to provide a more inclusive portrait of the author but also to expand the critical assessment of her work. Dove's auctorial stand mediates afresh between art and artistic intention as well as between herself and those wishing to understand and enjoy her multilayered texts. The aim throughout *Crossing Color* is

3

the seemingly old-fashioned notion of "prodesse et delectare" (teach/inform and entertain) through an analytic and synthetic examination of Dove's poetic network.

After a long, historic absence of the author, the result of the formalists' New Criticism movement, deepened by Cleanth Brooks and Robert Penn Warren's influential 1939 textbook *Understanding Poetry*—"the text itself" said all (Perkins 1987: 79f)—the writer's voice is back: first in the confessional poetry that was the mainstay in the 1960s and 1970s, then in the aesthetics of the Beats and Black Arts Movement of the same period. And this, despite Dove's definition of "the ultimate reading," which still faintly testifies to the New Critics' or, in this instance, a young person's foregrounding of primary-sources-only: "I think the ultimate reading experiences are the kind one had as a child, when you don't really know, or care, for that matter, who the author is. . . . As we grow older and more savvy we get to know a little bit too much—too much literary theory and how it works, which gets in the way of the pleasure of the reading." (Walsh 1994: 145). The poem "Watching Last Year at Marienbad at Roger Haggerty's House in Auburn, Alabama" (*GN* 26) confirms: "The first time / for anything is the best, / because there is no memory / linking its regrets to drop / like bracelets in the grass." This study adds to these and other arguments by exploring more inclusively what it means to be a visual and formal poet who clears transcultural interstices of her own.

Crossing Color confronts the reader with a poetic concept crucial to Dove's writing: the sign of the cross, a capacity for "crossing over," "extending," "intersecting," "bringing into contact," if necessary, to "thwart" and "counteract," as well as to "hybridize" and "cross-fertilize" in "combining the qualities of two different things or types" as Webster's *New World Dictionary* indicates. These "different things" may range from skin color, class, and gender to various cultures, continents, and literary genres. "Ars Poetica" (*GN* 48), a "breakthrough poem" to Dove and a "self-conscious declaration of literary philosophy" (Walsh 1994: 150), illustrates her poetics of crossing. Through three stanzas she contrasts an unknown essayist in Wyoming and an Australian novelist who both penetrate and violate literal and literary territory while producing but little, with a lyrical self, who pursues a more modest, yet more elevated and elevating path. She but brushes against mystery in this tongue-in-cheek ars poetica:

What I want is this poem to be small
a ghost town
on the larger map of wills.
Then you can **pencil** me in as a **hawk**:
a traveling x-marks-the-spot.[1] (emphasis mine)

A long and arduous development lies behind Dove's artistic use of the crossing sign and its denotations and historically significant connotations: a "person or thing unknown or unrevealed," the "signature of someone who cannot write," particularly "a slave's anonymous hand," as in the memorial gestures of the poet Marvin X, or of the social activist of the sixties, Malcolm X, identification with the nameless and forgotten. The chiasmus, to follow Henry Louis Gates, Jr. (*The Signifying Monkey*, 1989: 128), is perhaps the most common rhetorical figure in slave narratives and is signified in the black vernacular tradition by tropes of the crossroads, that liminal space where Esu resides, the trickster figure who suggests double-voiced enunciations. Dove's crossing sign indeed is an ephemeral yet highly eloquent poetic marker on the move: hawk-like, she surveys human transience from above. Instead of a possessive claim, her poetry suggests and produces an essential insight: things, emotional states, creative processes, individual and collective narratives—History at large—cannot be fixed and reduced, taken in at once and forever. Her "traveling x-marks-the-spot" rather turns into a mathematic symbol for an unknown quantity or a variable, a power of magnification, one's choice or answer. It may as well refer to an innocent kiss in a letter, Christ's passion, even an X-rated motion picture. One may add an in-depth search, by means of X-rays, for the blind spot hiding ultimate truth; maybe the chiasmus signifies the Greek X (for Christ) or a German "Ich [I]."

Hence, "Ars Poetica" celebrates no permanent settlement but "a ghost town / on the larger map of wills," ready to invite and host the powers of imagination that will ensure communication between the Aristotelian 'intellectus agens' (knowledge) and the 'sensus communis' (experience). In *Playing in the Dark: Whiteness and the Literary Imagination*, Toni Morrison praises this particular ability of writers "to imagine what is not the self, to familiarize the strange and mystify the familiar" as the test of their power (1993: 15). Indeed, via her hawk image for the poet, Dove moves on international as well as national ground—"a ghost town / on the larger map of wills" might as well figure as the remains of Manifest Destiny out West—and at the same time stays true to her indigenous vernacular tradition: a "verna" is a homeborn slave. In *Blues, Ideology, and Afro-American Literature: A Vernacular Theory* (1987), Houston A. Baker, Jr., shows how the X-mark crosses "fixity as a function of power."[2] Not unlike Dove, he holds forth that those "who maintain place, who decide what takes place and dictate what has taken place, are power brokers of the traditional. The 'placeless,' by contrast, are translators of the nontraditional. Rather than fixed in the order of cunning Grecian urns, their lineage is fluid, nomadic, transitional. Their appropriate mark is a crossing sign at the junction" (202–3). Dove's and Baker's crossing sign then is the eloquent and powerful antithesis of a place marker, always signifying change, motion, transience, and process.

> "Do what you can," it demands. "Do what you can—right here—on this place-less-place, this spotless-spot—to capture manifold intonations and implications of fluid experience!" . . . The risk of situating oneself at the crossing sign is, of course, enormous. But the benefits are beyond price. The relinquishing of a self-certainty that strives to annul "otherness" and to masterfully fix its own place is meetly compensated. (202.)

Baker even sees the task of present-day scholars, in their "situating themselves inventively and daringly at the crossing sign" in order to materialize vernacular faces and works. If scholars are successful, he concludes, their response to literature, criticism, and culture in the United States will be "as wonderfully energetic and engrossing as the response of the bluesman Sonny Terry to the injunction of his guitar-strumming partner Brownie McGhee. Brownie intones: 'Let me hear you squall, boy, like you never squalled before!' The answer is a whooping, racing, moaning harmonica stretch that takes one's breath away, invoking forms, faces, and places whose significance was unknown prior to the song's formidable inscriptions" (203).

Dove's credo throughout her work, "I just don't believe in boundaries" (Kirkpatrick 1995: 57), does not preclude their existence but her and Edward Said's (1993: 336) disbelief in their limiting effect. Neither does she believe in color or being typecast by any particular experience. Her poem "Crab-Boil" (*GN* 13) explicitly thematizes "belief" as an independent decision even of an adolescent mind: a double "I don't believe . . . " is prompted by "I decide to believe this." From her earliest writing days she has consistently opposed "being classified as a black writer and then being assigned certain topics" or, worse, being "only compared to other black writers" (Johnsen and Peabody 1985: 6). Al Young served as an early role model to Dove in his individualistic expression of a variety of thoughts and feelings beyond African-American fashion and wrath: "He didn't write about just being Black—he wrote about a grandmother, an aunt, he wrote about simply being in love" (Waniek and Dove 1991: 262). By the mid-1980s, Dove considers the literary market as well as herself changed and relaxed enough. "After Toni Morrison and Alice Walker, it's possible for people to imagine that a black writer doesn't have to write about ghettos" (262). "Color" to her should represent merely the core definition of a "sensation resulting from stimulation of the retina of the eye by light waves of certain lengths," or "any coloring matter." Instead of the tainted concept of "a person's skin," most likely that of someone "not classified as Caucasian," one could indeed foreground a range of other semantic hues: "a healthy rosiness or blush," "the appearance of truth, likelihood, validity, or right; justification," a "general nature; character," or "vivid quality or character, as in a personality, literary work, etc.," "a trace of gold found in panning," maybe "a timbre, as of a voice or instrument." (*Webster's New World Dictionary*, 1976). Beulah, in *TB*, a Cherokee father's black daughter, perfectly illustrates the point. Though she is "Papa's girl," yellow does not refer to her mulatto skin color but to her leitmotif, a spot of golden brightness guiding her soul, externalized in the "yellow scarf" that Thomas wraps around her in courtship as well as in her canary singing behind the bars of domesticity. "If Black is the combined richness of all color," Houston Baker observes, "then Rita Dove is the singing blackness of blackness" (1990: 577).

Things then would no longer get so wrapped up in classifications of race, class, gender, and genre. "It's like the genre is making them, instead of them making literature," Dove protests in view of a victimized Zora Neale Hurston (Johnsen and Peabody 1985: 6). She "is a good example for someone who's suffered because of that. That's why she got lost for so many years. . . . On the one hand, she was accused of playing up to the whites, on the other hand, she did these wonderful anthropological studies of folktales in her book, *Mules and*

Men. A lot of the misunderstanding about Zora Neale Hurston comes from the fact that people were trying to fit her into some existing pigeonhole. And she resisted that." In "How It Feels to Be Colored Me," a chapter of her autobiographical writings in *I Love Myself When I Am Laughing,* Hurston, not unlike Dove, adheres to an almost transcendental view of herself:

> The cosmic Zora emerges. I belong to no race nor time. I am the eternal feminine with its string of beads. / I have no separate feeling about being an American citizen and colored. I am merely a fragment of the Great Soul that surges within the boundaries. My country, right or wrong. (1979: 155)

In terms of finding herself cast as a poet, fiction writer, playwright, or essayist, Dove is ready to fight similar preconceptions and misconceptions. She sometimes reacts with amused irony when people dovetail her into categories because she is not really concerned about how they perceive her. "I just want to keep writing. They can figure it out later" (Johnsen and Peabody 1985: 5).

Dove bridges gaps in a number of ways. Yet how and where does her "crossing color" position her synchronically, that is, in respect to contemporary writers and movements, and diachronically, in view of historical antecedents? How could she come to represent American poetry at large at this particular point? How does she fit into the African-American, U.S. and international scene? How does she use and blend cultures, and in what respect does her poetic vision differ from what Henry Louis Gates, Jr., calls "the nature of commodified postmodern ethnicity—which we could describe as the Benneton's model: 'All the colors of the world,' none of the oppression" (*Loose Canons* 1992: 186)? According to Gates:

> Every black American text [reflects] a complex ancestry, one . . . that is literary and vernacular but also one white and black. . . . Just as we can and must cite a black text within the larger American tradition, we can and must cite it within its own tradition, a tradition not defined by a pseudoscience of racial biology, or a mystically shared essence called blackness, but by the repetition and revision of shared themes, topoi and tropes, the call and response of voices, their music and cacophony. ("Whose Canon Is It, Anyway?" 1990: 73)

Hers is a double reaction to the Black Arts Movement of the 1960s: Dove picks up the political impetus, a sense of politics as the given starting point (for example, in "Parsley," *SP* 133–35; *DF*), but refuses and ironizes the clichéd political discourse and aesthetic dilettantism (see "Upon Meeting Don L. Lee, In a Dream," *SP* 12). Instead she seeks to link up with the strong modernist imagism of William Carlos Williams ("The Red Wheelbarrow") or Wallace Stevens ("Anecdote of the Jar"). Hence her aesthetic and thematic departure serves as a critique of the 1960s and offers a "politicalization of the modernist tradition" (Werner Sollors, personal conversation). In moving from the historically informed political occasion (for example, in "Belinda's Petition," "David Walker," "Parsley" *SP* 28, 30, 133f) to the most beautiful imagery, she ties herself to a sense of urgency yet at the same time keeps a safe distance from the limited and limiting essentialism of the black aesthetics. Hence, Dove opposes, even fights, tyranny both in a broader and more subtle way.

In 1986 Arnold Rampersad hailed the work of the 33-year-old Dove as "at least one clear sign if not of a coming renaissance of poetry, then at least of the emergence of an unusually strong new figure who might provide leadership by brilliant example" (52). At the time Rampersad deemed African-American poetry "in a state of inactivity not unlike a deep slumber" whereas earlier it had stood "so very close to the center of the movement for civil rights and black power" (52). However, he felt no poet was as effective in building "on his or her beginnings in the late sixties in anything like the way that Toni Morrison, Alice Walker, John Wideman, Gloria Naylor, and David Bradley, for example, have built on their own starts *in fiction* during the same period" (52, italics mine).

Indeed, both Rampersad and Dove herself perceive her poetic voice as singular. By far the youngest writer, born almost too late to join the established group, she rounds off an exceptional flowering of African-American female literary and critical talent since the mid-1970s. Novelists in this period, in addition to those mentioned above, include Toni Cade Bambara and Paule Marshall. And poets from Ai, Maya Angelou, Gwendolyn Brooks, Lucille Clifton, Jayne Cortez, Toi Derricotte, Mari Evans, Nikki Giovanni, June Jordan, Audre Lorde, Carolyn Rodgers, Sonia Sanchez, and Ntozake Shange to Margaret Walker remained active and successful. African-American feminist critics began to theorize their work and reconstruct literary history; these include Abena P. A. Busia, Hazel Carby, Barbara Christian, Mae Henderson, bell hooks (Gloria Watson), Gloria T. Hull, Deborah E. McDowell, Marjorie Pryse, Barbara Smith, Valerie Smith, Hortense J. Spillers, Claudia Tate, Cheryl A. Wall, Michele Wallace, Mary Helen Washington, Sherley Anne Williams, and Susan Willis. Where does Rita Dove, born in 1952, fit in? Asked "whether she felt generationally accompanied in her work and her exploration of language," she pointed out "the diversity of her generation's writing as well as this drive toward narrative that has come up" as a "response to a very heady kind of disembodied lyric" (Vendler 1993: 29).[3]

> I don't feel particularly accompanied by anyone in my generation, though there are people whose work I admire and follow; I think we're all kind of stumbling along. I feel accompanied by earlier generations. Rilke accompanies me. Derek Walcott accompanies me in a funny kind of way, and Toni Morrison does, and Heinrich Heine does, and that kind of list goes on. (29)[4]

In her interview with Patricia Kirkpatrick Dove comments on the choice certain poets had to make in the 1950s and 1960s between traditional formalism and autobiographical writing with a confessional touch. Dove considers herself fortunate that her generation could avoid these choices up front:

> Sometimes I feel like getting down on my knees and saying thank you because these battles have already been fought. And these are not easy battles—

between confessionalism and beat poetry and formalism, or whether poetry adheres to gender or not, or whether it adheres to whatever black aesthetics. These discussions have been on the table. We haven't had to clear the path first before writing. (1995: 37)

Nonetheless, Dove long hesitated to publish and enter the arena of discourse in the late 1970s because she wanted to be absolutely honest to her work and to herself and that excluded addressing a limited and limiting agenda of women or blacks or black women: "To think on that level at all was death to the writing"(56). Owing not only to her youth but above all to her unusual individual stand, her all-inclusive boundary crossing had to await its day for a few years. What particular agendas prevented or rather postponed her singular new voice? In Vendler's words, "Dove entered a literary scene where both assimilation and separatism have had powerful voices. But she arrived not only with her own formidable talent, but with an education ideally constructed to let her talent have its fullest expansion" (1993: 29).

> She is freer than her black predecessors—to write poems many of which explore specifically black subjects, while many others take on subjects available to anyone. She can include black speech or not; she can write as a black woman or not. This freedom helps to insure that poems can follow their own inclinations, discover their inner shape, without feeling a distinct obligation always to reflect either the female or the black "experience." . . . It is in fact the artist's only obligation, as Dove understands it, to be faithful to the actual, and to show, by refusing sentimentality, that one has seen the world as it is. (29)

Indeed, the year 1976 marked a juncture in African-American culture (Johnson and Johnson 1994: 369).[5] It signaled the end of the Black Arts Movement and the emergence of a new literary period. Whereas the texts of the 1970s and 1980s were enabled at least partly by the civil rights movement and feminist activism of the 1960s, Dove's literary freedom is the result of the subsequent political and cultural reorientation into what we may casually call a "fin-de-siècle" trend toward a mainstream pluricultural national identity after decades of racial oppression. This may "manifest itself . . . as an intensified reflection on history as event and on historiography as a problematic science" (Vendler, *Soul Says* 1995: 245).

Dominated by a white feminist movement on the one hand and by male black power on the other, African-American women were long denied a sense of presence, place, and voice. Nonetheless, they refused to be silenced and turned their writing into fierce political statements, as in the verse of Nikki Giovanni, Sonia Sanchez, Jayne Cortez, Audre Lorde, June Jordan, and Sherley Anne Williams, or in the activism of Angela Davis and Michele Wallace. During the 1960s and early 1970s the Black Arts Movement had advocated the "Black Aesthetic," which meant art as propaganda and a literature exclusively by, about, and for blacks. Yet by the mid-1970s, as Abby Arthur Johnson and Ronald Johnson note (1994: 369), African-American writers of both sexes were already beginning to explore a plurality of theoretical approaches. In so doing they set a new course for black literature. African-American cultural and literary periodicals have both shaped and documented this change, as they did in earlier decades (369). With the death of its journal, *Black World,* in February 1976, the Black Arts Movement ceased to dominate in African-American literature. The cultural shift however, began several years earlier. As the Black Arts Movement of the 1960s and early 1970s unraveled, the black revolutionary journals also lost their constituency. Most of them—*Black Dialogue* (1964–1970), *Liberator* (1961–1971), and *Journal of Black Poetry* (1966–1973)—ceased publication at the turn of the decade. Attempts by Hoyt W. Fuller, the most influential editor and black aesthetician next to Addison Gayle, Jr., to revive the movement's spirits in the late 1970s, were largely unsuccessful.

Times had indeed changed. The year 1978 experienced a marked impetus toward more consciously literary and theoretically based analyses of African-American texts with the publication of a seminar on "Afro-American Literature and Course Design" held at Yale University in June 1977. Both the Modern Language Association and the National Endowment for the Humanities endorsed what was published in 1978 as *Afro-American Literature: The Reconstruction of Instruction,* edited by Robert Stepto and Dexter Fisher. The title reflects the seminar's intention to revise both the field and its analytical tools. Reconstruction was required to free the critical literary discourse from "fundamentally ideological or sociological methodologies that tended toward the naively reductive" (Mason 1994: 15–16). These attempts to ground African-American literary theory and criticism both in a vernacular as well as in a broader Euro-American critical discourse are documented by the emergence of two literary-cultural journals that have served as major outlets for contemporary African-American writers: *Black American Literature Forum,* founded in 1967 and reconfigured in 1976 with Joe Weixlmann's editorship, and *Callaloo,* established by Charles H. Rowell in 1976 as a southern black literary magazine. Dove is on the editorial board of *Callaloo* and published her 1985 short story collection *Fifth Sunday* in the *Callaloo* Fiction Series. Both *Black American Literature Forum* and *Callaloo* emerged as primary platforms for a new African-American critical literary discourse. In 1974 *Hambone,* edited by Nathaniel Mackey of Stanford University, joined their effort (Johnson and Johnson 1994: 371).

In the early 1980s, the spirit of the black vernacular tradition associated with the Black Arts Movement lived on in the work of Houston A. Baker, Jr. Though his 1981 essay "Generational Shifts and the Recent Criticism of Afro-American Literature," published in *Black American Literature Forum* (*BALF*), acknowledged "blatant weaknesses in the critical framework that actually accompanied the postulates of the Black Aesthetic" (11) Baker kept blaming the new African-American criticism for being too far away "from the context of black life and depend[ing] unduly on the theories of white critics" (9). This attack was countered by the Winter and Spring 1981 issues of *BALF,* guest-edited by Henry Louis Gates, Jr. In his 1981 "Introduction: Criticism in de Jungle," Gates, signifyin(g) on—referring to something or someone in the humorous way of the African-American tradition—Geoffrey Hartman, whose chapters two, three, and four of his 1980 *Criticism in the Wilderness* bear the title "The Sacred Jun-

gle," advocated a "close reading of any intellectual complexion" within "a plurality of readings," including formalist, structuralist, and Marxist approaches
from both black and white contributors. The debate reached its climax in 1984
when three major voices advanced their views in three books. In *Daggers and
Javelins* Amiri Baraka (LeRoi Jones), a protagonist of the Black Arts Movement,
declared himself "a Marxist-Leninist," favoring a "complete social change."
Baker, in *Blues, Ideology, and Afro-American Literature*, which included his essay
"Generational Shifts and the Recent Criticism of Afro-American Literature,"
supported a contextualizing of African-American art in black life, and Henry
Louis Gates, Jr.'s *Black Literature and Literary Theory*, containing eight articles
previously published in *BALF* from 1981 to 1982, favored a theoretical pluralism
and openness that also welcomed women writers and critics. In its Winter 1984
issue *BALF* indeed featured the works of contributors such as Toni Morrison,
Alice Walker, and Michele Wallace, and its introductory article was Calvin
Hernton's "The Sexual Mountain and Black Women Writers," which he later
expanded into a book of the same title (1987). To redress the female talent he
felt was oppressed by the Black Arts Movement, Hernton (1984: 139–45)[6] iden-
tified four generations of female authors: "Old Timers" who were writing before
the 1960s, such as Paule Marshall, Gwendolyn Brooks, Margaret Walker, Margaret Danner, and Sarah Wright; women emergent in the 1960s, including
Maya Angelou, Toni Cade Bambara, June Jordan, Audre Lorde, Toni Morrison,
Sonia Sanchez, and Alice Walker; the "Late Bloomers," who had been writing
in the 1960s and 1970s but were first published in the 1980s, such as Barbara
Masekala, Hattie Gossett, Regina Williams, and Barbara Christian; and the
"prodigious progeny of new black women authors"—Lorraine Bethel, Gloria
Hull, Hillary Kay, Thylias Mos, and many others.

Assimilation finally marked the path of the figureheads who represented
the fields of vernacular tradition and theoretical pluralism: Houston A. Baker,
Jr., and Henry Louis Gates, Jr. In his 1988 landmark study *The Signifying Monkey: A Theory of Afro-American Literary Criticism*, Gates fused Euro-American
theoretical concepts with an African-American signifying trope—the Yoruba
concept of Esu-Elegbara, or the Signifying Monkey—while Baker moved from a
profoundly contextualized understanding of African-American texts still palpable in his books *Blues, Ideology, and Afro-American Literature*, (1987), *Modernism and the Harlem Renaissance* (1987), and *Afro-American Poetics: Revisions of
Harlem and the Black Aesthetic* (1988) to a more "hybrid" view in *Workings of the
Spirit* 1991.[7] Though still reluctant to fully adopt what he called "reconstruc-
tionist" approaches to African-American literature (1987: 90f), he could then
embrace Gaston Bachelard's *Poetics of Space*, which is of interest for our study.
In retrospect, Dove considers the Black Arts Movement's racial essentialism and
its aftermath:

> a necessary overkill, especially in terms of black literature—a time when, in
> order to develop black consciousness, it was important to stress blackness, to
> make sure the poems talked about being black. 'Cause it had never really been
> talked about before—it wasn't predominant, except in the Harlem Renais-

sance, sure, but then we had, in a certain way, forgotten about that. So I think it was necessary and the pendulum had to swing back. (Johnsen and Peabody 1985: 6)

When the pendulum swung back from a position of African-American separation to one of assimilation and increasing recognition of hybridity inherent in any cultural form by the end of the 1980s, this was the result not only of Gates's and eventually Baker's critical stance, but also of Hazel Carby's influential *Reconstructing Womanhood* (1978) and bell hooks's *rethinking of reconstruction and feminist theory*. Carby, attacking black feminist criticism for its identification with bourgeois humanism (7–19), at the same time unmasked the critical neglect of middle-class African-American writers such as Jessie Fauset and Nella Larsen as a curtailed construction of African-American identity and as romanticizingly rural:

> Afro-American cultural and literary history should not create and glorify a limited vision, a vision which in its romantic evocation of the rural and the folk avoids some of the most crucial and urgent issues of cultural struggle—a struggle that Larsen, Petry, West, Brooks, and Morrison recognized would have to be faced in the cities, the home of the black working class. (175)

Carby's notion of class as a fundamental critical category against an ahistorical essentialism was complimented by bell hooks's agenda. Already in her 1979 study *Talking Back: Thinking Feminist, Thinking Black,* hooks advanced a theorizing stance as fundamental to feminist practice and condemned an opposition to theory as a form of anti-intellectualism (38–39).

Two recent periodicals reflect the openness within the African-American intellectual community to critical and theoretical concerns worldwide: *Reconstruction,* founded in 1990 by Randall Kennedy, a law professor at Harvard University; and *Transition,* which had originated in Uganda in 1961 and then was reissued in 1991 under the editorship of Henry Louis Gates, Jr., and Kwame Anthony Appiah, also at Harvard, by Oxford University Press. How and where did Dove grow into a writer of the *Callaloo, Reconstruction,* and *Transition* period?

The two fundamental speeches Dove delivered at the Library of Congress as part of a poet laureate's duty envision both "the poet in the world" (PW 1995: 13) and "the world in the poet" (43). This is a mutual correlation of acquiring and rendering perception and experience. Only by "stepping out" into any imaginable space beyond one's own confines can the poet gather and represent the world in "a handful of inwardness" (13–69). This material and spiritual growth, however, requires a nourishing environment. Dove likes to quote the African proverb "It takes an entire village to educate a child" and, she adds, "villages take many forms, from neighborhoods to global communities" (see, for example, the *Daily Progress* 30 Oct. 1993).

Dove was born in Akron, Ohio, in 1952, the daughter of a scientist who in the 1950s broke the race barrier by becoming the first African-American chemist at the Goodyear Tire and Rubber Company, the only industry in town. Ray Dove gave his daughter his chemist's sense of science, and her mother, Elvira, a housekeeper, gave her a gift for storytelling. With two younger sisters and an older brother, Dove grew up protected, in a loving, supportive, but stern environment.

Her grandparents were blue-collar workers who had moved north from the South during the Great Migration. A first-generation sense of responsibility "to do the best you can inside out," as her grandmother advised, prompted Dove to carry that earned respect a little further. "You had to do your best; there were no excuses" (Walsh 1994: 145). In the spirit of that kind of newly educated and upwardly mobile family, she was encouraged to read a lot and took advantage of and refuge in the opportunity. From comic books to Louis Untermeyer's *Treasury of Best Loved Poems*, Rita devoured everything with little discrimination. Her favorite reading included *King Arthur, Black Beauty, Treasure Island, Kidnapped, A Christmas Carol, Tales of Shakespeare* and Shakespeare's *Complete Works*, Hans Christian Andersen, Raggedy Ann and Raggedy Andy's adventures, *Little Women, Robinson Crusoe, Aesop's Fables,* and *A Thousand and One Nights,* as she revealed in her Keynote Address to the American Library Association (ALA: Chicago, 24 June 1995). Color and space, two major concepts in Dove's poetics, originate and join in a volume she particularly loved: Crockett Johnson's *Harold and the Purple Crayon* (1955), a picture book featuring a little boy with a purple crayon, still Dove's favorite color, who would draw things he could then enter. Books were "companions rather than adversaries," and she grew to regard them "as illuminators and boosters of Life rather than mere arbiters of moral or cultural tastes." A trip to the public library or to the book-filled solarium at home "was not an act of desperation or courage, but a yearned-for-reward" (ALA: Chicago, 24 June 1995).

In 1970 Dove was invited to the White House as a presidential scholar, one of the two best high school graduates of the state of Ohio. When word got out that the group of "the 100 most outstanding high school graduates in the United States" had prepared a petition protesting the Vietnam War, President Richard Nixon delivered his speech without shaking hands with the winners. In the fall of 1970 Dove enrolled as a "pre-law" National Achievement Student at Miami University in Oxford, Ohio, as was expected of her, but changed her major four times: from prelaw to psychology, then German, and finally English. Already in seventh grade she began learning German in order to understand a book of poems by Friedrich Schiller titled "Das Lied von der Glocke" (The Song of the Bell)—a "meditation on the difficult art of achieving a pure tone" (Walsh 1995: 146)—and the books her father kept. During World War II he had mastered Italian and German, "to know the language of the enemy" (Vendler 1990: 482). Yet Dove's dialogue between German thought and historicality ("Geschichtlichkeit") and an African-American double consciousness facing modernity stands well in a tradition established by two of the most venerable figures of the community: Frederick Douglass's more than thirty-year-long influential exchange with the German journalist Ottilie Assing has been investigated by Maria Diedrich (Münster), whereas W. E. B. Du Bois's admiration for

German nationalism and the achievement of the Prussian state in particular, which preceded his studies in Berlin, is well known. This integral racial culture, Paul Gilroy notes (1993: 135), is something Du Bois consistently figured in the feminine gender, and rightly so in our case. In December 1973 Dove graduated summa cum laude with a degree in English and worked as a secretary for a contracting firm before heading to Germany in June 1974. At the Goethe Institute in Schwäbisch Hall she prepared for her year as a Fulbright scholar at the University of Tübingen, where she studied with the noted author-critic Walter Jens among other topics Paul Celan, Rainer Maria Rilke, and expressionist drama. Speaking in terms of craft, Dove told Helen Vendler and Steven Bellin (1995: 25) how her knowledge of the German language has been one of the biggest influences on her work: "Put the verb on the end of a sentence and you've got to suspend everything until then and then revelation comes in a rush. Epiphany is really easy in German" (Vendler 1990: 484). Gradually she began to appreciate how German syntax "kept the sentence energized. Could an English sentence be stretched to sustain suspense like that? Could she work it so that everything clicks together at the very end of the poem?" (Bellin 1995: 25).

When she was still in high school, an encounter with John Ciardi, poet and translator of Dante's *Divine Comedy*, convinced Dove that authors did and could exist in real life. Later, Milton White, an inspiring substitute professor in college, made all the difference. Upon her return to the United States in the summer of 1975 she joined the highly competitive Writers' Workshop, founded by Paul Engle, at the University of Iowa, where she earned her Master of Fine Arts degree in 1977. Her teachers included Stanley Plumly, Marvin Bell, Louise Glück, Bill Matthews, and Carolyn Kizer.[8] One of the most positive and influential impacts on Dove at Iowa was the International Writing Program: "Twenty-five professional writers from all different countries . . . gave a seminar every week! A two-hour talk about their literature, the literature of their country. It was just all there" (Johnsen and Peabody 1985: 4). The false pride of being "the only writers in the world" she found "a kind of arrogance she did not like (4). While Dove still considers the creative writing regimen "one of the best things that's ever happened for the sake of culture" in the United States, a country that denies substantial and consistent government support of the arts (Walsh 1994: 143), she ultimately feels "poetry shouldn't be taught, it should just be there" (Kirkpatrick 1995: 57).

In 1976, her second year as a graduate student at Iowa, Dove met the German writer Fred Viebahn on his first day in the country. Eager to keep up her German, she accepted the invitation to act as his translator. As luck or fate would have it, the title of Viebahn's first novel translates *The Black Doves*.[9] After Dove received her M. F. A. in the spring of 1977, she was offered a tenure-track assistant professor position at Florida State University but turned it down to join Viebahn at Oberlin College in Ohio, where he taught German literature and directed plays. Dove took classes in modern dance and silversmithing; sewed their wedding outfits; completed her first book of poems, *The Yellow House on the Corner*; and began writing the short stories that were published later in *Fifth*

Sunday. During the summer of 1978 the couple wrote in and around Dublin, Ireland, where Dove began her work on what would become *Through the Ivory Gate* and Viebahn finished *Die Fesseln der Freiheit* [The Chains of Freedom]. They were married in 1979. The two years in Oberlin and the two years immediately following, spent in Israel and Berlin, where they intended to earn livings as free-lance writers, Dove jokingly refers to as her "salad days." She was able to travel and began writing her second book, *Museum*. Worried about losing her English, "the precise tone of a phrase," she commenced writing prose where "the damage was more manageable." In 1981 Dove accepted a tenure-track position as assistant professor for creative writing at Arizona State University in Tempe. In 1983 their daughter, Aviva Chantal Tamu Dove-Viebahn, was born. A sabbatical leave in 1987–1988 and a Rockefeller Foundation Residency at Bellagio in 1988 led them back to Europe (Yugoslavia, Germany, Italy) and to a 1987 international poetry festival in Mexico City, which was featured in *Mother Love*. The years 1988–1989 were spent at the National Humanities Center in North Carolina. Dove's allergy problems and longing for seasonal change prompted the couple's move to Virginia in 1989. Since then she has been on the faculty of the University of Virginia in Charlottesville, holding a chair as Commonwealth Professor of English. Charlottesville is a place where many American myths and dreams intersect and where a healthy and vibrant arts community keeps in touch with the university Thomas Jefferson built. Although Dove has been living in Virginia for several years, she has not written a poem about its spirit of place, hoping to avoid a "tourist piece." In her rare spare time, she enjoys playing the viola da gamba, a seventeenth-century string instrument related to the cello, and her classical voice training; occasionally she performs with the University of Virginia's Opera Workshop.

Appearances in national magazines and anthologies had already won Dove wide acclaim when she published her first poetry collection, *The Yellow House* on the Corner, with Carnegie-Mellon University Press in 1980. It was followed by *Museum* (1983) and *Thomas and Beulah* (1986), both also with Carnegie-Mellon. *Thomas and Beulah*, a collection of interrelated poems loosely based on her grandparents' life, earned her the 1987 Pulitzer Prize, making her the second African-American poet (after Gwendolyn Brooks in 1950) to receive this prestigious award. Other publications by Dove include her book of short stories *Fifth Sunday* (1985), the poetry collection *Grace Notes* (1989), the novel *Through the Ivory Gate* (1992), and *Selected Poems* (1993). A verse drama, *The Darker Face of the Earth*, was published in book form by Story Line Press in 1994; it was work-shopped by the Oregon Shakespeare Festival in Ashland, Oregon, in August 1994. Its first full-scale production took place during the 1996 season at both the Oregon Shakespeare Festival and at the Crossroads Theatre in New Brunswick, New Jersey, where a staged reading of the *The Darker Face of the Earth* was produced on 24 May 1995, followed by a 92nd Street Y theater reading, directed by Derek Walcott, in New York City on 20 November 1995. The work was subsequently produced, among other places, at the Kennedy Center in Washington, D.C., and at the National Theatre in London. In the fall of 1994 Dove's poem "Lady Freedom among Us," first read by the poet at the ceremony commemorating the two-hundredth anniversary of the U.S. Capitol and the restoration of the Freedom Statue on the Capitol's dome in October 1993, was published by Janus Press as a limited edition. *Lady Freedom among Us*, commissioned by the University of Virginia libraries, became the four-millionth volume in their collections. Norton released Dove's poetry collection *Mother Love* in early May 1995, and simultaneously the Library of Congress published a book of her laureate lectures under the title *The Poet's World*. Her song cycle *Seven for Luck*, with music by John Williams, was first performed with the Boston Symphony Orchestra at Tanglewood in 1998. In March 1999 her poetry collection, *On the Bus with Rosa Parks*, was published by Norton.

Dove's poetry has earned her fellowships from the International Working Periods for Authors in Bielefeld (1980), the National Endowment for the Arts (1978 and 1989), the Guggenheim Foundation (1983–1984), and the National Humanities Center (1988–1989), among others. She was granted a Portia Pittman Fellowship from the National Endowment for the Humanities as writer-in-residence at Tuskegee Institute in 1982; was chosen by Robert Penn Warren—then the first U.S. poet laureate—for a 1986 Lavan Younger Poet Award from the Academy of American Poets; received a 1987 General Electric Foundation Award, the 1988 Ohio Governor's Award in the arts, and a Literary Lion citation from the New York Public Library in 1990; and was awarded honorary doctorates from Miami University in Ohio, Knox College in Knoxville, Tennessee, Tuskegee University in Alabama, the University of Miami in Florida, Washington University in St. Louis, Case Western Reserve University in Cleveland, and the University of Akron in Ohio. Honorary degrees from Arizona State University and Boston College followed in May 1995, and from Dartmouth College—with President Bill Clinton as commencement speaker—in June 1995. Spelman College in Atlanta and the University of Pennsylvania in Philadelphia, as well as Columbia University and others, brought Dove's total of honorary degrees to sixteen as of Spring 1999. She was named one of the "Outstanding Women of the Year 1993" by *Glamour* magazine, and that same year the National Association for the Advancement of Colored People honored her with its Great American Artist Award. In 1994 she received the Folger Shakespeare Library's Renaissance Forum Award for Leadership in the Literary Arts, a Golden Plate Award from the American Academy of Achievement, and the Carl Sandburg Award from the International Platform Association. In 1996 she received both the Heinz Award in the Arts and Humanities and the Charles Frankel Prize/National Medal in the Humanities. In 1997 she was honored with the Sara Lee Frontrunner Award and the Barnes & Noble Writers for Writers Award.

Dove has read her poetry at a White House state dinner and was featured on NBC's *Today Show*, in a one-hour Bill Moyers's *Journal* on PBS television, on the *McNeil-Lehrer News Hour* (in an interview with Charlayne Hunter-Gault), PBS's *Charlie Rose* show, and Dennis Wholey's *This Is America*. She hosted and produced, in collaboration with the Virginia Center for the Book, *Shine Up Your Words: A Morning with Rita Dove*, a nationally televised one-hour video program with elementary school children about poetry, filmed a segment with Big Bird for *Sesame Street*, and appeared several times on Garrison Keillor's public radio program *A Prairie Home Companion*. In April 1995 she welcomed, together with former president Jimmy Carter, an unprecedented gathering of nobel laureates in literature to Atlanta, Georgia—hosted by the Cultural Olympiad of the Atlanta Committee for the Olympic Games. In June 1995 Dove presented a tribute to Billie Holiday for what would have been the jazz singer's eightieth birthday, produced by National Public Radio in Washington, D.C.

Dove is a past president (1986–1987) of the Associated Writing Programs, the association of creative writers in American academia. As previously mentioned, she serves as associate editor of *Callaloo*, the preeminent magazine for African-American arts and literature, and as advisory editor to the literary periodicals *Georgia Review, Gettysburg Review, Ploughshares,* and *TriQuarterly* and to the feminist magazine *Iris*. She is a member of the advisory board of *Civilization*, the magazine of the Library of Congress. Since 1988 Dove has been a commissioner of the Schomburg Center for Research in Black Culture at the New York Public Library, and in 1994 she was appointed to the Council of Scholars at the Library of Congress and elected to a six-year term as a senator of the national academic association Phi Beta Kappa.

In 1993 the "world in the poet" turned "poet in the world," when President Clinton and Librarian of Congress James H. Billington appointed Dove to the position of U. S. poet laureate and consultant in poetry at the Library of Congress, making her the youngest person—and the first African American—to receive this highest official honor in American letters. In 1994 the appointment was renewed for a second year—the maximum permitted by law. In 2000 she returned for the bicentennial anniversary of the Library of Congress.

What matters to Dove beyond the grid of an official biography[10] may be summed up in the following questions: "How do you hold on to your dreams with dignity? How do you know when you should listen to others and when to follow your own hunches? How can you remain connected to that innermost spiritual hunger while negotiating the necessary commerce of living?" (*UVA Alumni News* Jan./Feb. 1994: 24). "Part of my political/personal mandate," she states elsewhere, "is to represent life in all of its complexities, in its fullness. That means that if I'm writing a poem in which I notice a flower, if I felt it was important to talk about this flower, I would be dishonest not to do it just because I thought it wasn't directly about being black and a woman. Besides, how do I know it ISN'T about being black or a woman?" (Lloyd: 1994: 1). "Anyone who feels the need to connect the outside world with an interior presence must absorb the mysterious into the tangle of contradictions and longings that form each one of us. That's hard, ongoing work, and it never ends," Dove testifies in "The Epistle of Paul the Apostle to the Ephesians" (1990: 174).

Dove is represented in major anthologies[11] and is widely taught.[12] Yet critical investigation of her work, apart from short articles, reviews, and interviews,[13] has been scarce in relation to her high public acclaim.

Critics have brought out early Dove's developing interest in history, displacement, and fragmentation, in the exotic and the domestic, in reticence and disclosure (Gregerson 1984; *The Norton Anthology of American Literature* 1989;

Georgoudaki 1991) on one hand, and her equilibratory search for wholeness and all-inclusiveness, her "universal appeal,"[14] on the other (Smith 1982; Hernton 1985; Vendler 1986; Grosholz 1987; Steinman 1987; Harris 1988; Georgoudaki 1991; Sample 1994). Her concerns include the reconstruction of a familial and cultural past (Gregerson 1984) and the underside of History, meaning history in terms of overlooked events (Georgoudaki 1991; Stein 1995). Attention also has been drawn to Dove's emphasis on the continuity of human experience, longing for the complete freedom of imagination, and her determination to break new ground (Rampersad 1986), to her visionary montage technique (McDowell 1986; Costello 1991), and to the dramatic fascination and force of her cycles of poems (McDowell, Rampersad, Vendler, all 1986). Critics with an eye for the formal and rhythmic qualities of language, notably Vendler, who was among the first influential voices highlighting Dove's talent, have observed her techniques of fierce concision and rhythmic pulse through modulated syntax and sound, her crosscutting elliptical jumps as her chief stylistic signature. Her suggestive juxtapositions replace explanatory passages (Vendler 1986–1995; Shoptaw 1990). *Thomas and Beulah* shows a strikingly brilliant sequence (Vendler 1986) in which men and women's voices complement each other (Harris 1988), or tell of segregated lives, bifurcations, and divisions (Shoptaw 1990), thus forming a chorus in the history of the private, black, "other" America. Stein (1995) also elaborates on Dove's awareness of flux and plurality, her intersecting vision of public and private history as motion itself, and her production of multiple perspective and various vantage points. The multitude of poetic variations with which Dove semanticizes, for example, her black awareness is the subject of Vendler's essays, "Blackness and Beyond Blackness" (1994) and "Rita Dove: Identity Markers" (*The Given and the Made* 1995). Baker (1989) sees race in Dove's work "poetically transformed into an uncommon commonality." Her linguistic artistry seems occasionally too controlled for Arnold Rampersad as he wishes for "more wayward energy that springs naturally out of human circumstance" (1986) or, in Vendler's words, "a relaxation of her tense drama into an occasional digressiveness" (1988). Vendler (*Soul Says* 1995) attributes this taut control of language and emotions to an anxiety that has so far "precluded certain forms of the comic, the genial, or the insouciant; but her poems know reproach, irony and a terse impatience very well. They also know a surprising surrealism, which turns out to be realism." (166–67). "Isn't Reality Magic?" asks the title of Walsh's 1994 interview, but Dove's search for the magical in our contemporary lives and her devotion to myth have been noted before (McDowell 1986). The vital aspects of Dove's linguistic artistry are brought out in two different contributions: Kirkland C. Jones (1992) particularly emphasizes the energy of the vernacular in Dove and Yusef Komunyakaa, while Patricia Wallace (1993), in her essay on "three minority writers" (Cervantes, Dove, Song), examines the forces of language and culture, its barriers and breaks (the literary) that evoke the ineffable (the literal).

Helen Vendler's "The Black Dove: Rita Dove, Poet Laureate" (*Soul Says* 1995) portrays "an unusual mind," "acute, well-read, observant, reflective, formal. It refuses naiveté, and prefers a scalpel to a paintbrush. It is not a comfortable mind: aloof, watchful, it scrutinizes its readers and demands an answering intensity in return for its own." Walt Harrington's miraculous empathy for Dove's creative process (1995) allows the reader to grasp the "shape of her dreaming" through his sensitive depiction of a poem in "statu nascendi": "Sic itur ad adstra" (14–29).

In 1978 Rafael Lozano became the first European to acknowledge Dove in his portrait of twelve young American poets. Yet, apart from a 1982 German review by Heide Hoge noting the absence of love poems in her work, Dove did not receive critical recognition in Europe until a decade later, from Aristotle University in Thessaloniki. Ekaterini Georgoudaki's *Race, Gender, and Class Perspectives in the Works of Maya Angelou, Gwendolyn Brooks, Rita Dove, Nikki Giovanni, and Audre Lorde* serves as an introduction for first-year students and includes two chapters on Dove: "Black and White Women in Poems by Angelou, Brooks, Dove, Giovanni, and Lorde: Complex and Ambivalent Relationships" and "Rita Dove: Crossing Boundaries," an essay originally published in *Callaloo* 14.2 (1991). According to Georgoudaki, Dove's stylistic polish not only sets her apart from contemporary African-American poetry, but it may also explain why she has had only modest success within her own ethnic group, another reason being the hermetism of poetry as a genre. Particularly convincing is Georgoudaki's analysis of Dove as an intercultural mediator of many lyrical voices that explode all barriers.

A collection of essays (1993) edited by Wolfgang Karrer and Barbara Puschmann-Nalenz is one of the most definitive German-language publication on studies in Afro-American literature. In the foreword to *The African American Short Story. 1970–1990*, Dove is merely mentioned as meriting "a closer look."

What Vendler (*Soul Says* 1995) noted as so far absent from Dove's repertoire—"personal hatred, marital jealousy, shame of inadequate motherhood" (165)—is revealed, not in the first but certainly in the third person, in various protagonists:[15] see, for example, *Fifth Sunday* ("Second-Hand Man," "Aunt Carrie"), expanded in *Through the Ivory Gate*, and *The Darker Face of the Earth*, an Oedipal tragedy, also bears witness to personal hatred or marital jealousy, and the sonnet cycle *Mother Love* clearly touches on the shame of inadequate motherhood. What is missing in view of these more recent works is in-depth investigation. Except for short reviews, *Fifth Sunday* (McGraw 1986; Wade-Gayles 1987), *Through the Ivory Gate* (Cherry, Ostrom, Ryman, Smith, all 1992; Foreman 1993; Hull 1994), *The Darker Face of the Earth* (Throne 1995), and *Mother Love* (Bagby, Barker, Chappel, Love, Silberg, Tarasevich, Vendler, all 1995; Booth, Cushman, Lofgren 1996; Proitsaki 1997) have not yet received detailed critical attention. Though Geta Leseur, in her 1995 investigation on the black bildungsroman, *Ten Is the Age of Darkness*, mentions Dove as poet laureate (33), *Through the Ivory Gate* is not dealt with at all.

It follows that Dove obviously resists being typecast under a mantra of race, class, and gender. She is no nature poet, no regionalist, no feminist, neither a representative of one particular group, nor a trader of all worlds. Her individual stance speaks as a poet, historian, geographer, astronomer, archaeologist, sociologist, psychologist, mythologist and mythmaker, traveler in body, mind, and fantasy space. With modernist spareness she traces events and feelings that provoke a response beyond conventional limitations. Not unlike Albrecht Dürer (1471–1528), who keeps inspiring one of her forthcoming lyric cycles, her positionality mirrors the mediating role of "one of the most interesting examples of an inquisitive mind" (Gates, *Reading Black* 1990: 484–85):

> He was an artist really poised . . . between two eras, who sensed that the Renaissance was happening and that Germany was somehow behind and that the dark kind of iconic representations in medieval German art were going to change. He didn't know what was coming after that but he was willing to move outside of art, in his case, and go into philosophy and mathematics. He was willing to move out of his cultural frame and try to figure out, to stretch himself. That of course is one of the things that always interests me when an historical character occurs to me. . . . (485)

To do justice to the various stretchings and strains of inner and outer dislocation and emplacement, both in Dove's writing and in her liminal position as a fin-de-siècle artist on the threshold of a new millennium, and to explore the questions raised by the gaps in critical reception, the following concerns need to be pursued: How do we define literary space in a crosscultural interface? To what extent is Dove's "universality,"[16] which is thematically entailed in "crossing boundaries," really a written factor, and how, if at all, is cultural difference inscribed in a universal model? Is the alien assimilated and defused in the process, or accentuated in a strain of magic realism that could eventually transform the categories and enclosures of the mind? To what extent do such concepts as "place," "displacement," and "emplacement," in other words, a cultural reorientation and reterritorialization generated by dislocation, eventually mark Dove's oeuvre as postcolonial or as emergent within U.S. mainstream tendencies?[17] To what extent is there a congruence between approaches developed in a European setting (translatability, dialogicity: Bakhtin, Lachmann; poetics of space: Bachelard, Bronfen, Lefebvre) and African-American theory (for example, Henderson's *Speaking in Tongues*, Baker's *Workings of the Spirit*)?[18] Are performative aspects also intrinsic in Dove's work?[19]

Concentration on her worldmaking beyond cultural fixations, which allows in its transference a revised artistic freedom, necessarily excludes a closer look at other strands that define the aesthetic and eth(n)ic essence of Dove's writing: for instance, the magic of an intricate imagery as a unifying principle and her use of birds, wings, scars, flowers, trees, water, color, or music as leitmotifs; a consistent exposition of themes such as motherhood, children, dolls, traveling, or the polyphony of voices overriding an African-American "double consciousness." This concerns not only Dove's positionality in spite of her *Crossing Color*, but also remains, though not extensively dealt with here, an important aspect. For decades, literary figures and theoreticians like W. E. B. Du Bois have spoken of the the "two-ness" of black authors. In her paper on Derek Walcott ("Either I'm Nobody, or I'm a Nation:" 67), Dove forcefully evokes this split in black consciousness, a veil accented by public acknowledgment.

The fate of any member of a minority who "makes it" is double-edged. As a model, he or she must be perfect; no slip-ups or "you've let us down." As a special case, he or she is envied, even reviled. Move away from the home court and you're accused of being "dicty": return and you're a prodigal. Write about home and you blaspheme; choose other topics and you're a traitor.

Decisive for our investigation is the revolutionary territory that grows out of these culturally ambivalent interstices, which are renegotiated by authors of an ethnic minority. It is there that art, between borders and beyond incommensurable cultures, nationalities, or rationalities, creates a homeplace of coexistence for both writer and reader. This is how Dove's major concern for "rooted displacement in art" not only legitimizes but also invites an investigation of space.

The first chapter, therefore, sets out the prerequisites and dimensions of spatiotemporal relations in Dove's oeuvre. As a working hypothesis it will chart a topology of her worldmaking distinguished by physical, mental, and cultural enspacements, as well as boundaries and movements between. In a broader perspective of relevant critical theory, Dove's poetics of space as it emerges from her writing will be put to test in an analysis of "In the Old Neighborhood," the prefatory poem of *SP*. Primarily in conjunction with her poetry (*YH*, *M*, *TB*, *GN*, and *ML*), Chapter 2 explores in depth the various enspacements, movements, and boundaries particularly in terms of the hybrid cultural ground Dove envisions beyond confinements. Chapter 3 then examines the web of relational semantics in the sequence of *Thomas and Beulah*, where circular structures interact with a linear movement. As one cannot deny a text's spatiality one cannot abrogate its temporality as a constituent part of a meaningful whole. Chronology, particularly in *TB*, *IG*, *DF*, and *ML*, plays an important part in a sequential understanding. At the same time these chronologically ordered texts produce simultaneity and reversibility in their nonsequential allusions and connections, narrative spaces the reader has to reproduce while following the linear course. These issues are further investigated in the subsequent chapter as it foregrounds the particular linear and circular movements of the Bildungs- and Künstlerroman *Through the Ivory Gate* developing out of *Fifth Sunday*. The penultimate fifth chapter continues this line of argument, with a particular focus on form as artistic enspacement, as mythic realms of Greek tragedy are at stake. The Oedipal conflict of incest and murder in the context of slavery in *DF* and the Demeter-Persephone cycle of death and renewal in *ML* prove their perpetuity in a contemporary setting. The book concludes with a critical assessment and an outlook in the form of a conversation with Dove.

The narrative format of *Crossing Color* reflects the poetic construction of the ghazal: Each chapter is a separate piece, yet the text develops sequentially as well. The guiding principle of a spiral circling around a focus of interest might foreground various aspects of the same poem in different chapters. I have chosen representative poems and explored them as a whole whenever possible, since the movement and the structure of the poem is important in its spatiotemporal development.

Two aspirations I would like to share with readers before they embark on a voyage that expands from a transatlantic dialogue to the pluricultural polylogue that I would like this book to represent. The first is to (re)design a poetics of space and spatiotemporal relations not only informed by and apt to highlight a particular work but also able to serve as an interpretive model. The second is, in spite of the first, my desire that Dove's and this book's plea against the closure of categories that prevent us from growth will not go unheard. In "The Fish in the Stone" (*SP* 69) Dove reminds readers that "the fish in the stone / would like to fall / back into the sea. / He is weary / of analysis, the small / predictable truths. / He is weary of waiting / in the open, / his profile stamped / by a white light." For whereas the form and content of her poetry are sophisticated and finished, their implied message yields a course of lessons as "to the instability and mutability of identities which are always unfinished, always being remade" (Gilroy 1993: xi).

O N E

RITA DOVE'S MACRO-POETICS
OF SPACE

Cultural space is most likely the only place deserving the uncanny name of home, where artist and reader, as creating and recreating subjects, uncontestedly remain "masters in their own house."

Sigmund Freud

The macro-poetics of space approaches Rita Dove's oeuvre as a whole. It examines the sequence of sections within a single work, as well as the development of themes and strategies of space throughout her work, rather than individual units dealt with in the micro-poetics of Chapter 2.

In the present study of a poetic representation and revision of space and time, Immanuel Kant's concepts outlined in his "Transcendental Aesthetic" are of continuing interest: Space, Kant maintains, is in no sense a property of things in themselves, nor in relation to one another. It is pure perception and presents itself to our consciousness as an infinite, undivided magnitude. The seeming plurality of spaces stems but from limitations of the whole. Time, to Kant, is neither an empirical, objective conception, nor an independent substance but a form of inner sense. How we perceive ourselves and our inward state determines the way we define time. In itself, or apart from the time-conscious subject, time is nothing at all (22–35).[1] "Does the cosmic/space we dissolve into taste of us, then?" asks epigraph by Rilke to Dove's "Ozone" (*GN* 28). Space and time are *how* things appear to us; they are not things themselves. They are intuitive, negotiable. The beggar's time is not the merchant's time, the daughter's not her mother's, the mourner's not the lover's. How time travels when no clock is around is explained by Rosalind to her beloved Orlando in Shakespeare's *As You Like It:*

> Time travels in divers paces with divers persons. I'll tell you who Time ambles withal, who Time trots withal, who Time gallops withal, and who he stands still withal. . . . Marry he trots hard with a young maid, between the contract of her marriage and the day it is solemnized. If the interim be but a se'nnight, Time's pace is so hard that it seems the length of seven years. (III.2.302f)

Because time has no shape of its own, we resort to analogies and metaphors drawn from space. We are running out of time. "Moments slip by like worms" or "morning is still a frozen / tear in the brain," Dove writes (*SP* 12, 16).

As space often merges with place in experience, space needs to be defined further. It is more abstract than place, which I equate with location.[2] Indiscriminate space, however, becomes place as soon as we endow it with a particular name or meaning. "There is no place like home," Dorothy exclaims in *The Wizard of Oz*. In their 1993 collection of essays, *Space and Place: Theories of Identity and Location*, Erica Carter, James Donald, and Judith Squires reinforce the way space becomes place:

> By being named: as the flows of power and negotiations of social relations are rendered in the concrete form of architecture; and also, of course, by embodying the symbolic and imaginary investments of a population. Place is space to which meaning has been ascribed. (xii)

This, of course, does not preclude space from gaining significance of its own without being pinned down and located. Quite the reverse. The aim of this investigation is precisely an analysis of the creation and meaning of cultural[3] space, understood as a space that has been seized upon and transmuted by imagination, knowledge, or experience. How radically the powers of imagination and reasoning are capable of reshaping cultural space is shown in Dove's poem "Geometry" (*SP* 17):

> I prove a theorem and the house expands:
> the windows jerk free to hover near the ceiling,
> the ceiling floats away with a sigh.
>
> As the walls clear themselves of everything
> but transparency, the scent of carnations
> leaves with them. I am out in the open
>
> and above the windows have hinged into butterflies,
> sunlight glinting where they've intersected.
> They are going to some point true and unproven.

In Dove's color-oriented creative realm, "Geometry" is one of those few poems to emerge from a clear folder, which holds very little and is "reserved for pure thought, the perfect, clear, pure lyrical poem" (Harrington 1995: 15). The speaker proves a theorem and is out in the open. How could this experience be expressed through visual and verbal imagery? Two slightly different readings are imaginable. Either the house metaphorically portrays the mind, or the mind-blowing expansion blasts the house apart. Whatever the case: "windows jerk free . . . going to some point true and unproven," "the ceiling floats away with a sigh," "the walls clear themselves of everything / but transparency" and "the windows have hinged into butterflies." This liberating move from the initial "prove" to the final "unproven" not only obliterates sensory and olfactory remnants ("sigh," "scent") but also metamorphoses the wallbound window-frames like earthbound caterpillars into butterflies. On Psyche's wings the pure mind reaches out for truth in the unproven magnitude of infinite cultural space where nothing is proven except the magic of the poetic and intellectual process.

In "Building Dwelling Thinking," Martin Heidegger, whose notion of building equals being and thinking, epitomizes this act of poetic clearage and expansion as follows:

> A space is something that has been made room for, something that is cleared and free, namely within a boundary, Greek *peras*. A boundary is not that at which something stops but as the Greeks recognized, the boundary is that from which something *begins its presencing*. . . . Space is in essence that for which room has been made, that which is let into its bounds. (1975: 154)

This is precisely how Dove treats and reinterprets cultural space throughout her work. In view of the sociohistorical context of her writing I shall employ space instead of place not only as the more inclusive term but also as the one less imbued with notions of slavery. Whereas in an African-American context place always connotes the displacement and commodification of human bodies in the "Middle Passage," space does contain options for a cultural reterritorialization of a lost homeplace. The ideas of space and place, however, always require each other for definition as we can equally discuss the spatial qualities of place as well as the locational qualities of space. "The Island Women of Paris" (*GN* 65) illustrate the point as they:

> skim from curb to curb like regatta,
> from Pont Neuf to the Quai de la Rappe
> in cool negotiation with traffic,
> each a country to herself
> transposed to this city
> by a fluke called "imperial courtesy."
>
> The island women glide past held aloft
> by a wire running straight to heaven.
> Who can ignore their ornamental bearing,
> turbans haughty as parrots,
> or deft braids carved into airy cages
> transfixed on their manifest brows?
>
> The island women move through Paris
> as if they had just finished inventing
> their destinations. It's better
> not to get in their way. And better
> not look an island woman in the eye—
> unless you like feeling unnecessary.

Nobody enhances the spatial qualities of place more strikingly than the island women of the West Indies, Polynesia, or Africa as they drag postcolonial space[4] into Paris, the place. In their 1989 study, *The Empire Writes Back*, Ashcroft, Griffiths, and Tiffin define the term "postcolonial" "to cover all the culture affected by the imperial process from the moment of colonialization to the present day" (2). They argue that a major feature of postcolonial literatures lies in their "concern with place and displacement" and, therefore, the development of an "effective identifying relationship between self and place" (8–9). Indeed, a "fluke called 'imperial courtesy'" has brought the island women to France. Throughout Paris's colonial and postcolonial period the center of civilization where it was assumed racism was less prevalent has attracted islanders as well as African Americans (from Josephine Baker to James Baldwin, from Richard Wright to Sidney Bechet and Maya Angelou).[5] "Each a country to herself" in "ornamental bearing, / turbans haughty as parrots," the island women hence testify to the locational qualities of space. Islandlike, they "move through Paris / as if they had just finished inventing / their destinations" and compensate for their dislocation on a horizontal level with an extraordinary verticality aloft "by a wire running straight to heaven." Their rootedness stretching from hair into air, their "cool negotiation with traffic," their "manifest brows" warning us "not to get in their way" turns these women into avatars whose presence and stamina make it advisable not to look them "in the eye— / unless you like feeling unnecessary." Their determination and pride embody and highlight an empowered marginal space within the center of French civilization. Right there they command respect and reclaim a cultural niche of their own.[6]

A fusion of varied cultural spaces arguably promotes the use of the term "multicultural" instead of "cultural." Yet, defined as a space that has been seized upon and transmuted by imagination, knowledge, or experience, cultural space not only subsumes multiculturalism. The term also has less in common with Dove's concepts of boundary crossing than with the current American canon debate. Coined in 1970, in a Canadian report that advocated bilingualism and biculturalism, "multiculturalism" came largely to describe the demographic change produced by an increasing number of immigrants from various parts of the British Commonwealth since then. In 1988 a law concerning the cultural contribution of the other (non-French-or non-English-speaking) inhabitants was passed (Hutcheon 1994: 159).[7] Multiculturalism's rapid dissemination and ideological ambivalence after 1987 is based on the U.S. debate on syllabi, ethnicity, and affirmative action (Ostendorf 1994: 8). It denominates a program of intercultural education within the normative creed of complete assimilation on one hand, and a *bricolage* of various discourses of postmodernism, postcolonialism, and deconstruction on the other.[8] Multiculturalism's retreat into the politics of minorities and categories of difference may very well be in reaction to the failure of universal[9] models such as the enlightenment, communism, or Panafricanism.

Dove, however, "balances opposites, bridges conventional divisions . . . . and transcends boundaries of space and time. . . . She speaks with the voice of a world citizen who places her personal, racial, and national experience within the context of the human experience as a whole" (Georgoudaki 1991: 430). She not only writes beyond postmodernism and multiculturalism but also revalues a transethnic universalism in view of a revision of the past, present, and future.[10] No longer distrustful of "universality" as a "hegemonic European tool wielded to designate 'inferior and superior cultures'" (Ashcroft et al. 1989: 149), Dove embraces the notion of crossculturality, a cultural syncretism also inherent in Wilson Harris's (149) or Derek Walcott's work. Yet hers is no disabling harmonization of alterities, as Etheridge Knight criticizes in "On Universalism" (Henderson 1973: 330).[11] Beyond the example of "The Island Women of Paris" I will discuss how her universality, which is thematically entailed in crossing boundaries, is really a written factor, and that diversity is inscribed in her universal model. To what extent does Dove's cultural reorientation and reterritorialization generated by dislocation eventually share traits with "emergent" literatures within or beyond U.S. mainstream tendencies?[12] Homi Bhabha's vision of a new nation space theorizes important characteristics of Dove's poetic network. What emerges, in Bhabha's words, "is a turning of boundaries and limits into the *in-between* spaces through which the meanings of cultural and political authority are negotiated" (1993: 4).

THE MACRO-POETICS OF CULTURAL SPACE

How do we map out literary space in view of a crosscultural interface that includes the private and the public, the near and the far? To what extent is the macro-structure, the sequence of sections within a single work, as well as the development of themes and poetic strategies throughout Dove's work, a statement in itself? Rita Dove's work sets the pace and lends the grid. From the first piece she kept, an unpublished novel called "Chaos,"[13] about robots taking over the earth, till her 1995 sonnet cycle *Mother Love*, which takes us to the underworld, the shaping of personal and public cultural space consistently centers her writing. "Stepping Out—the poet in the world," her first laureate lecture, subtitled "house and yard," opens with a remarkable statement:

> All of my books but one bear titles concerned with matters of definable space—*The Yellow House on the Corner* is wistfully specific; *Museum* evokes that specially prepared space for contemplation of significant achievements of the past. Although *Thomas and Beulah* is not a place, the two names establish a condition—these two protagonists are to be regarded as a unit, the title seems to say, a unit that becomes irrevocably wedded to a defined and also *confined* place, Akron, Ohio—much in the same way other famous moniker-teams evoke specific milieus—Barnum and Bailey, Sacco and Vanzetti, Frankie and Johnnie, Jack and Jill, Liz and Richard, Adam and Eve. The title of my collection of short fiction, *Fifth Sunday*, does a similar thing by calling attention to the alteration in the normal run of days in the week—since a month with five Sundays is a break with the ordinary, the fifth Sunday is automatically imbued with a metaphysical and moral significance. My novel *Through the Ivory Gate* connotes a place that exists in order to be moved through: it is a passage, a transient space. And the title of my verse drama, *The Darker Face of the Earth*, finally locates us in the beyond, since to see the face of the earth implies a distance, an estrangement, from our world. (*PW* 1995: 15–16)

The titles of her books reflect Dove's tendency to use private and public space—in the 1980 poetry collection *The Yellow House on the Corner*, followed by *Museum* (1983), *Thomas and Beulah* (1986), and *Mother Love* (1995)—and to detect the extraordinary within the commonplace—1985 in the short story collection *Fifth Sunday*, 1989 in the lyric collection *Grace Notes*. Though omitted from the list above, *Grace Notes*, like a fifth Sunday, testifies to those moments added to the basic melody of life that "break with the ordinary" but make all the difference. Repeatedly, she reflects the trauma of slavery—directly in single poems or in the verse drama *The Darker Face of the Earth* (1994–1996), indirectly in the thwarted social rise of *Thomas and Beulah*. The fundamentals of artistic enspacement are most markedly evident in the Bildungs- and Künstlerroman *Through the Ivory Gate* (1992) and in the sonnet cycle *Mother Love* (1995).

However, the "definable space" addressed in her poet laureate essay and the concepts that emerge from her crosscultural interface are only revealed implicitly, or, as Dove puts it, they are "wistfully specific." *The Yellow House on the Corner*[14] sits ambiguously "in-between" in terms of neighborhood boundaries and ethnic affiliation. A "yellow" African American is one accused of sellout, one who has been compromised by too much currency in a white world (Gregerson 1984: 46). The cover photos of *YH* document an intriguing development from the personal to the public. The first edition, in 1980, shows a photograph of the author full front in monochromatic yellow that acts as an interface between reader and text; the 1989 reprint shows a yellow house. Interestingly, the content of the collection, divided into five sections, reflects and confirms the first impression evoked by both pictures: autobiographical parts about growing up in the U.S. Midwest (I, II, IV) and traveling (V) frame the central sequence (III) of segregation in African-American slave narratives as if a ghost long gone were overshadowing the psychic comfort of a sensitive young woman. Thus the poet not only evokes a painful reality carefully shielded from her by her parents but at the same time succeeds in creating a crosscultural imaginary realm. While *YH* travels timewise in remembering and reconstructing African-American history, it moves through space via travelogues that capture images of postwar Germany, Mexico, or the Sahara. A migrating body and mind counteract and expand the enclosures of history (slavery) and geography (Akron, Ohio) with an extraordinary openness and curiosity about the unknown, heightened by imagined participation in another's experience. This is how the world expands with artifacts marking momentous events.

Art may even translate and emplace nothing into being. Dove explicitly designates her *Museum* as a space "for contemplation of significant achievements of the past." Yet choice and absence determine the selection and reading of these frozen images. This public display of meaningful private sites and moments is more closely structured than *YH* and focuses largely on European settings, with the First World and ancient China serving as storehouses of myth (part I: "The Hill Has Something to Say"). Beulah, an ancestor-figure shaped on Dove's maternal grandmother, presides over the collection as *M's* curator and the protagonist of the introductory poem, "Dusting," repeated in *TB*. She keeps dusting, the archaeologist's task of clearing away layers of dirt and oblivion and bringing both beauty and historical accuracy to view (Rubin and Ingersoll: 238). Beulah, however, is dusting someone else's house, working, as she has all her life, serving others. Thus the reconstructions of *M* highlight social histories, small vignettes of lives and moments easily ignored like the epitaph on a "tombstone near Weimar, Texas." The epigraph of part I, with the telling title "The Hill Has Something to Say," reads: "Here lies / Ike Tell: / Heathen. / No chance of Heaven, / No fear of Hell." Weimar is no longer Goethe's town but the poet's choice for cultural twist and transfer. Yet Dove's own major dislocation—*M* emerged during her second stay in Europe—also allows for superb flashbacks on the recent and more removed American past (part II: "In the Bulrush"). Her artistic detachment from her father in the third part, "My Father's Telescope," where she develops her own voice and personae, generates a new book. This Primer for the Nuclear Age contemplates History (public) and history (private) worldwide. Facing possible nuclear extermination, we should be able to read the warning scripture that faintly echoes S. T. Coleridge's sublime "Rhyme of the Ancient Mariner": "At the edge of the mariner's / map is written: 'Beyond / this point lie Monsters.'" Archaic perceptions of the world—the old mariner who feared he would fall off the world's edge if he went too far—and recollections of childhood—primers are part of anyone's basic education—mingle to prepare us for contemporary threats. "'Beyond / this point lie Monsters'": Primer for the Nuclear Age indeed concludes with a monstrous act, the killing of 20,000 Haitians, in one of Dove's best known poems, "Parsley." Thus the lyrics of *M* collect and exhibit, as museums do, artifacts without a connecting narrative. Wandering from one room to the next, the visitor must act as a chronologist or archaeologist assembling and reconstructing a forgotten or unknown story. Cultural space emerges as an enlightening dialogue between poem-picture and reader-beholder. Dove gives us an instructive map to follow in the penultimate poem and also in the opening of part IV: "The Sailor in Africa" presents an adventurous voyage as an allegory for racial and colonial domination, a common theme discretely yet consistently evoked throughout *M*. The requested admission ticket to *M* is to consider and reconsider the obvious and the hidden. "This alone is what I wish for you: knowledge," Demeter tells Hades in *ML* (63).

In her 1985 article "Telling It Like It I-S *IS*: Narrative Techniques in Melvin Tolson's *Harlem Gallery*" (109–117), Dove highlights Tolson's narrative strategy, also at the core of her own work, with a quote from Geneva Smitherman:[15]

> The relating of events (real or hypothetical) becomes a black rhetorical strategy to explain a point, to persuade holders of opposing views to one's own point of view. . . . This meandering away from the "point" takes the listener on episodic journeys and over tributary routes, but like the flow of nature's rivers and streams, it all eventually leads back to the source. Though highly applauded by blacks, this narrative linguistic style is exasperating to whites who wish you'd be direct and hurry up and get to the point. (114–115)

In various ways *M* elaborates on themes and strategies developed in *Harlem Gallery*, for which Tolson planned five books but finished only the first, entitled "The Curator."[16] Dove considers the timing "bad for such a complex piece"

(109) because the Civil Rights, Black Consciousness, and Black Arts Movements were at their peak in 1965 and barely ready for this curator/narrator, "a Mulatto of 'afroirishjewish origins' and ex-Professor of Art" (111). Her dusting curator Beulah awaited a better day.

Akin to *YH*, the cover of *Museum* shows a striking transmutation from an initial auctorial portrait, albeit in the likeness of a Madagascan snake charmer, to a less personal prospect. While the 1983 edition displays the 1929 painting by German artist Christian Schad, *Agosta the Winged Man and Rasha the Black Dove*, the 1992 reprint features a group of students in front of a medieval scene of nativity. A treacherous trace of the author's depersonalization[17] remains: the second edition still thanks "Bettina Schad for her kind cooperation" for the reprint of her father's painting. "Negative capability," however, the self-renunciation that John Keats avowed William Shakespeare, rather than self-effacement, is responsible for Dove's disappearance from the title pages. Her presence in absence is in tune with her texts, which allow her to move in a polyphony of voices, manifold refractions of perspective and valuations. Thereby she expands languages, culture, and seemingly opposing concepts like oral and written speech not only in an American-European dialogue but also among various ethnicities. Correspondingly, her motto for *M* reads *for nobody / who made us possible*, (nobody hinders our finding and creating a fitting identity), and to this nobody *M* is dedicated. Human identities, Kwame Anthony Appiah reminds us *In My Father's House* (1992: 174), are always "invented histories, invented biologies, invented affinities . . . ; each is a kind of role that has to be scripted, structured by conventions of narrative to which the world never quite manages to conform."

Spacewise, the public *M* offers a well-framed homeplace for a diversity of displacements and dislocations. The near and the far, reticence and disclosure, provide artistic coherence beyond the homely grid of a neighborhood. "*M* was much more about art and artifact, and attempts to register personal human experience against the larger context of history," Dove said (Schneider 1989: 115). Indeed the sweep and scope of the spatiotemporal expansion is impressive. From Argos to Alexandria, from Munich to Tel Aviv and Delft, from the deep South to China, from the Dominican Republic to Eastern Europe and back to native Ohio, *M* moves through time in harboring saints (Catherine of Alexandria, Catherine of Siena), writers (Shakespeare, Boccaccio, Hölderlin), and historical and biblical figures (Nestor, Liu Sheng, Banneker, Trujillo, Moses). Aristocrats (Baroness Erpenberg, Prince Liu Sheng) and commoners (Ike from Weimar, Texas), a writer's muse (Boccaccio's Fiammetta), painters (Schad), musicians (Champion Jack Dupree), and family (father, grandfather) gather with anonymous killers, vegetarians, readers, and translators. This is the larger argument of self-presentation via poetic representation in *M*, where autobiography and history merge. African-American identity (for instance, Banneker's, Rasha's) is not explicitly addressed but embedded in the world and a key to understanding difference, diversity, and excellence. Thus *M* ultimately turns into a homeplace for exiles and guestworkers of various origins such as the Madagascan Rasha or the Russian aristocrat Katja. Dove not only houses the strange and displaced in her poetic museum but also recurrently points to the uncanny in the ongoing fiction called "home." When "Tou Wan Speaks to Her Husband, Liu Sheng" (*SP* 77f) she addresses the corpse of her faithless husband in dignified irony: "I will build you a house / of limited chambers / but it shall last / forever: four rooms / hewn in the side of stone / for you, my / only conqueror." Surviving, she is empowered to furnish a traditional mausoleum enriched with offerings, where next to a statuette of his most frequently coveted palace girl she entombs her own longings and frustrations.

In the two earliest lyric collections the African-American past emerges piecemeal (from the slave narratives in *YH* to the paternal lineage of grandfather, father, and brother in part III of *M*), but in *Thomas and Beulah* it takes centerstage. Foregrounded are their imagined lives after the great migration of black southerners to find work and peace in the industrialized, more liberated North. Their journey up from Wartrace, Tennessee, and Rockmart, Georgia, to Akron, Ohio, and the thwarted attempt to show off their car back home in Tennessee mark significant cycles of personal and public U.S. history and cultural space. Although more varied in subject matter and tone, *YH* and *M* seem to function but as a prologue to the unearthing of a lost black heritage in *TB*. "The two names establish a condition . . . a unit that becomes irrevocably wedded to a defined and also *confined* place, Akron," Dove describes her Pulitzer Prize-winning cycle of forty-three poems, to be discussed in detail in Chapters 2 and particularly 3.

The eight short stories in *Fifth Sunday* are small in volume but large in their spatiotemporal command. "A month with five Sundays is a break with the ordinary, the fifth Sunday is automatically imbued with a metaphysical and moral significance," Dove specifies. Indeed each story leads us straight into a world of decision-making, judgment, heartbreak, and eventual redemption. As in Shakespeare's romance plays, the protagonists brush against tragedy but are granted a second chance. From the innocence of a church sanctuary where a girl is wrongly accused of a shameful pregnancy in the title story to the concluding experience of "Aunt Carrie," an incident of incest told in a nursing home, the stories always hold a surprise. Dove's global version of Edgar Lee Masters's *Spoon River Anthology*, a collection of portraits, moves from the confinement of a small town into the roaring realm of a motorcycle gang. The "Zulus" soaring "on the dark edges of adventure and superstition . . . "had been to all these places which belched along the glittery soiled neckline of North America" (10). "The Spray Paint King," set in Germany, is "an intriguing journey into the mind of a racially and sexually confused German 'war baby' who spray paints white buildings" (Wade-Gayles 115). In the end the Spray Paint King, who is the narrator, resumes his ars poetica: "I put the stain back on the wall—no outraged slogan, no incoherent declaration of love, but a gesture both graceful and treacherous, a free fall ending in disaster—among the urgent scrawls of history, a mere flick of the wrist" (*FS* 22). "The Second-Hand Man" shares an American background with the other story dealing with male-female relationships. "Damon and Vandalia" explores a difficult love triangle, whereas "The Vibraphone" traces the past of a successful musician from an

Italian perspective. A homeless woman in an American shopping mall, "Zabriah," redefines cultural space most successfully.

Several of these apprenticeship stories, especially "Second-Hand Man," "Damon and Vandalia," and "Aunt Carrie," are further developed in the Bildungsroman *Through the Ivory Gate*, "a place that exists in order to be moved through; . . . a passage, a transient space," as Dove states. In a nutshell, *IG* is a lyrical novel that correlates the needs of a young girl's growing up with the child's need for surrogate artistic mothering. Virginia King, a gifted young African American, returns as "artist-in-residence" to an elementary school in her hometown of Akron, Ohio. Her homecoming recalls a series of painful memories: early experiences with racial prejudice, an unhappy love, a strict community and family life, unexplained tensions between her parents, a sudden move to Phoenix, Arizona, coupled with Aunt Carrie's dark secret, which she begins to discover. Virginia King's sweeping inner and outer journey as a puppeteer from Akron, Ohio, to Phoenix, Arizona, to New York and back to Akron, yet with Oberlin as her way out, will be discussed in depth in Chapter 4. Interesting at this point is the change of directions in the family's journeys. Whereas Thomas and Beulah moved vertically from South to North and back, two generations later Virginia King moves horizontally East-West-East-West.

Chronologically, *Grace Notes* follows *FS* but precedes *IG*. *GN*, whose ornaments heighten the basic melody of life, is linked to *TB* and *M* not only as their thematic expansion—more intimate ("Pastoral"), more cosmic ("Ozone"), and lighter—but also through Beulah's presence. "Summit Beach, 1921," the prologue, resurrects her unnamed as her Papa's golden girl. The year 1921, we know from *TB*'s chronology, was the year of Thomas's arrival in Akron. Beulah, who "could wait, she was gold" for the right man while others danced on the Negro beach, is retrospectively shown as a young woman. Ready to explore her own life, she presides over five sections of various stages of growth in *GN*. The reluctant dancer who "refused / to cut the wing, though she let the boys / bring her sassafras tea and drank it down / neat as a dropped hankie" is portrayed as an imaginative girl already before she met Thomas's smile like "music skittering up her calf / like a chuckle" (*GN* 3). She could eventually turn into the hankie emblematic of her father and fly away as she had tried to earlier while stepping off "the tin roof into blue, / with her parasol and invisible wings" (*GN* 3). Is the cycle of hope and disillusion from *TB* reiteration? No, the poem "Crab-Boil (Ft. Myers, 1962)" features a much more confident voice that decides what to believe and what not to believe.

Part I, "largely a 'remembrance' of the 'buckeye state'" (Baker 1990: 575), sets out with peaceful intimate moments of growing up and into a family and town ("Silos," "Quaker Oats," "Fifth Grade Autobiography," "Flash Cards"). Both epigraphs of part II prepare for a world of experience after the fall; the second, by Hélène Cixous, reads: "To inhabit was the most natural joy when I was still living inside; all was garden and I had not lost the way in." The first poem, "Mississippi," indeed takes a biblical stance: "In the beginning was the dark / moan and creak."[18] The avowal of guilt (over a friend's death in "Mississippi") and of mortality ("Your Death," "The Wake") introduces the aftermath of the forbidden fruit followed by the wastelands of "Watching *Last Year at Marienbad* at Roger Haggerty's House in Auburn, Alabama" ("What / a shabby monstrosity spring / actually is!") and of "Dog Days, Jerusalem" ("Exactly at six every evening I go / into the garden to wait for rain"). The series of places in part II, from Mississippi to Auburn, Alabama; Jerusalem; and back to Manhattan, act as "memorials for the ended life and poetical grief at the section's close" (Baker 1990: 576). In part III, however, fertility and a frame of home and homecoming in the first and last poems ("The Other Side of the House," "Backyard, 6 A.M.") provide the setting as if to turn a homeplace for the erring and dying human beings of part II into a womb. Femininity indeed is revealed and fulfilled in the motherhood poems "Pastoral," "The Breathing, the Endless News," "After Reading 'Mickey in the Night Kitchen' for the Third Time before Bed," and "Genetic Expedition." Without false sentimentality or shame, we participate in the intimate moments of breastfeeding and explore with the "cream child" of a white father the vagina of a black mother and discover afresh with the three year old: "We are rosy and the rosiness is within us." The childish hours of sexual enlightenment abruptly grow from the physical and psychic intimacy into the supra-personal. Motherhood past, part IV moves on to a different kind of knowledge. "I know the dark delight of being strange, / The penalty of difference in the crowd, / The loneliness of wisdom among fools." Claude McKay's epigraph leads us to a world of artistic and academic learning, "The freedom of fine cages!" (GN 47), ending "In a Neutral City." In between lie stretches of cultural self-assertion ("Ars Poetica," "Stitches," "Medusa") and a critique on academia ("Arrow"), dry museum space ("In the Museum"), and classical allusions ("And Counting"). In her finest wit and irony Dove probes herself in these lines written in Bellagio, Italy: "I came here / to write, knock a few poems off the ledger / of accounts payable—only to discover / pasta put me under just as neatly as sambuca / would catapult me into telepathic communication" (GN 53). Section V of GN, the ultimate wisdom, is devoted to the castaways and lost in society, the "Saints" also addressed in "Lint": "What to do with this noise / and persistent lint, / the larder filled past caring? / How good to revolve / on the edge of a system— / small, unimaginable, cold" (GN 68). Genie, "a man born too late for / *Ain't-that-a-shame*" (GN 61) teams up with Billie Holiday in "Canary": "Fact is, the invention of women under siege / has been to sharpen love in the service of myth. / If you can't be free, be a mystery" (GN 64). The collective of "The Island Women of Paris" ("better / not look an island woman in the eye— / unless you like feeling unnecessary" [GN 65]) is compared with a lonely crying woman in "A l'Opéra" (GN 66). African-American adolescence in the beginning ends in the dark demonic sides of life containing differing skin colors, ages, and death, a theme carried into the Middle Eastern and Jewish worlds of "The Royal Workshops," "On the Road to Damascus," and "Old Folk's Home, Jerusalem," as if Dove wanted to overcome "the current impasse in black-Jewish relations" (West 1993: 109) and remind the opposed Christians and Muslims of their mutual becoming, being, and vanishing into nothing: for they all labor in the "Royal Workshops," the king's dye-house. Offering ways of resistance and coping with wounds—from the initial "scar on [Beulah's] knee" to "Stitches" (GN 51) and the resilience of "The Island Women of Paris"—these lines fade out in untranscendable surrender. In view of the great leveler, death, color no longer matters, and "Old Folk's Home, Jerusalem," the final poem in *GN*, fades out laconically: "Everyone waiting here was once in love."

"And the title of my verse drama, *The Darker Face of the Earth*, finally locates us in the beyond, since to see the face of the earth implies a distance, an estrangement, from our world" (*PW* 1995: 15–16). Thus Rita Dove introduces her Greek myth verse play, continued, in the opposite direction, in *Mother Love*. The story of Persephone's abduction into the underworld by Hades and her mother Demeter's painful loss and consent to her biannual return to the upperworld, as well as the Oedipal conflict transposed to a southern plantation in *DF*, will be dealt with in Chapter 5.

THEORETICAL CONCEPTS OF CULTURAL SPACE

Rita Dove's "poetic consciousness of occupied space—of the space we inhabit, of the shape of thought and the pressure of absence" (*PW* 15) was inspired if not instigated by Gaston Bachelard's *The Poetics of Space*,[19] a book Dove considers exemplary. One sentence stayed with her: "The houses that were lost forever continue to live in us" (*PW* 15). She returns to Bachelard in her second laureate address "A Handful of Inwardness—the world in the poet":

> Words—I often imagine this—are little houses, each with its cellar and garret. Commonsense lives on the ground floor, always ready to engage in "foreign commerce," on the same level as the others, as the passers-by, who are never dreamers. To go upstairs in the word house, is to withdraw, step by step; while to go down to the cellar is to dream, it is losing oneself in the distant corridors of an obscure etymology, looking for treasures that cannot be found in words. To mount and descend in the words themselves—this is a poet's life. To mount too high or descend too low, is allowed in the case of poets, who bring earth and sky together. (Bachelard 147; *PW*: 18, 45f)

Dove's mapping of interior and exterior space calls for an extension of Bachelard's primordial categories of "1: The House. From Cellar to Garret. The Significance of the Hut; 2: House and Universe;[20] 3: Drawers, Chests and Wardrobes; 4: Nests; 5: Shells; 6: Corners; 7: Miniature; 8: Intimate Immensity; 9: The Dialectics of Outside and Inside; 10: The Phenomenology of Roundness." Her own inventory of inhabitable space in *PW* takes up the significance of the dynamics of inside v. outside (*PW* 19) and comprises back-, front-, and side-yards (*PW* 19–23); back doors and screen door (*PW* 24); front-doors (*PW* 25); space atmospherically changed by bad news, fear, and death (*PW* 25–26); or the state of being in two places at once and not there at all (*PW* 24). She adds kitchens (*PW* 27), porches (*PW* 28), stoops (*PW* 29), as well as the poet laureate's office (*PW* 33f). The predominance of interiors shown on American TV screens, which she discusses in her second laureate lecture (*PW* 38), leads her to embrace Ludwig Wittgenstein's more inclusive first precept of his *Tractatus*

Logico-Philosophicus (1922) as an epigraph: "The world is everything that is the case" (*PW* 40, 43), so that the title of her second lecture, borrowed from Rainer Maria Rilke's line "A Handful of Inwardness," goes hand in hand with her "Stepping Out" into the world (*PW* 51). These concepts, developed to systematize and analyze parts of her poetry as well as the work of others,[21] need to be expanded and regrouped in view of her entire work. The following divisions and subdivisions drawn from her oeuvre suggest only definable, physically inhabitable, traversable space, although opposites such as open-closed, private-public, near-distant, above-below, one's own-foreign, past-present, here-there, allowed-forbidden are always already inscribed. The subsequent table is the cultural topology inherent in Dove's worldmaking[22] as a perceptive process.

1. Physical Space (receptacles, containers, confinements, enclosures)

   —house, cellar, upstairs, kitchen, dinner table, library, solarium, bedroom, bathroom, bathtub, window, (back) door, screen, threshold, stoop, porch, patio, garden, front-, side-, backyard, lawn, street, lookout, street, road, park, bulrush, swamp, desert, stone
   —neighborhood, small town, ghost town, (neutral) city, church, palace, classroom, office, workplace, workshop, nursing home, artist's studio, museum, concert hall, cinema, restaurant, shop, shopping mall
   —riverboat, car, cage, zeppelin, factory, silos, pithos
   —world (specified cities, countries, continents), sky, cosmic space, underworld
   —local, national, international, transnational worlds

2. Borders, Boundaries[23]

   —dividing line
   —area of contact/conflict
   —unilateral: traversable only in one direction
   —brink or edge
   —threshold

3. Movements

   —journeys, quests
   —sightseeing
   —travelogue
   —flight
   —flying
   —water/liquefaction
   —routes (instead of roots)

Before I move on toward the significance, that is, the psychotopology, of these spaces in Chapter 2, Gaston Bachelard's works must be seen in a broader context. *La Poétique de l'espace* (1957) and *La Poétique de la rêverie* (1960), published toward the end of his career, reflect his wish to liberate himself from the philosophy of science as well as from a psychoanalytic or psychologic predetermination of the poetic image.[24] Rather than being laden with conceptual manipulation, the poetic image should belong to a sphere of *pure sublimation*, far from regulated experience but close to an unmediated creative domain where space is primary. Dove's artistic intention seems in tune with Bachelard, who declares:

> the attempt to attribute antecedents to an image, when we are in the very existence of the image, is a sign of inveterate psychologism. On the contrary, let us take the poetic image in its being. For the poetic consciousness is so wholly absorbed by the image that appears on the language, above customary language. (1994: xxix)

Bachelard is well aware that the immediate message of a poetic image does not lie in its measurable geometry alone. On the contrary, "It is often this *inner immensity* that gives . . . real meaning to certain expressions concerning the visible world" (185). The *immensity of the forest*, as his example goes, has less to do with geographical information than with a body of impressions, images of the mind, reaching deeper into a limitless world.

Dove "stumbled across" Bachelard as an "anxious and quite Romantic (with a capital R!) graduate student" (*PW* 15). Does the mature poet relativize her youthful enthusiasm as essentialist positivism? And if so, why? *The Poetics of Space* is deliberately modest in compass, focusing on the anthro-cosmology of the house, a western concept, I argue, which precludes not only apartments but also especially nomadic forms, the tent, the igloo, and the caravan, from being considered home. Yet out of the ur-cell of domesticity, out of universally shared concepts such as "house," "hut," "nest," "shell," "corner," "miniature," "intimate immensity," "outside vs. inside," "roundness," grows an understanding of the universe, of an intimacy and immensity also prevalent in Dove's boundary-crossing work, moored in her poet's cabin adjacent to her home. Bachelard's humanism connects with the poet's wish of inclusion. He reads images afresh, without preconceived ideas, and is conscious of something other than himself, and this "other" changes him (Jones 1991: 9). This confirms both his humanism as well as his refusal of idealism. Bachelard's love for language, a wide range of evidence found in poetry and fiction (of French, German, and American origin), folktale, (Jungian) psychology, even modern ornithology, make his topology occasionally seem arbitrary, even contrary to a systematic methodology. Yet this crosscultural plenitude and structural leanness, I argue, turn the *The Poetics of Space* into a particularly apt theoretical backdrop for a polyvocal supranational poet who seeks articulation at the threshold of the twenty-first century. "Primer for the Nuclear Age" reads section IV of *M*.

This apparently simplistic yet universal appeal of a poetics of space that shares basic crossculturally known concepts and does not attempt a theorization beyond applicability helps to explain its interdisciplinary influence. Not only in architecture, photography, and film theory[25] but also in the African-American criticism of Houston A. Baker, Jr., Bachelard remains influential. In his 1991 study *Workings of the Spirit. The Poetics of Afro-American Women's Writing* (38f) Baker argues that the inter- and intracultural appeal and aesthetic transfer of *The Poetics of Space* reach "beyond the tangible in search of meta-levels of explanation." Moreover:

> The "poetics of Afro-American women's writing" signals, then, a theory that seeks to arrive at the guiding spirit, or consciousness, of Afro-American women's writing by examining selected imagistic fields. Space, as considered by Bachelard, is an imagistic field. . . . We come to know space through an examination of such images. (61)

The epigraph Dove chose to introduce the second laureate lecture, Ludwig Wittgenstein's "The world is everything that is the case" (PW 43), leads to yet another theoretical source of her world-expanding poetics. Wittgenstein's definition of the notion of contingency indeed summarizes her concerns: 5.634 of his *Tractatus Logico-Philosophicus* reads: "Everything we can describe at all, could as well be different. There is no a priori order of things." And in 6.43 he continues: "If good or bad will changes the world, it can only *change the boundaries* of the world, not the facts; not that which can be expressed by language. In short, the world must become different. It needs, so to speak, to decrease or increase as a whole: *"The boundaries of my language* are the boundaries of my world"* (Wittgenstein 1993: 5.6; italics and translation mine). It is indeed the poet's expanding consciousness and voice that reshape the world for herself and for her audience. Rita Dove's poem "The First Book" (Moyers 1995: 119) confirms: "It's not like it's the end of the world— / just the world as you think / you know it."

A discussion of textual expansion harks back to Lessing's *Laokoön* (1766) and his fundamental distinction between art in space (sculpture, architecture) and art in time (music, literature). Whereas spatial art is three-dimensional, simultaneous, and essentially reversible, temporal art is one-dimensional, progressing, and essentially irreversible. A sculpture or a building may be altered, a tune or a text performed is past. Expansion in terms of language means expansion in terms of time. Yet—and this is the crux—time must be expressed spatially, as syntactic sequence or spatial metaphor. Apparent temporal metaphors from the most temporal of the arts, music, such as pause, interstice, bar, and silence are spatial as well. Thus the single "arrow of time" in the syntactic order contrasts the two- or three-dimensionality of the space created, evoked or alluded to by linguistic means. "The finest specimens of fossilized duration concretized as a result of long sojourn, are to be found in and through space," Bachelard argues in *Poetics of Space* (1994: 9). Such a metaphoric spatialization of time, however, leads to a more static if not petrified quality of time. According to Aleksandrov (in Lotman 1993: 312f), this static textual space could be defined as "the totality of homogeneous objects (phenomena, circumstances, functions, figures, values of variables, etc.) interconnected by relations which are comparable to usual spatial relations (continuity, distance, etc.)." In other words, former events and spaces expressed in language—not simply referred to as, for example, "Once upon a time"—must be recollected through the poetic process of layering where spatial metaphors of time interconnect with metaphorical space. It is interesting to note that in the theory of relativity the three space coordinates are mixed with the one time coordinate when events are being described by observers moving at high speed with respect to eachother.

A semantics of cultural space, however, develops within the two types of coordinates,[26] time and space. Language posits time on the vertical, or diachronic, axis, and space on the horizontal, or synchronic, axis. Whereas the diachronic dimension investigates changes occurring over a period of time in language, mores, or history, the synchronic dimension deals with simultaneous phenomena at a given point, disregarding historical antecedents. Between the vertical axis of pressed and pressing time and the simultaneity of space(s) at a given point the plane of cultural space develops. "The Island Women of Paris" (*GN* 65) illustrates the point. On the vertical axis they are linked with colonial time, while on the horizontal axis they simultaneously represent colonial space within a contemporary Parisian setting. Given these coordinates, the imaginative mind (re)creates the cultural space beyond the visual clues of their "ornamental bearing, turbans haughty as parrots." A comparable cultural space opens up when a text refers back to earlier texts, as in the rewriting of myth in *DF* or *ML*.

Bakhtin (1992: 251), who highlights Lessing's leading role in establishing the temporal character of the literary image, its "chronotopicity"—its "time-space"—presents this intertextual reference as the contrast between a monologic, static (centripetal) and a dialogic, active (centrifugal) force ("being and becoming"). Dialogue to Bakhtin means "communication between simultaneous differences."[27] Roland Barthes (1985) follows Bakhtin when he distinguishes a distributional (horizontal) axis geared toward heterogeneity from an integral (vertical) axis geared toward homogeneity in the generation of meaning in a representatory system. In view of the questions I wish to explore, Edward W. Said and Homi K. Bhabha's twist of the axial reference in postcolonial discourse is of interest. Here we are dealing with a conflict-laden economy, described by Said as a "tension between the synchronic panoptical vision of domination—the demand for identity, stasis—and the counter-pressure of the diachrony of history—change, difference" (Bhabha 1994: 86). "The Island Women of Paris" embodies this twist as well. The women's presence in Paris precisely marks "the counter-pressure of the diachrony of history—change, difference" against "the synchronic panoptical vision of domination" in the capital's representation of grandeur.

A quickened attention given to the status of space and time as a complicity of strategies leads to a concluding look into the past and the future to trace the continuous interest and impact of the subject of relational semantics.

The mental image or representation of art as a distinctly marked space, narrower or wider—a poem's *stanza,* Henry James' *House of Fiction,* William Shakespeare's "all the world's a stage" (*As You Like It* II.4)—has its classical locus in the art of memory. At a banquet given by the Thessalian nobleman Scopas, the poet Simonides of Ceos (c. 556 to 468 B.C.) read a poem, was summoned away, and upon his return found the guests buried under a fallen roof. The corpses were unidentifiable, yet Simonides remembered the seating order. He inferred that for the training of the faculty of memory we "must select places and form mental images of the things . . . and store those images in the places, so that the order of the places will preserve the order of the things, and the images of the things will denote the things themselves" (Frances Yates 1995: 17).

What suggests, even vindicates, a poetics of space at the threshold of the twenty-first century? Michel Foucault offers a striking explanation:

> The great obsession of the nineteenth century was, as we know, history: with its themes of development and suspension, of crisis and cycle, themes of the ever-accumulating past, with its great preponderance of dead men and the menacing glaciation of the world. . . . The present epoch will perhaps be above all the epoch of space. We are in the epoch of simultaneity: we are in the epoch of juxtaposition, the epoch of the near and far, of the side-by-side, of the dispersed. We are at a moment, I believe, when our experience of the world is less that of a long life developing through time than that of a network that connects points and intersects with its own skein. (1986: 22)

As we enter a new century, Foucault's premonitory observations on the emergence of an epoch of space and simultaneity indeed reflect the development of the current digital communication. Though a globalized communicative network seems to restructure physical space—the Internet is said to be fundamentally *antispatial* (Mitchell 1995: 8)—Dove's poetics relates to virtual space in two way. First, the concept of a defined, ascribed, and potentially limited identity is negated in both realms. Whereas the poet seeks to establish a multiple self, with the possibility to exercize or exorcize all personalities, the Internet also eliminates traditional dimensions of civic legibility (Mitchell 10). Virtual space has no *where* telling *who* you are. Geography is no longer destiny. Creating one's own virtual identity or identities and then refashioning the self according to one's needs offers opportunities similar to Rita Dove's poetic enspacements. Second, and even more crucial, the poet's *and* the Internet's imagining new mental or for that matter virtual spaces cannot avoid falling back on spatial metaphors when it comes to expressing their locality or, rather, lack of locality. Brand names such as Windows or Worldwide Web and cyberspace venues like home, garden, or hospital prove the a priori quality of space: the unknown or uncanny can only be portrayed in terms of the known and familiar. Although Mitchell describes the Internet as *antispatial,* he actually relies heavily on spatial metaphors and similes:

> The Net . . . will play as crucial a role in twenty-first-century urbanity as the centrally located, spatially bounded, architecturally celebrated agora did (ac-

cording to Aristotle's *Politics*) in the life of the Greek polis and in prototypical urban diagrams. (Mitchell 8)

That these netscape communities are occurring in disjunctive time and place is interesting to theorists, but in practice the online agora is as natural and familiar as a townhall or classroom meeting. Dove created her own digital agora in April 1994, when she projected poetry into electronic space in hosting and producing the nationally televised one-hour program, shown to elementary school children in thousands of U.S. classrooms, *Shine Up Your Words: A Morning with Rita Dove*. Not only does she create poetic spaces but she also skillfully translates a closeted, hermetic genre into large contemporary rooms.

CULTURAL SPACE "IN THE OLD NEIGHBORHOOD"

Rita Dove's autobiographical signature poem, "In the Old Neighborhood"[28] (*SP* xxii–xxvi), concludes this chapter and provides the transition to the micro-poetics of Chapter 2, which includes a close analysis of the function and meaning of boundaries, movements, and transcultural space beyond. Dove's careful spatial structuring of her home borrows its title from an epigraph by Adrienne Rich, "Shooting Script": *To pull yourself up by your own roots; / to eat the last meal in your own neighborhood.*[29] It precisely enacts the conflict-laden economy, described by Edward Said as a "tension between the synchronic panoptical vision of domination—the demand for identity, stasis—and the counter-pressure of the diachrony of history—change, difference" (1978: 240), and explores, in Gaston Bachelard's plain terms, "the dialectics of outside and inside" (*Poetics of Space*, chap. 9). Both in Heidegger's and Bachelard's writings dwelling still passes for a special, quasi-religious, almost absolute space of thinking and being (Lefebvre 1994: 121).

The "physical topography as well as the spiritual and aesthetical terrain" (*SP* xxi) of the poem—fifteen stanzas of varying length—suggest the intact world the poet elsewhere attributes to the sonnet form (*ML* xi). The poem's position, however, is ambivalent. As a prologue to *Selected Poems*, it marks a formal artistic departure, with creativity seen as spatialization of time, while the subject matter celebrates a homecoming, a simultaneity of disparate events past and present. The poet returns to celebrate her sister's wedding, yet another liminal event between stasis and movement, inside and outside, containment and complicity. As if to counteract the impending transience inherent in this rite of passage, domestic space is clearly assigned to individuals: the mother is worrying and cooking in the kitchen, the matron of honor moves between kitchen and library, the sister is in her bridal apartment, the brother is rummaging upstairs, and the father is out on the lawn consoling his roses. At first glance the spatial rhetoric of gender distinctions is strikingly conservative: male mobility outside, opposed to female stasis and control of knowledge inside. Yet the matron of honor as poet is on the move.

At this point she lingers "indoors, pretending / to read today's paper." Though educated to concentrate, the poet transgresses the linear order with her mind "snared between datelines," a superb image to connote an outside space that, despite the concrete place markers *Santiago,* / *Paris, Dakar,* remains as "unreal as the future / even now." The past, however, closes in like the Chinese box principle: from neighborhood to house, to library, to mind, her memory encompasses an increasingly significant transcendental private space that, marks yet another threshold between two levels of being: one real, one imaginary. At this triple doorsill of binary oppositions, real v. imaginary, past v. future, inside v. outside, we are reminded of Gaston Bachelard's refusal of clearcut demarcations:

> you feel the full significance of this myth of outside and inside in alienation, which is founded on these two terms. Beyond what is expressed in their formal opposition lie alienation and hostility between the two. And so, simple geometrical opposition becomes tinged with aggressivity. Formal opposition is incapable of remaining calm. (1994: 212)

> Outside and inside are both intimate—they are always ready to be reversed, to exchange their hostility. (1994: 217–18)

How does the poet's home-again self, snuggling up to her paper and books in the library and to her mother's chatter in the kitchen, yet ready to depart on her own journey as a writer, express this precarious equilibrium between present and past ("stacked platters high" like layers of memory), inside and outside, the horizontal and the vertical axes? It is her mother's "pressure cooker [that] ticks / *whole again whole again now*" in stanza eight. Like a time bomb ready to explode, the sense of wholeness is so condensed at this moment that it can hardly wait to diffuse into the outside world. Yet this potentially explosive mixture of here *and* there is already invoked by the epigraph. "Shooting Script," "To pull yourself up by your own roots," "last meal," "old neighborhood," all suggest contending forces right from the start: the vertical rootedness from which "shooting" and "pulling up" allows one to (horizontally) leave the stasis of the old place called home. The tension between a move into the unknown and a static simultaneity of well-known spaces is palpable from the beginning ("Raccoons[30] have invaded the crawl space / of my sister's bridal apartment") till the end ("I am back / again, . . . I wrap bones and eggshells / into old newspapers for burning"). A "matron of honor" as well as an observer and chronicler in this rite of passage, the poet symbolizes a choice beyond marriage: not pronouncing "I will," just "nodding *yes,*" she assists her sister but also performs the significant ritual of wrapping "bones and eggshells / into old newspapers." Out of eggshells springs new life; bones are the remains of human existence. Wrapped only in words, old and new, by a journalist or a poet, life is put into perspective and acquires meaning.

The tension between the vertical and horizontal axes reveals another interesting pattern of contending forces. The epigraph's "pull yourself up" is taken on by the "raccoons" of the first stanza, yet in the reverse direction, for they "have invaded the crawl space" from above. Chiefly carnivorous and active largely at night, they threaten the bridal apartment with animalistic appetites. Afraid of the "too ferocious and faggy" raccoons, the landlord "insists they're squirrels / squirrels he'll fight." Like *Alice in Wonderland*, Dove enters her home sliding past a bridal apartment until she lands in the kitchen of her mother's "sudsbath / of worries." Her mother's devotion to detail focuses on a candle that could "accidentally ignite / the reverend's sleeve." And no firebrand should entice or jeopardize the clergy.

The guiding principle of opposites, of inside-outside, upstairs-downstairs, stasis-motion, male-female, old-young, animal-human, married-unmarried, canny-uncanny, and vertical-horizontal—perfectly embodied in the warp and woof of the crossword puzzle in stanza eight.[31]—recalls Bachelard's topoanaly-sis of the house: "A house," he states, "is a privileged entity for a study of the in-timate values of inside space, provided, of course, that we take it in both its unity and its complexity, and endeavor to integrate all the special values in one fundamental value" (Poetics of Space 3). "For our house is our corner of the world. As has often been said, it is our first universe, a real cosmos in every sense of the word" (4).

> A house constitutes a body of images that give mankind proofs or illusions of stability. We are constantly re-imagining its reality: to distinguish all these im-ages would be to describe the soul of the house; it would mean developing a veritable psychology of the house.
>
> To bring order into these images . . . we should consider two principal connecting themes: 1) A house is imagined as a vertical being. It rises upward. It differentiates itself in terms of its verticality. It is one of the appeals to our consciousness of verticality. 2) A house is imagined as a concentrated being. It appeals to our consciousness of centrality. . . . Verticality is ensured by the polarity of cellar and attic . . . they open up two different perspectives for a phenomenology of the imagination. (*Poetics of Space* 17)

The horizontal dimension comes into perspective in stanza three, where the poet envisions her father outdoors. Unlike Alice Walker (*In Search of our Moth-ers' Gardens*), Dove persistently searches her father's garden (*SP* 105, 106, 115f). Hers is a double identification: both with the nurturing female realm and the male outside world. Her poetic voice assumes an androgynous power as she moves, in Jacques Lacan's terms, from the imaginary into the symbolic order, from the traditionally female object level into the male dominated subject posi-tion. Thus she shares in and reformulates the "law of the father," understood as any absolute self-determining power.[32] The poet's father too is androgynous in pursuing a traditionally female role. While the women are inside he "prefers a more / reticent glory. He consoles / his roses—dusts them / with fungicide, spades in / fortified earth." In brandishing "color / over the neighborhood, year after year producing / lovelier mutants: these / bruised petticoats, for instance, / or this sudden teacup / blazing empty, its rim / a drunken red smear," father performs a double duty. While the landlord refuses to fight the carnivorous rac-coons, he responds to lice and worms with fungicide, thus consoling his ersatz-daughters outside, his roses not yet plucked, as he perceives their beauty threatened by the ancient image of phallic penetration. Powerless in regard to his daughters, he fortifies his virility outdoors as he engenders and spreads "lovelier mutants" into a multicolored neighborhood. [33]

Flowers—tea roses, a few carnations, baby's breath, and maybe ferns— reappear in the final stanza, no longer wildly dispersed but bunched into a bridal bouquet. Such is the frame of nature, animal and floral, in a poem signifying growth on hold. The title is and is not what the reader expects: "In the Old Neighborhood" presents a real home but represents a spatial metaphor of compressed and unfolding layers of imaginary time, the cultural inner space of Dove's own Bildungsroman in a nutshell. Her casual reading of today's paper in stanzas four and five leads to a different kind of ferocious appetite, that of a serious reader put into relief by the threefold anaphoric "I": "I skip to the daily horoscope. / I've read every book in this house, / I know which shelf to go to / to taste crumbling saltines . . . and the gritty slick of sardines / silted bones of no consequence / disintegrating on the tongue." This is the stuff that *Romeo and Juliet*'s dreams are made of, with their salty tears signifying nothing. The voracious artist as a young girl has a characteristic snack for every piece of literature, a compressed edible timespace traceable as an ironic comment and material imprint between pages:

> stuffed green olives
> for a premature attempt at *The Iliad.*
> Candy buttons went with Brenda Starr, [34]
> Bazooka bubble gum with the Justice
> League of America. Fig Newtons
> and *King Lear,* bitter lemon as well
> for Othello . . .
> But Macbeth demanded dry bread.

Rita Dove's spiritual and material appetite feeds the ur-cell of significant cultural space. While she retreats into her sanctuary her brother is looking for something upstairs. At the end of her search, also his "rummaging's stopped. Well, / he's found it, whatever it was." Rita's memory of their rivalry is activated: "*Bee vomit, he said once, / that's all honey is,*" countered by his sister 's dwelling on the anatomy of a strawberry in return: "each select seed / chose to breed in darkness, / the stomach's cauldron / brewing a host of vines / trained to climb and snap / a windpipe shut." What first appears to be but a competitive bantering is linked to personal and literary growth: "Cauldron" harks back to the drama last mentioned: *Macbeth.* Out of vomit well digested, out of darkness well groomed, nature's raw material emerges into the becoming-space of life and art.

Leaving the sanctuaries of the library and mother's kitchen behind, the poet joins the male world of danger and casualties outside. More remote layers of memory reveal two instances of growth from innocence to experience (stanza nine f). First, father had his two children put to a test of Eagle Scout toughness by having them sleep in a tent outside. While brother succeeds with bravado, sister keeps weeping. An even deeper buried memory returns "when Dad switched on / the attic fan" and a bird was caught in the blades. Books are also dropped when a lawn mower chops up a pebbly toad. Eros and thanatos, roots and routes, as the epigraph suggests, are part of growing close and apart. Thus Dove's homecoming includes comforting and uncanny memories and becomes an expressive prelude for the *Selected Poems*. Oscillating between "home" and "exile," they will explore what is already laid out "In the Old Neighborhood." This co-dependency between the notions of inside and outside often entails a border journey into the memory and imagination that negotiates between old and new, past and present, self and other, safety and danger—an idea put forward by Edward W. Said in his 1984 essay "Mind of Winter: Reflections on Life in Exile":

> In a secular and contingent world, homes are always provisional. Borders and barriers which enclose us within the safety of familiar territory, can also become prisons, and are often defended beyond reason or necessity. Exiles cross borders, break barriers of thought and experience. (54)

Yet "In the Old Neighborhood" reflects not only Bachelard's and Said's concepts of the house as a real and virtual homeplace for human experience. The poem also evokes the Bakhtinian concept of the *chronotope*, literally the "time space" (1981: 84) that determines our conditions of experience by changing visions of distance and proximity in an "intrinsic connectedness of temporal and spatial relationships": public and private, stasis and motion, dreams and disillusions. In short, "In the Old Neighborhood" *is* the shooting script for Dove's future transcultural enspacements moored in her homeplace. Her autobiographical exploration of major impulses in her childhood shows how she pulled herself up by her own roots and became herself.

The poetics that I have proposed so far entail but the single gesture of looking at Dove's work from the specific angle of space. Space, as the titles of her works and her reference to Gaston Bachelard's *Poetics of Space* in PW reflect, has always played an important role in her writing. Space and time are a priori concepts of life and art. You cannot ignore space. If you did, you would have to ignore yourself, which precludes a self to think space. We do not get the notion of space and time from looking at things. Apart from measurements in meters and minutes, time and space are subjective forms of intuition and negotiation. Space is, in the Kantian sense, an undivided magnitude; time has no shape of its own and must be expressed by analogies and metaphors drawn from space. Space as a mental image has long informed the art of memory. The most recent development in digital communication, though said to be antispatial, nonetheless relies on spatial metaphors in its terminology.

Cultural space, as distinguished from place and location, is a space that has been seized upon and transmuted by imagination, knowledge, or experience. How radically the power of the imagination paired with the power of reasoning is capable of reshaping cultural space is shown in Dove's poem "Geometry." Her crosscultural syncretism in "The Island Women of Paris" suggested the use of the term multicultural. Cultural, however, is retained as the more inclusive and less restricted generic term, an independent variable.

The macro-poetics of space, defined as the sequence of sections within a single work, as well as the development of themes and strategies of space throughout Dove's work, has led to a closer analysis of those books that will not be treated as a whole in separate chapters: *YH, M, GN*. In order to assess a topology of Dove's worldmaking, I divided inhabitable, traversable space into physical space, borders, boundaries, movements, and cultural space by drawing and enlarging on the categories developed by Bachelard in *Poetics of Space*.

Dove's autobiographical signature poem "In the Old Neighborhood," less abstract than "Geometry" but nonetheless addressing house-expanding strategies, yields a range of poetic enspacements that cannot be separated from the level of significance, except for didactic purposes. We must now move on to an in-depth analysis of the micro-poetics of cultural space, which, according to Freud, is "most likely the only place deserving the uncanny name of home."

T W O

RITA DOVE'S MICRO-POETICS
OF SPACE

*Space that has been seized upon by the imagination cannot remain
indifferent space.*

> Gaston Bachelard,
> *The Poetics of Space*

Our interest in lieux de mémoire *where memory crystallizes and
secretes itself has occurred at a particular historical moment, a turning
point where consciousness of a break with the past is bound up with the
sense that memory has been torn—but torn in such a way as to pose the
problem of the embodiment of memory in certain sites where a sense of
historical continuity persists.*

> Pierre Nora, "Between Memory and History:
> *Les Lieux de Mémoire"*

Crossing Color examines cultural space, a single subject that embraces three levels: first, it focuses on *borders* and *boundaries* that decide inclusion and exclusion; second, it explores *movement;* and third, it concentrates on the nature of
cultural space. We best picture these levels as concentric circles. To be at the center of meaningful cultural space then is to be, simultaneously, at the center of
all three,[1] "for our house is our corner of the world" (Bachelard 1994: 4).

Nonetheless, it is useful to discuss a micro-poetics of space on various levels and from different perspectives, particularly in view of Rita Dove's extraordinary boundary crossing and fusion of cultural realms. The decisive structures
and the process of layering will come alive in representative poems.[2] How does
she envision a psychotopology of transcultural enspacements? How does she
renegotiate spatiotemporal relations in the history and geography she revises to
illuminate a hybrid cultural ground at the century's edge? How does she recreate the past—in the Ghanaian notion of *sankofa* which roughly translates as
"return to the source and fetch"[3]—while concurrently envisioning the future?

Who are her dramatis personae, and what are their intentions in "crossing borders"? How do these intentions in turn affect the barriers they are inclined to break?

BORDERS, BOUNDARIES

In a world of increasing global communication and movement, borders and boundaries seem to lose their impact as dividers. Yet in the segregated world in the aftermath of slavery, outer and inner, that is, internalized boundaries still loom large as *dividing line; area of contact and conflict; unilateral division, or brink; edge;* and *threshold.* In the following I shall rely on Fritz Gysin's principles of boundary distinction, which he developed particularly in view of recent African-American writing.[4]

Dove "does not believe in boundaries," yet borders and barriers prevail in various ways in her work. They mark the periphery of the possible and discuss the problematic of inside and outside, of the framer and the framed. Boundaries are there for her to revise, overcome, or enliven with new meaning. The act of crossing boundaries thus accrues poetic, even political, power. In his 1984 essay "Mind of Winter: Reflections on Life in Exile," Edward Said straddles the contrasting, at times contradictory, notions of belonging and exile, of being here and there, in a mind-opening twist:

> In a secular and contingent world, homes are always provisional. Borders and barriers which enclose us within the safety of familiar territory can also become prisons, and are often defended beyond reason, or necessity. Exiles cross borders, break barriers of thought and experience. (54)

In "Building Dwelling Thinking," Martin Heidegger also specifies and enlarges the boundary's function as a starting point:

> A boundary is not that at which something stops but as the Greeks recognized, the boundary is that from which something *begins its essential unfolding.* That is why the concept is that of *Horismos,* that is the horizon, the boundary. (1977: 332)

The experience of displacement, of living in at least two different worlds and seeing things with double vision, consistently informs Dove's imagination. Rather than the political division, however, it is the ethnic boundary, that is, the mental, cultural, social, moral, aesthetic, and not necessarily territorial boundary-constructing processes that brand Dove's work most.[5] Janus-faced, these processes are both markers of identity and belonging and the reverse, exclusion of the other. Let us first examine the boundary as *dividing line* that connotes "stranded," "confined," "fossilized," "a kind of wall put up between two contiguous realms, cultures, forms of behavior" that it separates or is supposed to keep apart. "Crab-Boil *(Ft. Myers, 1962)*" in *GN* (13) illustrates the point:

Why do I remember the sky
above the forbidden beach,
why only blue and the scratch,
shell on tin, of their distress?
The rest

imagination supplies:
bucket and angry pink beseeching
claws. **Why** does Aunt Helen
laugh before saying "Look at that—

a bunch of niggers, not
a-one get out 'fore the others pull him
back." **I don't believe** her—

just as **I don't believe** *they* won't come
and chase us back to the colored-only shore
crisp with litter and broken glass.

"When do we **kill them**?"
"**Kill 'em**? Hell, the water does *that*.
They don't feel a thing . . . no nervous system."

I decide to believe this: **I'm hungry.**
Dismantled, they're merely exotic,
a blushing meat. After all, she *has*
grown old in the South. If
we're kicked out now, **I'm ready.** (emphasis mine)

The parenthetical information in the title, *(Ft. Myers, 1962)*, immediately puts a private picnic into historical perspective. The place of action is a "forbidden beach" in the South (Florida).[6] The time, one year before the March on Washington, breathes with the Civil Rights Movement's heightened black consciousness. The first stanza's elemental question in variation—"Why do I remember the sky / . . . why only blue and the scratch, / . . . of their distress?"— ushers in the dream of boundless freedom beyond or, rather, above lethal confinement. The image of the crabs scratching their shells against their tin prison instantly evokes the calamity of the Middle Passage during which slaves were suffering from comparably stifling circumstances. The ship's hull and the pot's enclosure equally contain despair and destruction.[7]

At once the leisurely horizontal expansion of the beach turns upright into a vertical fight for survival for those crabs that seek to escape the boiling pot. After this strong recollection from childhood, "The rest / imagination supplies." A number of emphasized reiterations at decisive spots reflects the dualities that hound the child, who must find a way between competing worlds, opinions, and impulses: children versus adult, animal versus human, black versus white, black versus black, exclusion versus inclusion, fear fighting courage, innocence becoming experience. "Why . . . why . . . Why?"; "I don't believe . . . I don't believe"; "I decide to believe this"; "kill them? / Kill 'em?"; "I'm hungry . . . I'm ready" formally mirror the speaker's growing confrontation with a range of complex realities. This includes Aunt Helen, who denigrates her own race in comparing the crabs to "A bunch of niggers, not / a-one get out 'fore the others pull him / back."

It is this internalized black self-deprecation, this self-censuring confinement of pulling someone down who seeks escape that the young speaker rejects: "I don't believe her— / just as I don't believe *they* won't come / and chase us back to the colored-only shore / crisp with litter and broken glass," a ghetto of shattered identities and potential injuries. The young persona is as certain in refusing internal limitations as she is about the impending danger of being evicted from the "whites-only" beach. In a flash of self-affirmation, however, the speaker no longer believes what Aunt Helen says about blacks or about whites but seeks to accelerate matters: "When do we kill them?" Aunt Helen's self-deceiving answer, "Hell, the water does *that*. / They don't feel a thing . . . no nervous system" again links the crabs to black people. In the age of scientific racism African Americans, too, were said to feel no pain. Aunt Helen's insensitivity, then, is also a product of black self-hatred due to white racism.

The final stanza—the crabs are done, the mind is made up—features a secure self who decides "to believe this: I'm hungry. / Dismantled, they are merely exotic, / a blushing meat." The poet extends the image of "light meat beneath" to two other poems in *GN*, her own injured skin in "Stitches" (51)—"So I *am* white underneath"—and "After Reading 'Mickey in the Night Kitchen' for the Third Time before Bed" (41), when she and her three-year-old daughter inspect each other's vaginas only to find *"We're pink!"* "Crab-Boil" demystifies all that has come to symbolize black self-hatred, white oppression, and, more broadly, all of the fears of entrapment the speaker learns to reject (Costello 1991: 435). This leads to a deeper understanding of Aunt Helen's callousness—"After all, she *has* / grown old in the South"—where she internalizes white attitudes about blacks to the point of developing a hard-boiled courage of trespassing white space. Her readiness to endure ultimately colors the young speaker's growing self-confidence: "If / we're kicked out now, I'm ready." She is ready to fight back, endure, twist, reinvent, overcome limitations; the reader's imagination and the speaker's future will provide the answers. Dove's ambiguously graceful and witty play on inner and outer divisions presents an individuated speaker now apt and ready "to cross a few lines of her own and laugh off the lurking fear always present" (Vendler 1993: 31).

"Elevator Man, 1949" (Moyers 1995: 122–23) is a monument, or *lieu de mémoire* (Pierre Nora), to the racial discrimination endured by Dove's father, a pain he translated into music.

> *Not a cage but an organ*:
> if he thought about it, he'd go insane.
> Yes, if he thought about it
> *philosophically*,
> he was a bubble of bad air
> in a closed system.

He sleeps on his feet
until the bosses enter from the paths
of Research and Administration—
the same white classmates
he had helped through Organic Chemistry.
A year ago they got him a transfer
from assembly line to Corporate Headquarters,
a "kindness" he repaid

by letting out all the stops,
jostling them up and down
the scale of his bitterness
until they emerge queasy, rubbing
the backs of their necks,
feeling absolved and somehow
in need of a drink. *The secret*

he thinks to himself, *is not*
in the pipe but
the slender breath of the piper.

The elevator man does not suffer, like Aunt Helen does, from describing or feeling internalized self-hatred. With music he transcends his literal and symbolic
enclosure in a moving cage that contains his self-image as a "bubble of bad air
in a closed system," which cannot interact and inhale life-sustaining oxygen
across the racial barrier. There he plays "the scale of his bitterness" like an
"organ" and turns "bad air" into music. The philosopher, superior student of
organic chemistry, and reader of poetry evokes a Yeatsean tone in reminding
himself and us that "*The secret /* . . . *is not / in the pipe but / the slender breath of*
the piper." He fills his instrument—a "pipe" with buttons and stops—with his
own breath in an inner exile that keeps him alive even while "He sleeps on his
feet." Nonetheless, he jolts his white classmates who made it to the top without
him into consciousness, or into a bit of motion sickness, by "jostling them up
and down / . . . until they emerge queasy, rubbing/the backs of their necks, /
feeling absolved and somehow / in need of a drink."

Turning racial pain into music is also Billie Holiday's art of survival in "Canary" (GN 64). Her "burned voice / had as many shadows as lights." . . . Fact
is, the invention of women under siege / has been to sharpen love in the service
of myth." Her secret: "If you can't be free, be a mystery." For Dove, Holiday embodies "the notion of the singing bird in a cage," a woman who did not play up
to the myth of what women were supposed to be: delicate, elegant, submissive.
"Holiday" demanded her pedestal while showing that she was tough, too"
(Moyers 1995: 114).

In Moyer's interview Dove also illuminates her father's "mystery," which
he kept from his family for many years:

He had been one of the top students in his graduating class—he had a master's degree in chemistry—and all of his classmates got jobs as chemists with
the tire and rubber industry in Akron, but he was hired as an elevator opera-

tor. So for years while he was raising his budding family he was ferrying his former classmates up and down on this elevator. One of his professors from the university kept bugging the administration at Goodyear: "This is absurd. You have this incredible student employed as an elevator operator!" Finally my father became the first black chemist in the entire rubber industry.

But I knew nothing of all that until I was in college. When I thought that my father was insisting too much that we do it on our own, my mother would sometimes say, "Your father really means best for you. He knows what it's like. Just trust me on this." (122)

Dove pursues and questions borders and boundaries in a range of poems beyond the color line. "The Fish in the Stone" (*SP* 69) opens *M* and in a more general sense testifies to Dove's and Bachelard's "dialectics of outside and inside" (1994: 211–31).

The fish in the stone
would like to fall
back into the sea.

He is weary
of analysis, the small
predictable truths.
He is weary of waiting
in the open,
his profile stamped
by a white light.

In the ocean the silence
moves and moves

and so much is unnecessary!
Patient, **he drifts**
until the moment comes
to cast his
skeletal blossom.

The fish in the stone
knows to fail is
to do the living
a favor.

He knows why the ant
engineers a gangster's
funeral, garish
and perfectly amber.
He knows why the scientist
in secret delight
strokes the fern's
voluptuous braille. (emphasis mine)

This fossilized "Fish in the Stone" is entrapped not in color but in time.[8] Yet right at the beginning of the collection of poems entitled *M*, the petrified animal—emblematic for the frozen and framed artifacts, the still lifes on display—"is weary / of analysis, the small / predictable truths" that come from curators, visitors, critics, or scientists. "He is weary of waiting / in the open, / his profile stamped / by a white light." However, even from this most rigid and paradoxical state of enclosure by exposure—invisibility under scrutiny is an experience not unknown to African Americans—he declares his independence through action. He "would like to fall / back into the sea." "In the ocean . . . he drifts/until the moment comes / to cast his / skeletal blossom." With his ossification liquefied, "the small predictable truths" give way to a deeper knowledge of life and himself. His failure, he knows, does "the living / a favor." He is available for viewing: an object of beauty and scientific scrutiny as well as an example of life-in-death survival. This is why "He also knows" about the fate of the ant caught in amber. "He knows" why the scientist, with eroticized gaze and fingers, "strokes the fern's / voluptuous braille" back to a life of its own.

Michel Foucault argues that the fossil, with its mixed animal and mineral nature, is the privileged object of resemblance required by the historian of the continuum. "The fossil is what permits resemblances to subsist through all the deviations traversed by nature; it functions as a distant and approximative form of identity" (1994: 156–57). Fossils, I agree, represent time enshrined in space. But whereas for Foucault the antidote against the fossil is the monster "who ensures the emergence of difference" (156), Dove's counteracting power of mutual change is no subversive creature attacking from the outside but a force within the fossil, an earlier state of life. All it has to do is to return to its natural habitat. To be in process for Dove is not to be threatened by monsters but to lose any overdetermined identity and to disappear from sight by falling back into the sea. Moving from Foucault's line of argument in *The Order of Things* to Kirsten Holst Petersen and Anna Rutherford's "Fossil and Psyche," therefore, seems like moving from "small / predictable truths" to knowledge itself.

> Fossils like "living" beings contain restrictive as well as explosive rooms or spaces. The fossil value of our human and non-human antecedents can either act as positive forces or can become prejudices, hideous biases, leading to implacable animism. So in fact one half of our "fossil value" is constantly combating the other half. (1995: 188).

Holst Petersen and Rutherford's investigation of "architectonic fossil spaces" in Wilson Harris[9] proves particularly meaningful in view of Dove, as this Caribbean author also achieves a vivid syncretism of worlds following the notion of *sankofa*, that is, by "returning to the source and fetch." If one becomes aware of how ambivalent fossils are, new possibilities of transformation emerge even out of deadlock rigidity. This process generates Harris's "architectonic," a procedure that reflects profound creativity in reconstructing the world. Whenever patterns of "rest" begin to assume an idolatrous function of "changelessness," Harris suggests that the institutions and models at stake begin to hide from the body politic itself "creative" or "digestive" response to problems or conflicts ("Fossil and Psyche," 188).

Despite the fish's regained fluidity turned knowledge at last, "The Fish in the Stone" closes with a scientist's erotic and aesthetic scrutiny of a primeval fern leaf's "voluptuous braille." Any moment of understanding, the final stanza asserts, requires the arrest of flux, the fixing of movement in some conceptual image or snapshot. The poem advocates both liquefaction and formal containment; that is, borders and boundaries cannot and should not be thoughtlessly discarded. Instead, they need to be constantly examined and revalued in order to remain meaningful creative measures of support and understanding.

"Often it is from the very fact of concentration in the most restricted intimate space," Bachelard concludes, "that the dialectics of inside and outside draws its strength" (1994: 229). Between the two states Bachelard's and Dove's focus is clearly on "dialectics," no matter how rigid the divisions and barriers appear to be.

Let us move on to borders and boundaries as *areas of contact and conflict.* This second form, Fritz Gysin (ibid.) asserts, is

> closer to the actual cultural situation; it represents a zone of ethnic interaction and is characterized by cultural clash, superimposition, cross-fertilization, fusion, etc. The most concrete example is the territorial border, i.e. a line or band on a horizontal plane, where citizens of adjoining nations exchange or oppose customs or ideas. Minority existence often entails the experience of this kind of boundary. (unpublished lecture, 1994, ms. p. 23)

Placed near the closing of *TB* (*SP* 198–99), "Wingfoot Lake," subtitled (Independence Day, 1964), offers interesting parallels with "Crab-Boil (*Ft. Myers*, 1962)." Both poems feature a picnic on the waterfront (shore and beach), segregation, and a new black consciousness. The poem mentions two events of the previous year, according to the appended chronology (*SP* 203–4): Thomas's death and the March on Washington, which Beulah watched on televison. Beulah, who makes her single entrance into American History in one of her final poems, attends the Goodyear Company picnic, to which her family has "dragged" her, as Thomas had dragged her through the white neighborhoods of the rich in 1940:

> On her 36th birthday, Thomas had shown her
> her first **swimming** pool. It had been
> his favorite color, exactly—just
> so much of it, **the swimmers' white arms** jutting
> into the **chevrons of high society**.
> She had rolled up her window
> and told him to drive on, fast.
>
> Now this *act of mercy:* Four daughters
> dragging her to their husbands' company picnic,
> **white families on one side** and **them
> on the other**, unpacking **the same**
> squeeze bottles of Heinz, **the same**

waxy beef patties and Salem potato chip bags.
So he was dead for the first time
on Fourth of July—ten years ago

had been harder, waiting for something to happen,
and ten years before that, the girls
like young horses eyeing the track.
Last August she stood **alone** for hours
in front of the T.V. set
as **a crow's wing moved** slowly through
the white streets of government.
That **brave swimming**

scared her, like Joanna saying
Mother, we're Afro-Americans now!
What did she know about Africa?
Were there lakes like this one
with a rowboat pushed under the pier?
Or Thomas' Great Mississippi
with its sullen silks? (There was
the Nile but the Nile belonged
to God.) Where she came from
was the past, 12 miles into town
where nobody had locked their back door,
and Goodyear hadn't begun to dream of a park
under the **company symbol, a white foot
sprouting two small wings**. (emphasis mine)

As in "Crab-Boil," tension arises between title and subtitle. Not until the final stanza do we learn that "Wingfoot Lake" is Goodyear's "park / under the company symbol, a white foot / sprouting two small wings." This is the symbol of Mercury, inventor of the lyre, god of thieves and merchants, and guide of the dead souls to Hades. Yet does the swift dominant emblem of white economic supremacy allow and protect the freedom and pursuit of happiness evoked by "Independence Day" rhetoric for everyone? Whose good year is it? From the first symbol of stasis, the swimming pool, to "Wingfoot Lake," both artificial still waters,[10] Beulah, an old woman poised before a period of social unrest and before death, focuses on her life's journey in a series of flashbacks that expand and contract telescopically through space and time ("On her 36th birthday" [1940], "Now this *act of mercy*" [1964], "he was dead for the first time / on Fourth of July" [1963, 1964], "ten years ago // had been harder, waiting for something to happen" [1954], "ten years before that, the girls / like young horses eyeing the track" [1944], "Last August" [1963], "Where she came from / was the past" [before Goodyear's park]).

The main event, the company's Fourth of July picnic, presents a living picture of separate but equal conviviality.[11] Four daughters—in "Compendium," Thomas's disappointment over the lack of a son is visualized in the laconic cluster "Girl girl / girl girl" (*SP* 158)—dragged her to the site where "white families on one side and them / on the other" unpack "the same / squeeze bottles of

Heinz, the same / waxy beef patties and Salem potato chip bags." Whereas the notion of "the same" is epiphorically corroborated, the gap of "difference" is equally highlighted by the cut of the enjambment: whites are "on one side and them / on the other." This "*act of mercy*" is framed by two similarly disturbing experiences of segregation due to race and class as the white wings of Mercury and "the swimmers' white arms jutting / into the chevrons of high society"[12] of the first stanza turn into a black [Jim] "crow's wing" of marchers in Washington in the third. Within three decades the African-American couple's touring a white neighborhood by car grows into a river of African-American activism, moving "through / the white streets of government." Yet that "brave swimming // scared her" as much as Thomas's sightseeing did in 1940 and upsets her far more than the segregated picnic. Her idea of freedom is private: "Where she came from / was the past." The river in Washington for her becomes first "Thomas' Great Mississippi" and then turns into the Nile ("but the Nile belonged / to God"). The roots of "Africa" do not trigger Panafrican longing but the more remote past of her childhood in Rockmart, Georgia, a place away from town "where nobody had locked their back door." This is her idea of social peace. Beulah, the biblical figure who is supposed to lead the masses into the Promised Land, remains aloof from the Civil Rights Movement and tied to her own time and fate. She may not know where the crow's wing of social protest is flying or swimming, yet the two small wings that bear her to this lake and its concealed ferry ("a rowboat pushed under the pier") are those of Mercury the Messenger, bearing Beulah to the Styx, the Nile of her past, the last water to cross.

What do boundaries and barriers come to mean for a poet who maintains critical distance from both Black Arts ideologies (cf. *SP* 12) as well as religious notions of suffering transcended through faith? Is Beulah's tendency to withdraw into her own physical and mental space an individual trait of meditation, of "overcoming" in the African-American tradition, a reluctance to mingle with politics and people, or rather a result of oppression and segregation? The first stanza's flashback already shows her aloof, and further evidence is offered as we move back into her childhood in "Summit Beach, 1921." The epigraph of *GN* (3) features her anonymously sitting at the "Negro beach." As in "Wingfoot Lake," wings and water provide pervasive images of motion throughout the poem: "sweaters [are] flying off the finest brown shoulders / this side of the world." Yet, in the midst of segregated festivities Beulah, whose "knee had itched in the cast," sat by the fire and "did not care to dance." "So she refused / to cut the wing . . . She could wait" until the "right man smiled." Then she "could feel / the breeze in her ears like water, / like the air as a child when / she climbed Papa's shed and stepped off / the tin roof into the blue, // with her parasol and invisible wings." Beulah accepts her scars and wings with equal stoicism and courage, "till she grew mean from bravery." She embraces her limitations as well as her opportunities without edifying traditional beliefs and attitudes. Her "truer way" is family oriented, apparently endless and aimless, but justified nonetheless as she counterbalances an eerie sense of displacement—of not belonging—with an extraordinary poise and self-protection. The dignity of her individual choices cannot be measured against the public efforts of a new generation. "Although that poem revolves around recognizable historical events, the world arena is peripheral to the details of the picnic. Human beings do not live for history; they may live under its thrall or in spite of it, even in it—but not because of it," Dove says of "Wingfoot Lake" (1996: 43).

Borders and boundaries in Dove's poetry are warp and woof in a tightly woven fabric of private preordination, or tenacity, and public determination. This is also the case in a seemingly simple *unilateral* division. According to Fritz Gysin, it is:

> an asymmetrical variant including elements of the first two forms. The *unilateral boundary* is pervious a) from one side only, b) in one direction only, c) for agents of one side only. It can be illustrated by a situation in which people of one group have access to, or control of, the living space of the other group, but not vice versa. (unpublished lecture, 1994, ms. pp. 23–24)

"Parsley" (*SP* 133–35), a meditation on a death sentence and one of Dove's best-known poems—as poet laureate she read it at the White House—reports an incident at the Haitian-Dominican border, which in the 1930s was de facto traversable for Dominicans but closed to Haitians.[13] De jure, the case was even more complicated. Not clearly delimited since 1844, the border was redefined in 1929 when thousands of Haitians already lived abroad. In 1937,[14] to stop the influx of immigrants, the unilateral border, though officially still "open," was brutally enforced. The narrative poem in two parts deals with the massacre of approximately 20,000 Haitians, paradoxically guest workers on Rafael Trujillo's sugarcane plantations on the Haitian border. There the psychopathic dictator (1930–1961) determined the destiny of the needed and undesirables in his land by having the potential victims pronounce the shibboleth *perejil*, Spanish for "parsley." Creole speakers of French, he certainly knew, would inevitably fail the test." Standing at bayonet point, those who could not roll an "R" in *perejil* were condemned as Haitians and sentenced to death.

Most important for the genesis of Dove's work in general, and for "Parsley" in particular, is the German cultural background. It was Hubert Fichte's study *Petersilie*[15]—the epilogue features a prose version of the "Parsley"story—that served as a starting point for the poem.[16] Fichte's text as a prose foil for the poem also reveals intriguing parallels with Dove's own poetics of boundary crossing. In his 1994 essay "Das Heterogene, Das Werk," Hans-Jürgen Heinrichs[17] describes Fichte's anthropological aesthetics as an "open literature," his associative imagining as less confined in its use of heterogeneity than a thematically bound and restricted writing. In Zora Neale Hurston's footsteps, Hubert Fichte collects anthropological material in the Caribbean, including folktales, myths, and political vignettes. This is precisely Dove's point of departure and the aim of her transcultural enspacements in poetry, but she does more than merely articulate the heterogeneous and unadjustable as Heinrich's term *"Erkenntnispoesie"* [poetry of recognition] stipulates.

In short, with precise images and scurrilous details, Dove evokes Trujillo's perverted reverence of language. Embodying this frightening testimony in the exqusite form of a villanelle[18] in the first part only intensifies the horror.

1. *The Cane Fields*

There is a parrot imitating spring
in the palace, its feathers parsley green.
Out of the swamp the cane appears

to haunt us, and we cut it down. El General
searches for a word; he is all the world
there is. Like a parrot imitating spring,

we lie down screaming as rain punches through
and we come up green. We cannot speak an **R**—

out of the swamp, the cane appears

and then the mountain we call in whispers *Katalina.*
The children gnaw their teeth to arrowheads.
There is a parrot imitating spring.

El General has found his word: *perejil.*
Who says it, lives. He laughs, teeth shining
out of the swamp, the cane appears

in our dreams, lashed by wind and streaming.
And we lie down. For every drop of blood
there is a parrot imitating spring.
Out of the swamp the cane appears. (emphasis mine)

"Parsley" not only shows language at the threshold of life and death but also deconstructs oppressive political patterns by revealing the dictator's psyche. Dove highlights in the opening lines his grotesque mimicry of his mother's pronunciation with their "imitating parrot" and reiterated jarring "Rs," a sound cage with "a kind of a growl to it even in English, a subdued growl I suppose in American English" (Rubin and Ingersoll 1986: 231). The anonymous workers in this dictator's hand can only counteract the machine gun–like iteration of "Rs" with four waves of natural greenery: "Out of the swamp the cane appears."[19] "Spring" and "appears," the two recurring rhymes of the villanelle, are paired in the concluding lines, where the artificial greenery of an "imitating spring" encounters the fast growing green of "the cane [that] appears." Whereas the first part, *The Cane Fields,* is a villanelle where enjambments and iterations combine to mirror formally the rolling cane fields, the second, *The Palace,* opposed to the open fields in its enclosures, consists of seven stanzas of seven or eight lines each that are followed by a detached, conclusive line "to be killed / for a single, beautiful word."

The second part reveals an inner world of the obsessive-compulsive (Vendler 1994: 12), a Freudian repetition compulsion mirrored in the ubiquitous letter "R." Deranged since his mother's death, and hearing the parrot, or the field workers call her name—"*Katalina,* they sing, *Katalina,/mi madle, mi amol en muelte*"—he feels vexed by the presence of people who cannot "roll an R like a queen. Even a parrot can roll an R." For the General who lives in the continuous anxiety of being ridiculed "The knot in his throat starts to twitch" and relief comes by killing. Obsessed with language as any poet is and still neurotically bound to his mother, he kills to defend his and her honor (Vendler 1994: 12). Perversely, the cultural symbol of newborn life, "Parsley," turns into its contrary: a death sentence. Yet, paradoxically, the parrot who lives in the dictator's deceased mother's curtainless room is also a "migrant worker" who "traveled all the way from Australia in an ivory cage." In his double enclosure of a cage and a palace, he lives doubly removed from his natural habitat. "Coy as a widow, practising spring," he does so in mimicry of El General and his dead mother who "collapsed in the kitchen while baking skull-shaped candies for the Day of the Dead." With "its feathers parsley green," only "imitating spring," he is associated with mimicry, that is, "life-in-death" and "bright feathers arch in a parody of greenery." A range of contrastive imagery emphasizes the gap between form and content: the palace's artificial enclosure contrasts with the open swamp, out of which waves of fast-growing sugarcane come to threaten the single walking cane planted at the General's mother's grave. In an ironic imitation of spring, this act of "love in death" stolidly produces "four-star blossoms" in honor of the four-star generalissimo. Within the palace, the beautifully contained parrot in his ivory cage contrasts with the skull-shaped candies the General's mother was preparing before she collapsed. His hatred for sweets and for those who grow and cut its raw material, cane, is already linked with his emptiness accentuated by his mother's death. The beautiful "pastries brought up for the bird" are "dusted with sugar on a bed of lace." An image of incestuous refinement reflecting the son's love for his dead mother vies with the "mud and urine as a soldier falls at his feet." From this palatial wasteland, however, the General "sees fields of sugarcane, lashed by rain and streaming," a lavish abundance of water set against his single "startled tear [that] splashes the tip of his right boot." Beautiful form and painful content—the singing on the verge of disaster and the killing—conjoin stretto-like in the General's final perverse reversal of the folk gesture of wearing "tiny green sprigs" to honor the birth of a son into his order to kill "for a single, beautiful word." In the end, the shibboleth *perejil* is no longer mentioned but metonymically referred to.

> *My mother, my love in death.*
> The general remembers the tiny green sprigs
> men of his village wore in their capes
> to honor the birth of a son. He will
> order many, this time to be killed
>
> for a single, beautiful word.

Yet since the days of the Conquistadores the master language Spanish itself would replace an "R" with an "L" and produce "Katalina" for "Katharina" (Fichte 1988: 46).[20]

The biblical tradition reports "shibboleth" as an irrevocable password used by the men of Gilead to distinguish the escaping Ephraimites who pronounced the initial [ʃ] as [s] (Judges 12: 4–6). Crucial for the genesis of "Parsley," however, is the German cultural background that is not only palpable in Paul Celan's extensive use of the shibboleth as a racial marker[21] but also in Hubert Fichte's study *Petersilie.* Dove's poem transforms the German prose into a transcultural icon.

Her aim—as revealed by the poems discussed here—is a synthesis of antithetical moments, a fusion into something whole and new. In choosing Fichte's anthropological vignettes and a Spanish shibboleth, Dove enacts a double transatlantic cultural passage: as an African American who came to study "expressionist drama, Rilke and Paul Celan" in Tübingen in 1974 (Vendler 1989: 482), she relocates a token of Judeo-Christian European poetic tradition[22] in the Caribbean. Art has finally created a memorial, a home for those killed in the name of a master language.

A boundary understood as *brink or edge* represents "the outskirts of a familiar, known, accepted area, beyond which it is difficult or dangerous to go," traits shared with previous categories. "Depending on the nature of that other side," Fritz Gysin continues,

> the boundary may be seen as locking in or locking out. A No-Trespassing Sign, it nevertheless invites adventure and exploration, usually at a high risk. This is the form of boundary which in the Puritans' imagination divided their settlements from the "howling wilderness" of uncivilized nature. But the most typical boundaries of this sort are of the metaphysical kind; they separate this world from the next. Stories of closure and (less frequently) of quest operate with this form of boundary. (unpublished lecture, 1994, ms. p. 24)

I will focus on the notion of closure as protagonists confront loss, guilt, and death. Examples are numerous and varied, particularly in Thomas's section of *TB* ("The Event" *SP* 141f; "Variation on Pain" *SP* 143; "The Stroke" *SP* 169; "Thomas at the Wheel" *SP* 172; or in Beulah's section "The Oriental Ballerina" *SP* 201f) to be dealt with in chapter 3. Therefore, the spotlight will be on Part II of *GN* (23–33), which prepares for a world of experience after the fall, on the *brink or edge.* The first poem, "Mississippi," indeed takes a biblical stance: "In the beginning was the dark / moan and creak . . . We were standing on the deck / of the New World, before maps: / tepid seizure of a breeze / and the spirit hissing away"). The avowal of guilt over a friend's death in "Mississippi" and of mortality ("Your Death," "The Wake") introduces the aftermath of the forbidden fruit followed by the wastelands of "Watching *Last Year at Marienbad* at Roger Haggerty's House in Auburn, Alabama" ("What / a shabby monstrosity spring / actually is!") and of "Dog Days, Jerusalem" ("Exactly at six every evening I go / into the garden to wait for rain"). The poems in Part II act as "memorials for the ended life and poetical grief at the section's close" (Baker 1990: 576).

Yet "Your Death" (*GN* 32) joins the converse liminal experiences of birth and death—a pregnancy confirmed at grandfather's demise—as if to recall how even the mutually exclusive remains intertwined: "On the day that will always belong to you, / lunar clockwork had faltered / and I was certain. Walking / the streets of Manhattan I thought: *Remember this day.* I felt already like an urn, filling with wine." The only homeplace after a great loss, when "Your absence distributed itself / like an invitation," lies in one's innermost resources as "The Wake" (GN 33) suggests. There "I lay down in the cool waters / of my own womb / and became the child / inside / innocuous / as a button, helplessly growing." This regressive tapping of one's own spring is the necessary survival habit for "The Fish in the Stone" as well, because not even the universe provides a safe protective womb anymore. The hole in "Ozone" (GN 28) is a cosmic wound that invites ultimate questions to be explored beyond the personal and the human. How do we protect ourselves if "the dome of heaven" is perforated?

> . . . *Does the cosmic*
> *space we dissolve into taste of us, then?*
> Rilke, *The Second Elegy*

Everything civilized will whistle before
it rages—kettle of the asthmatic,
the aerosol can and its immaculate awl
perforating the dome of heaven.

We wire the sky for comfort;
we thread it through our lungs for a perfect fit.
We've arranged this calm, though it is constantly
unraveling.

> *Where does it go then,*
> *atmosphere suckered up*
> *an invisible flue?*
> *How can we know where it goes?*

A gentleman pokes blue through a buttonhole.

> *Rising, the pulse*
> *sings:*
> *memento mei*

The sky is wired so it won't fall down.
Each house notches into its neighbor
and then the next, the whole row scaldingly white,
unmistakably as a set of bared teeth.

> *to pull the plug*
> *to disappear into an empty bouquet*

If only we could lose ourselves
in the wreckage of the moment! Forget
where we stand, dead center, and
look up, look up,
track a falling star . . .

now you see it

now you don't

Ozone, an unstable, pale-blue gas with a penetrating odor, is a form of oxygen, formed usually by a silent electrical discharge in air. It is used as an oxidizing, deodorizing, and bleaching agent and in the purification of water. The perforated womb of heaven, however, is a region in the upper atmosphere, about 15 to 30 kilometers (10–20 miles) in altitude, containing a relatively high concentration of ozone that absorbs solar ultraviolet radiation in a wavelength range not screened by other atmospheric components. If this protective dome is damaged by pollution, such as overuse of aerosol, ultraviolet radiation is no longer filtered, leading to a temperature increase with serious consequences. Dove renders this doomsday scenario as a dialogue of two voices intertwined. One strand of pressing elegiac questions grows out of Rilke's subtitle " . . . Does the cosmic / space we dissolve into taste of us, then?" "*Where does it go then . . . How can we know where it goes?*" The other construes visual and verbal irony around self-produced existential threats and vain attempts at fixing them. The second stanza resumes and ridicules these efforts in an anaphoric "We wire," "we thread," "We've arranged . . . for comfort," "for a perfect fit," yet without avail for "*atmosphere suckered up / an invisible flue . . . to disappear into an empty bouquet.*" The constructive and destructive components of "Ozone" connect toward an "ars poetica" that wonders what to do between momentary fixation and dissolution ("We've arranged this calm, though it is constantly / unraveling"). Stacked images of piercing penetration mark the mock ironic path of bad news: Out of a domestic kettle ready to blow its steam whistle before it explodes with boiling rage pops an aerosol can, a phallic "immaculate awl." The "dome of heaven's" gushing wound yields but the blue "A gentleman pokes . . . through a buttonhole." The casual aestheticism, another instant of perfect arrangement, immediately turns into the third image of powerful perforation. This is a poisoned environment that is now beginning to show signs of affecting the human family as a whole (or hole). Though the "sky is wired," an aggressive row of white houses bites the sky like "a set of bared teeth" (in "Silos" *GN* 7).

In line with notions of "house and universe" (38–73) and "intimate immensity" explored in *The Poetics of Space* (1994: 183–210), "Ozone" questions origin, destiny, and creation in terms of the local and familiar. Bachelard states that:

> In analyzing images of immensity, we should realize within ourselves the pure being of pure imagination. It then becomes clear that works of art are the *byproducts* of this existentialism of the imagining being. In this direction of daydreams of immensity, the real *product* is consciousness of enlargement. . . . Immensity is within ourselves. (184)

> But the problem under consideration...is that of a more relaxed participation in images of immensity, a more intimate relationship between small and large. (190)

The two kinds of space, intimate space and exterior space, keep encouraging each other, as it were, in their growth. (201)

"Ozone" is no occasional piece for the Environmental Protection Agency; rather, it is about artistic creation, because "Thinking to express feeling, they [artists] make a hole in reality" (Vendler 1991: 398). The final stanza with its conditional "If only" but varies "The Fish in the Stone"'s similar wish to arrest transience in a conceptual image or snapshot. "If only we could lose ourselves / in the wreckage of the moment!"

This "carpe diem" then would entail forgetting the "dead center" of the past while brushing against the mystery of creation. John Donne's imperative "Go and catch a falling star" turns into Dove's "track a falling star" visualized in the planet's tale pursued to its vanishing point

now you see it

now you don't

The final type of boundary to discuss functions as *threshold*, both in terms of closing the foregoing paragraphs as well as leading over to "Movement." In Fritz Gysin's terms, this

boundary zone acts as a locus of transformation. Again, depending on the nature of the "other" side, the boundary can be crossed (in which case the crossing entails the change) or it is experienced as an outmost region, from which one returns changed. Commonly related to the process of initiation, it manifests itself in psychological, social, cultural, and ethnic contexts, but it also frequently implies metaphysical dimensions. (unpublished lecture, 1994, ms. p. 24)

Threshold experiences permeate *TB*, *FS*, and particularly *IG*, which "connotes a place that exists in order to be moved through; it is passage, transient space" (*PW* 1995: 16). These works, however, will be discussed in chapters 3 and 4. In tune with Dove, I shall explore this particular boundary's function as *threshold*, as neutral territory, a state of merely being in transit. Bachelard (1994: 223) cites Michel Barrault's *Dominicale*, on the discovered majesty of the threshold within himself: "I find myself defining threshold / As being the geometrical place / Of the comings and goings / In my Father's House." In "Turning Thirty, I Contemplate Students Bicycling Home" (*GN* 30), Dove highlights the mood of a speaker who watches her students' youthful vigour as she herself moves from young adulthood into middle age ("This is the weather of change / and clear light"). In a setting of seasonal ("through the tired, wise / spring") and diurnal change (from "clear light" till "Evening"), the speaker diachronically compares past and future (from weather on its A side to "weather on its B side, / askew") and, synchronically, her transience against "the legs of young men / in tight jeans wheeling." Wheeling, a spatial metaphor for fleeting time, leaves her to see "the same thing / and for a long way."

This is the weather of change
and clear light. This is
weather on its B side,
askew, that propels
the legs of young men
in tight jeans wheeling
through the tired, wise
spring. Crickets too
awake in choirs
out of sight, although
I imagine we see
the same thing
and for a long way.

This, then, weather
to start over.
Evening rustles
her skirts of sulky
organza. Skin
prickles, defining
what is and shall not be . . .

How private
the complaint of these
green hills.

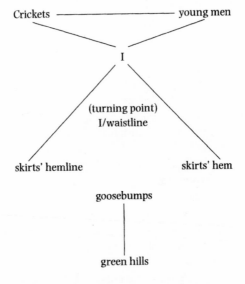

The speaker's quiet contemplation visualizes transience in a striking configuration of two triangles. Hourglass-like, their obtuse angles meet at the turning
point ("to start over") and are formed by hidden crickets, wheeling cyclists, and
the speaker in the center whose evening then unfolds like "skirts of sulky /
organza." The sensuous rustle causes skin to prickle, ripples echoed by nature's
"green hills."

This is how Dove's boundary crossing, explored in this paragraph, works
through form and striking imagery that lend a visionary clarity and precision
to the flow of her thought and imagination. After all, a poem's "charmed structure" may be the only "talisman against disintegration" (Preface, *ML*).

MOVEMENTS

Dove's poetics of space, which informs the tripartite structure of chapter 2, reflects a pattern of origins (borders, boundaries, barriers), including departure
(brink, edge, threshold), passage (movement), and arrival (transcultural enspacement); of human progress in general; and of African-American history
in particular. Safely moored in her hometown, Dove travels world and time.
"Silos" (*GN* 7) and "Lady Freedom among Us" (*PW* 11) symbolize these factual and spiritual roots. Both the smokestacks and grain silos of her Akron,
Ohio—"They were masculine toys. They were tall wishes. They / were the

ribs of the modern world"²³—and the Statue of Freedom in front of the U.S. Capitol in Washington, D.C., mark widening horizons: "no choice but to grant her space / crown her with sky / for she is one of the many / and she is each of us."

Movement as migration, or exile, together with the enunciation of borders and crossings, is also deeply inscribed in the itineraries of much contemporary reasoning and theory (Chambers 1994: 2). From Edward Said's 1984 landmark study, "The Mind of Winter: Reflections on Life in Exile," to Iain Chambers's poetic exploration of *Migrancy, Culture, Identity*, and of how our sense of place and identity is realized as we move through a myriad languages, worlds, and histories, journeys and passages acquire interrogative value as shifting nurseries of hope or dread. I am interested in the literary, historical, and imaginary journeys of a poet who is able and eager to travel in her mind and person. What cultural and human geography emerges from an honest and truthful recording of a world in transition? What kind of an ideal remains to be imagined beyond the millennial boundary? Movement, as it emerges from Dove's oeuvre, will be discussed under the headings of *travelogues and sightseeing, flights into freedom, quests and metamorphoses,* and *imaginary voyages.*

The category *travelogues and sightseeing* at first glance might be as misleading as offensive to a poet who abhors tourist pieces. Except for "The Sahara Bus Trip" (*SP* 55–56) and the atmospheric "Notes from a Tunisian Journal" (*SP* 54), where "Food's perfume" and "salt above eucalyptus fields" highlight a boy's movement against the stasis of the camels' "vague beauty— / at night they fold up like pale accordions," Dove's "Early Morning on the Tel Aviv-Haifa Freeway" (*SP* 124) and "Sightseeing" (*SP* 10–11) defy the very notion of visiting places but for pleasure and leisure. They portray acts of violence against animals and human beings.

Hers is a training to perceive things anew, in various perspectives, and in the vein of an apprenticeship text she cherishes, Rainer Maria Rilke's *The Notebooks of Malte Laurids Brigge:* "I am learning to see. I don't know why it is, but everything penetrates more deeply into me and does not stop at the place where until now it always used to finish. . . . I am learning to see," the young hero comments on his growing cognizance (1992: 14–15). Dove's signature poem "Sightseeing" entices the reader right to the site or sight: "Come here, I want to show you something. / I inquired about the church yesterday," the first of sixteen unrhymed couplets reads. Yet the meditation on the aftermath of World War II terminates on a single line: "to look at a bunch of smashed statues." In the role of the griot, the roving troubadour who sang his poetry to villagers, the speaker invites everyone to "the inner courtyard, also in ruin . . . after the Allies left." In this vignette of postwar Germany (cf. "The Bird Frau" *SP* 5), subtle parables of the universal and the particular entwine in "a kind of thinking tourist's meditation on internal exile" (Gregerson 1984: 47).

> . . . What a consort
> of broken dolls! Look, they were mounted

> at the four corners of the third floor terrace
> and the impact from the cobblestones
>
> snapped off wings and other appendages.
> The heads rolled the farthest. Someone
>
> started to pile the limbs together—
> from the weight of the pieces, an adult—
>
> a deserter, perhaps, or a distraught priest.
> Whoever it was, the job was interrupted,
>
> so to speak, in mid-step: this forearm
> could not have fallen so far from its owner
>
> without assistance. The villagers,
> come here to give thanks, took one look in
>
> and locked the gates: "A terrible sign . . ."

Though the villagers decided to leave the fractured statues, signifiers of war victims, as they found them after the Allies' retreat, destruction ("broken dolls," "snapped off wings and other appendages," "heads rolled farthest") pairs with reconstruction right away, for "Someone / started to pile the limbs together—." Unlike the community, the speaker realizes how civilized forces ("an adult— / a deserter, perhaps, or a distraught priest./Whoever it was") began to counteract chaos by secretly rearranging the ruins. This is the sight that triggers an inner journey of increasing discrimination and abstraction:

> But all this palaver about symbols and
>
> "the ceremony of innocence drowned" is—
> as you know—civilization's way
>
> of manufacturing hope. . . .

When the mind reassembles the broken symbols—freedom, equality, fraternity, peace, democracy—the speaker is also aware of the futility ("this palaver") of "civilization's way // of manufacturing hope." Even though the personal sightseeing opens up into public World War II and the individual meditation into the poetry of W. B. Yeats ("the ceremony of innocence drowned"), Dove's stance denies Yeats's "The Second Coming,"[24] that is, a second Christian redemption of evil. Instead she argues for a careful conciliation between forgetting and remembering. After all, each contains the other. Contingency that turns angels into monsters, or vice versa, is but a matter of perspectives.

> . . . Let's look
> at the facts. **Forget** they are children of angels
>
> and they become childish monsters.
> **Remember**, and an arm gracefully upraised

is raised not in anger but a mockery of gesture.
The hand will hold both of mine. The vulgarity

of life in exemplary size is why
we've come to regard this abandoned

constellation . . . (emphasis mine)

"Abandoned / constellation" is a key figure in this "Sightseeing" turned "ars poetica." For "The vulgarity / of life in exemplary size," the rigid normative view
that connotes Nazi Germany's ethnic cleansing as well as a stonemason's ab-
breviation of human features, must be counteracted by constant revisions of a
seemingly static reality, fragmented or perfectly intact. "Sightseeing" then is "to
regard this abandoned // constellation" and rebuild it through language from
as many angles as poetic imagination and prowess allow.

In "Corduroy Road" (*SP* 63) Dove writes "*The symbol of motion is static,
finite, / And kills by the coachload.*" According to Kevin Stein, "Meaning is not
just *reflected* in language but also something *produced* by it" (1995: 58–59). This
is why the ravaged sanctuary of the church turns into a memorial of ethnic
and ethic diversity preserved and enlivened through linguistic configuration.[25]
"Sightseeing" then as well as "The Fish in the Stone" show how a poem, insofar
as it considers historical and social phenomena, represents them as *failed*, as
ceasing to participate in the organic process by which they acquired significance in the beginning. Dove's failures however—fossils, broken statues, murdered laborers (*SP* 133f), mummies (*SP* 77), plague victims (*SP* 82), displaced
sideshow performers (*SP* 98), and, of course, African Americans suffering from
racial hypocrisy and segregation—present more authentic marks of both futility and intrinsic truth, strength, and beauty. Any historical character or
situation's not-being, before or after the frozen moment of a linguistic constellation, provides a conceptual outline for what is seen. Yet, while Dove foregrounds the form, the body within wins contours as well. It is Dove's preoccupation with boundary, movement, and enspacement that allows a type of social
reflection through lyric, an imaginative examination of the values of what is, or
was, or is not, or was not.[26]

Flights into freedom highlight the African-American past, as it appears in
section III of *YH*. This slavery sequence ("Belinda's Petition," "The House Slave,"
"David Walker (1785–1830)," "The Abduction," "The Transport of Slaves From
Maryland to Mississippi," "Pamela," "Someone's Blood," "Cholera," "The Slave's
Critique of Practical Reason," and "Kentucky" [*SP* 28–40]) is not an erratic
block of difference in an otherwise cross-culturally delineated volume; it is an
equally powerful chapter of history as World War II in Dove's weaving together
struggles of all worlds and times. Often she uses historical and elevated poetic
language, interspersed with authentic slave dialect. In "Pamela['s]" flight (*SP*
34) the speaker accompanies a slave on a tryst with freedom. While the surrepti-
tious departure in the first stanza and a moment of clandestine rest after the long
day's journey into the "White quiet" in the third provide a frame in verse, the big
move into tempting liberty is in prose.

*". . . the hour was come when the man must act, or forever be a
slave."*

At two, the barnyard settled
into fierce silence—anvil,

water pump glinted
as though everything waited
for the first step.
She stepped
into the open. The wind
lifted—behind her,
fields spread their sails.

There really is a star up there and moss on the trees. She discovered if she kept a
steady pace, she could walk forever. The idea pleased her, and she hummed
a hymn to herself—Peach Point, Silk Hope, Beaver Bend. It seemed that the
further north she went, the freer she became. The stars were plates for good
meat; if she reached, they flashed and became coins.

White quiet. Night pushed over the hill.
The woods hiss with cockleburs,
each small woolly head.
She feels old, older
than these friendly shadows
who, like squirrels, don't come too near.
Knee-deep in muscadine, she watches them coming,
snapping the brush. They are
smiling, rifles crossed on their chests.

After this delicate opening up of the world, horizontally into the north, and vertically into the sky, we suddenly see Pamela's action jeopardized by "them coming . . . smiling, rifles crossed on their chests." Again, failure is in the air and
renders her splash into freedom even more volatile and precious.

Another high point of manifold refractions of perspective and valuations
hampering and thwarting the escape into freedom is found in "The Transport of
Slaves from Maryland to Mississippi" (*SP* 32–33). An introduction explains the
internal monologue of a slave whose humanity triumphs over racial solidarity:

(*On August 22, 1839, a wagonload of slaves broke their chains, killed two white
men, and would have escaped, had not a slave woman helped the Negro driver mount
his horse and ride for help.*)

"*I don't know if I helped him up / because I thought he was our salvation / or not.
. . . his eyes were my eyes in a yellower face. / Death and salvation*—one accomo-
dates the other. / *I am no brute. I got feelings. / He might have been a son of mine.*" Are
we reminded of "Crab-Boil" where "A bunch of niggers, not / a-one get out 'fore
the others pull him / back?" Not in this case. The slaves betrayed the rebellion because the injured guardian could have been the slave woman's son. Death and
salvation do go hand in hand. "The flip side of this coin is that if you don't know
who your family is, everyone is your family," Dove told Wayne Ude (1993: 6).

"Three Days of Forest, a River, Free" (GN 92) is the only successful flight into freedom: "The way is free / to the river. Tell me, / Lord, how it feels / to burst out like a
rose. // Blood rises in my head— / I'm there." The speaker, however, pays a high
price in leaving a companion behind: "I think I lost you to the dogs, / so far off
now they're no / more than a chain of bells / ringing darkly, underground."

Yet Dove not only covers a range of female fugitives' experiences. In "David
Walker (1785–1830)" (*SP* 30) and "The Abduction" (*SP* 31) she recounts the
individual efforts of two historical male figures, David Walker and Solomon
Northrup. Both are free to travel, yet, in using their freedom, encounter
death and renewed confinement. Whereas Walker was too successful with his
pamphlets[27]—"his person (is that all?) found face-down / in the doorway at
Brattle Street [Cambridge, MA]"—Northrup falls prey to the treachery of his
new friends, Brown and Hamilton, and after a night of heavy drinking finds
himself "in darkness and in chains" again. His decreasing freedom is formally
enhanced by five stanzas winding down from five to four, to three, to two lines
with a single one punctuating his loss of liberty. A successful flight into academic freedom and public recognition, however, is possible for "Banneker" (*SP*
93–94). The subject is the black mathematician, astronomer, and architect
Benjamin Banneker (1731–1806), who helped outline the new plans for the city
of Washington, D.C. and surveyed the land. Here Dove elevates a counterfigure
to rival the icons of the founding fathers. Both, Benjamin Franklin, a publisher,
scientist, politician, and diplomat, and Thomas Jefferson, an architect, educator, inventor, farmer, scientist, and president of the United States (1800–1808),
signed the Declaration of Independence. Although he corresponded with Banneker, Jefferson never altered his conviction that the black race was inferior.
Banneker, neither this nor that, fills a pioneering liminal gap of creative activity
beyond firm inner and outer associations or conventional behavior:

> But who would want him! Neither
> Ethiopia nor English, neither
> lucky nor crazy, a capacious bird
> humming as he penned in his mind
> another enflamed letter
> to President Jefferson—he imagined
> the reply, polite and rhetorical.
> Those who had been to Philadelphia
> reported the statue
> of Benjamin Franklin
> before the library
>
> his very size and likeness.
> A wife? No, thank you.

Only at the end of the poem, which portrays an eccentric, does the capital
city take a visionary shape in Banneker's daydream and "he could see / a government's domed city / rising from the morass and spreading / in a spiral of
lights. . . . "

Quests and metamorphoses, of course, permeate *FS, IG, TB, ML,* and *DF.* "Nothing Down" in *TB (SP* 151–153) opens with *"flower / . . . blue flame."* Since the German Romantic Age the "blaue Blume," or "blue flower," is a motif and symbol for quests. Thomas and Beulah's journey back south to show off a sky blue Chandler, symbol of the American Dream fulfilled, opens ambiguously: no down payment was required, yet "down" in an African-American context also carries connotations of "primal tragic action, where fate and will can meet . . . the place of fulfillment; [that] implies the return not only to the native land but also to the native order" (Gates, *Figures in Black* 1989: 191–92). But the dream car breaks down "Eight miles outside Murfreesboro" and "A carload of white men / halloo past them on Route 231. . . . *The air was being torn / into hopeless pieces. Only this flower hovering / above his head / couldn't hear the screaming."* This is but another failure measured against immediate intention and the romantic hope symbolized by the "blue flower."

An extraordinary journey, whose title "On the Road to Damascus" (GN 71–72) has become synonymous with transformation, qualifies as both quest and metamorphosis.[28] A biblical epilogue (Acts 22: 6–7) and Dove's essay, "The Epistle of Paul the Apostle to the Ephesians" (1990), identify the otherwise anonymous hero. On the road in these tercets is the Roman Saul.

> They say I was struck down by the voice of an angel:
>   flames poured through the radiant fabric of heaven
> as I cried out and fell to my knees.
>
> My first recollection was of Unbroken Blue—
>   but two of the guards have already sworn by
> the tip of my tongue set ablaze. As an official,
>
> I recognize the lure of a good story:
>   useless to suggest that my mount
> had stumbled, that I was pitched into a clump
>
> of wild chamomile, its familiar stink
>   soothing even as my palms sprang blisters
> under the nicked leaves. I heard shouts,
>
> the horse pissing in terror—but my eyes
>   had dropped to my knees, and I saw nothing.
> I was a Roman and had my business
>
> among the clouded towers of Damascus.
>   I had not counted on earth rearing,
> honey streaming down a parched sky,
>
> a spear skewering me to the dust of the road
>   on the way to the city I would never
> enter now, her markets steaming with vendors
>
> and compatriots in careless armor lifting a hand
>   in greeting as they call out my name,
> only to find no one home.

The actual transformation of a bloody persecutor of Christians into the Lord's apostle does not intrigue the poet as much as the emotions and attitudes he reveals in his inner monologue and how the news is marketed. "Useless to suggest" what has truly happened when beholders and church officials need a good story. Dove's choice to base the poem on the biblical first person (Acts 22: 1–30) rather than on the third person account (Acts 9: 1–43), also points in that direction. "They say I was struck down by the voice of an angel" yet "My first recollection was of Unbroken Blue—" further enhances the divergent narrative positions right from the start. Blue, the color of hope and redemption throughout Dove's work (see, for example, Beulah's section in *TB*, "Crab-Boil," "Nothing Down"), cannot compete with the flames of official mythmaking. As a Roman realist and powerbroker, Saul, of course, acknowledges "the lure of a good story," but reality creates a considerable level of discomfort when he looks back onto a range of mishaps, the underside of His (s)tory: "my mount / had stumbled, that I was pitched into a clump," surrounded by "familiar stink," "blisters," "the horse pissing in terror." The new spirit has not yet entered him yet, only the Christian belief system, and it needs to disempower a persecutor by converting him. Dove's radical doubt in regard to this transformation (cf. also "Dialectical Romance," *GN* 54) is corroborated by her comment:

> Saul watched as Stephen was stoned to death; Paul was celibate in order to serve his Christ more ardently. Aren't these flip sides of the same coin? And if not, where did Saul go? Who, if anyone, was in the body that sat three days in darkness in Damascus, who spoke before the crowds, who crouched in that dark prison cell and built up the body of Christian thought into a white and pillared building? Did he remember Saul at all—or had he, as Paul, burned away his past self so completely that with it fled the childhood words for stone and bread? What initially fills the void when the old self is struck down and out—what rushes in before the light, what rides the arrow tip of redemption into the benighted soul? ("The Epistle of Paul the Apostle to the Ephesians," (1990: 170)

Dove seems to suggest the notion of a complex ambivalence, a dialectical synthesis rather than a binary opposition of before and after, for most renewals involve recombinations rather than absolute transformations. Saul and Paul, "the same sound but a different beginning" (170), to her are two aspects of the same personality, as contingency that turns angels into monsters, or vice versa, is but a matter of perspectives (cf. "Sightseeing"). The word Paul chooses for his move is *allagesometha*, "translation," which connotes barter and exchange (Hillman 1979: 86).

This poem too is about seeing sights in a new light. Not only Saul, who is terrified because his gaze, which could dwell unmoved on slain bodies, now fails him, but the poet also experiences a sudden conversion.

> When I was a teenager Paul seemed to be a hard man with an unrealistically severe code of sacrifice, a fanatic who devised silly laws of diet, dress codes, and impossible rules of behavior; an ideologue who equated belief with ethics and transformation with institutional rhetoric. (172)

Only later does she begin to recognize "that Paul's proclamations were demanded of him" because Christianity at that time was still a heresy within a larger tradition, a solid Roman world that eventually began splitting apart, "and he was falling into a mystery, bottomless and widening" (173). After years of doubt, Dove, upon looking at a "jewellike medieval painting of Saul on the way to Damascus,"[29] was suddenly able to perceive the individual's transformation beyond the system.

> Paul *was* a mystic. Only a mystic would address the newly converted with "And you *hath quickened*, who wee dwad in trespasses and sins." Or: "the fulness of him that filleth all in all." Devising a system for connecting and reflection, a guide for conducting a life of energized joy—this is Paul's abiding light. (173)

Saul's conversion to Christianity and Rita's conversion to Paul are both liminal experiences.

Anthropologist Victor Turner, drawing on his study of tribal ritual and Arnold van Gennep's *The Rites of Passage*, claims a space of "liminality" as the source of movement and change. This indeed provides a handy conceptual model for the study of exile—or border crossing "betwixt and between" countries, cultures, or denominations—as a processual rite. Turner's model of "liminality" usually refers to "the passage from one social status to another," and is often "accompanied by a parallel passage in space, a geographical movement from one place to another." This passage, according to Turner, involves the "literal crossing of a threshold which separates two distinct areas, one associated with the subject's pre-ritual or preliminal status, and the other with his postritual or postliminal status" (1982: 25). What is most interesting is how this ritualized move into liminality that we are calling border crossing becomes a site in which the border subject often discovers the cultural creativity and cultural authority to formulate "new models, symbols, paradigms" (28).

A new paradigm based on the experiences of the Middle Passage leads to the final form of movement discussed here: *imaginary voyages*. "The Sailor in Africa" (*SP* 119) presents an elaborate allegory for colonial conquest and racial oppression. A spinoff from a Viennese card game (c. 1910)—in the tradition of Pope's *The Rape of the Lock* and T. S. Eliot's *The Waste Land*—the poem unravels the adventures of the characters involved. The British and French have two white captains and two black pilots, while the Italian and Spanish crews consist of two white pilots and two black captains who become leading figures. Whereas the "Italian Moor" succumbs to a mutiny "on the western shore / of Madagascar," the "Spanish Moor" turns into a slave and then mutinously into the captain of the French vessel. En route to Brazil, he ends in a shipwreck, while the "Italian Moor" disappears into the Madagascan forests where he discovers great wealth in his isolation.

> At least one man happy
> to have lost everything.
> His crew will make it home
> with tales of strange lands

> and their captain's untimely
> demise.

Tales then are the timeless treasures brought back from an incompleted Middle Passage. Left but conked out is "the British captain and his swarthy pilot," who first appeared "stranded with an overladen [with slaves] ship / somewhere between the Ibos and / Jamestown, Virginia."

> In the Atlantic,
> windstill.
> The English vessel, so
> close to home, stalls.
> Nothing for them to do
> but pass the time
> playing cards.

Telling tales or playing games: With a reference to "the Suez Canal," Dove tellingly extends the colonializing traffic well into the nineteenth and twentieth centuries. Games continue on- and offshore: "Adrift in the Atlantic / again, the Englishman plays quoits with his pilot" and still does so at the end of the poem. Yet, through Dove's dramatic spatialization ("The captains, pilots, crews / commence / from the globe's four/corners. They share / a sun, a moon, and one / treasure. The goal / is Africa"), we too are "The Sailor in Africa" in this game of treasure hunting within the game of colonialization. In using European "flash cards," the African-American poet succeeds in holding up the mirror to generations of playful European gamesters, accomplices in the slave trade in the name of chance.

Dove's dramatic storytelling breaks new ground as a postcolonial rehearsal of colonialism, where only the superiors are distinguished through their skin color: "two white captains / and two Moors," while the crew . . . wear / identical motley." "Motley," the Shakespearean fool's garment, combines threads of various colors. A multicultural crew of colonizers sets out for Africa, a treasure house full of beautiful women, manpower, and "tales of strange lands." No single storyteller, only the motley crew, "will make it home." Only the artistic rendering of failure—adventure, shipwreck, mutiny, death—will survive. Cultural space is the only homeplace for the displaced.

SPACE BEYOND BORDERS AND MOVEMENTS

From *borders* and *boundaries* through *movement*, we shall now focus on the *(trans)cultural space* that unfolds beyond. *Cultural space* represents both a zone of arrival and new departures. Because no single frame is apt to cover all the spatial patterns arising from Dove's work, our micro-poetics of space will adopt terminological extensions that draw on and broaden Bachelard.[30] Momentous in *Crossing Color* is "the social character of space" not so much as "social product"

(Lefebvre 1974: 27) but as an interface of human interaction and experience both individual and collective. Cultural space, in short, is space that has been transformed by imagination. Art often serves as a code of this representational cultural space.

Hence, I will structure this section in three parts: *dreamscapes, mental expansion,* (intense felings, imagination, meditation, storyrelling, detachment, sensual and spiritual freedom) through renegotiated *social space,* as well as *transcultural enspacement.*

Dreamscapes as mind-expanding trajectories and alternative mappings of cultural space not only permeate Dove's work but Gaston Bachelard's as well. "There is always a line that sets you to dreaming," the poet explains her periodic returns to Bachelard (chapter 6). Her poetic declaration of independence from the Black Arts Movement cautiously takes the shape of a dream. In "Upon Meeting Don L. Lee, in a Dream" (*SP* 12), Dove reclaims creative territory for herself and her poetic sisters and expands it globally. Her groundbreaking stance is enhanced by the fact that this is her first poem to appear in Germany in 1979. Don L. Lee (later Haki Madhubuti), Sonia Sanchez, Nikki Giovanni, and Etheridge Knight are a group of "remarkable poets" who had a "constructively emotional impact on the collective racial ego of Black America" (Barksdale and Kinnamon 1972: 809). Committed to the cause of political, social, and moral revolution, they thought that all forms of artistic expression should serve the ends of revolution. Yet Dove moves clearly beyond black essentialism: "Black literature BY blacks, ABOUT blacks, directed TO blacks. ESSENTIAL black literature is the distillation of black life."[31] Also, while the celebration of black manhood was a political need to reestablish racial pride, the Black Arts Movement clearly marginalized feminist politics.[32] Dove distances herself from the movement in this programmatic poem dealing with one of its leaders, Don L. Lee. The third stanza of five reads:

> Moments slip by like worms.
> "Seven years ago . . . " he begins; but
> I cut him off: "Those years are gone—
> What is there now?" He starts to cry; his eyeballs
>
> Burst into flame.

She picks up the political impetus as the given starting point, that is, she is dealing with issues of race and gender, but she does not scream her message as propagandistically as Don L. Lee, whose "eyeballs / Burst into flame." Hers is rather a "politicization of the modernist tradition" (Werner Sollors), as she imbues perfectly composed poetry with subdued but powerful political messages.

"Chuckling as the grass curls around" her, the speaker, who is close to if not identical to Dove, turns into a spokeswoman for a phalanx of unnamed female poets. Her satire, dreaming and awake, is directed at the aesthetic dilettantism, the clichéd political discourse, and the credit card carrying militants with "caviar / Imbedded like buckshot between [their] teeth," those black poets who in spite of their credo always move "in the yellow half-shadows." Don L. Lee did dominate the scene.[33]

But that was "Seven years ago" and "Those years are gone." In alluding to "seven years" Dove may signify on Lee's poem "In a Period of Growth," which commemorates the beginning of the nationwide shift from "Negro" to "black" as a term of racial identification for African Americans in 1966: "like / if he had called me / black seven years ago, / I wd've— / broke his right eye out, / jumped into his chest, / talked about his momma, / lied on his sister / & dared him to say it again."

In Dove's poem, in the early 1980s enrobed women who "begin / To chant, stamping their feet in wooden cadences" confidently confront Lee in his once dominating, or domineering, version of the poet's role. The female challenge is couched in highly personal terms: A tearful, sapless, balding, and ultimately impotent poet who is unable to make love "To thin white boys in toilet stalls" suddenly faces singers floating away "Rustling on brown paper wings." This empowered female chorus, biblical seven years later, includes a chuckling lyrical self, ready to confront a burned-out, corrupted poet whose teeth are full of caviar, beads that contrast with the "beaded arms" of the women. "Among the trees, the black trees" they prevail and will as well endure those "Moments slip[ping] by like worms"—a phallic symbol of temptation and decay—until the poet condescends to meet their greeting. Emerging from a natural realm full of chanting, stamping, and "music [that] grows like branches in the wind," they counteract his increasingly static persona with a movement of their own. Whereas he turns from movement to stand still ("He comes toward me . . . always moving" till "He can only stand, fists clenched"), the women chiastically move from a standstill to movement ("Women in robes stand, watching. They begin / To chant, stomping their feet" till "the singers float away, / Rustling on brown paper wings"). Soundwise, he only "starts to cry" and "weep / Tears of iodine" while the women characterize themselves through a range of auditory effects, from chanting to "Rustling on brown [non-white] paper wings," a symbol of their creative ability. Their ethnic self-esteem no longer needs the mimicry of "yellow half-shadows." The new generation longs for the complete artistic freedom.

As Arnold Rampersad indicates (1986: 53), Dove radically departs from what has been considered quintessentially black verse. Instead of loose structures, she shows tight control; instead of reckless inspiration, one recognizes discipline and practice; instead of personal confession, she offers personal reference objectified; instead of an obsession with the theme of race, Dove repudiates black cultural nationalism in the name of a more inclusive sensibility. In these terms "Upon Meeting Don L. Lee, in a Dream" is both the ground and vanishing point for her transcultural enspacements.

In "Magic" (*SP* 176) Beulah combines similar willpower, imagination, and dreaming to escape the daily drudgery of her Great Depression household.

> *Practice makes perfect,* the old folks said.
> *So she rehearsed deception*

until ice cubes
dangled willingly
from a plain white string
and she could change
an egg into her last nickel.

things happened
to her. One night she awoke
and on the lawn blazed
a scaffolding strung in lights.
Next morning the Sunday paper
showed the Eiffel Tower
soaring through clouds.
It was a sign
she would make it to Paris one day.

Paris, the City of Lights, as a dream destination is deeply engrained in the African-American community as a privileged place of creative excellence, racial liberalism, beauty, and civilization. The "cherished experience of 'the Parisian moment' sometimes consists in the delighted discovery of a profound consonance between France and the Afro-American soul," Michel Fabre writes in "Paris as a Moment in African American Consciousness" (Sollors and Diedrich, eds. 1994: 126). Beulah's elaborations and linguistic and imagistic complexities attest to what Freud called "dreamwork" ("Traumarbeit").

Imagination, of course, works by forming and deforming at the same time. For Bachelard it is the *deformative activity of the imagination*.[34] The pathologized image in a dream, the disruptive, deformative elements, Bachelard insists, are vital and mobile new images for the imagination. Fusing his analysis with Bachelard, James Hillman in *The Dream and the Underworld* argues as well that:

> through the shock of deformation, especially the pathologized deformation which restores to an image its capacity to perturb the soul to excess that, by bringing an image close to death, concurrently makes it live again. For it is the shocking dream of which the nightmare is paradigm that we remember most, that most stirs the soul's *memoria*. (1979: 130).

Beulah, the day dreamer, also has nightmares about losing her kin. In "Mother-hod" (*SP* 185) her fear centers on "a white wolf" she has to kill to save her baby: "She dreams the baby's so small she keeps / misplacing it—it rolls from the hutch / and the mouse carries it home, it disappears / with his shirt in the wash. / Then she drops it and it explodes / like a watermelon, eyes spitting." In this concoction of dreaded loss, racial fear, and "Little Red Ridinghood" romance she turns into a hunter heroine "as she straddles / the wolf and circles its throat, counting / until her thumbs push through to the earth. / White fur seeps red." In "confusion and shame" over her ferocious fantasies, her evil shadow just shone through, she wakes up. We know she will fight to the very end. "Nightmare" (*SP* 197) has her worrying over her husband who barely recovered from a stroke. Two stanzas of twelve short lines assemble associations of the present and the past: salty sweat, greying hair, fear of loss, and childhood memories of shaming a mother's racial pride.

> She's dreaming
> of salt again:
> salt stinging her eyes,
> making pepper of her hair,
> salt in her panties
> and light all over.
> If she wakes
> she'll find him
> gone and the dog
> barking its tail off,
> locked outside in the
> dead of night.

Growing up and out of one's family engenders liminal, eroticized dreamscapes. A high point of poetically controlled exuberance for life is shown in the adolescent poems in *YH* in which the voices of prepubescent girls evoke the apprehensive taboos of an irresistibly growing sexuality. The scene of action or, rather, anticipation moves from the bedroom in Beulah's cycle to "behind grandmother's porch" ("Adolescence—I," *SP* 42), to the bathroom ("Adolescence—II," *SP* 43), and to "The dusky rows of tomatoes" ("Adolescence—III," *SP* 44). "As they glowed orange in sunlight / And rotted in shadow, I too / Grew orange and softer, / swelling out / Starched cotton slips. // The texture of twilight made me think of / Lengths of Dotted Swiss." Imaginary flights in striking visual representations are "tacked down again and again in homey details" (Rampersad 1986: 59). The young speaker now "dreamed how it would happen: / He would meet me by the blue spruce, / A carnation over his heart, saying, 'I have come for you, Madam; / I have loved you in my dreams.'" Less explicit but in precise vagueness "Adolescence—I" visually provokes a fluster of expectation over a boy's kiss. An extraordinary sequence of whirring sounds and a sense of explosive tension enhance the girl's excitement.

> A firefly whi**rr**ed **near** my **ear**, and **in** the distance
> I could **hear stree**tlamps ping
> **Into m**i**ni**ature suns
> Against a **feathery** sky. (emphasis mine)

If these adolescents or Beulah nonetheless can't "make it to Paris one day," there is an alternative: "Carrying dreams on into waking life, or what are called *waking dreams*" (Hillman 1979: 93). Whereas Hillman argues that this alternative does not move beyond feelings and is but another romantic variety, Bachelard testifies to the daydream's uplifting grandeur.

> Daydream undoubtedly feeds on all kinds of sights, but through a sort of natural inclination, it contemplates grandeur. And this contemplation produces an

attitude that is so special, an inner state that is so unlike any other, that the daydream transports the dreamer outside the immediate world to a world that bears the mark of infinity. (1994: 183)

However, daydreaming and poetic imagination are related as a way of inner life and survival habit for Beulah.

"Daystar" (*SP* 188) will open our discussion of *mental expansion* (intense feelings, imagination, meditation, storytelling, detachment, sensual and spiritual freedom) through renegotiated *social space*.

> She wanted a little room for thinking:
> but she saw diapers steaming on the line,
> a doll slumped behind the door.
>
> So she lugged a chair behind the garage
> to sit out the children's naps.
>
> Sometimes there were things to watch—
> the pinched armor of a vanished cricket,
> a floating maple leaf. Other days
> she stared until she was assured
> when she closed her eyes
> she'd see only her own vivid blood.
>
> She had an hour, at best, before Liza appeared
> pouting from the top of the stairs.
> And just *what* was mother doing
> out back with the field mice? Why,
>
> building a palace. Later
> that night when Thomas rolled over and
> lurched into her, she would open her eyes
> and think of the place that was hers
> for an hour—where
> she was nothing,
> pure nothing, in the middle of the day.

In a crowded life where both her children's and her husband's demands make her "feel like a public park instead of a human being" (Dove in Kirkpatrick 1995: 37), the speaker is capable of building castles in the air, even a palace populated with "the pinched armor of a vanished cricket, / a floating maple leaf," "field mice," or "her own vivid blood." Again, her imaginary state of being "pure nothing, in the middle of the day," is tied to "homey details" (Rampersad 1986: 59). This is how she has managed to negotiate her own social and mental space away from her kin, at least for a serene hour.

Dove and Bachelard equally treasure the "intimate immensity . . . within ourselves. It is attached to a sort of expansion of being that life curbs and caution arrests, but which starts again when we are alone. As soon as we become motionless, we are elsewhere" (Bachelard 1994: 184). Beulah's backyard room of her own shares with Bachelard's nests, shells and corners the notion of "a secluded space in which we like to hide, or withdraw into ourselves (136). This germ of a private mental space turns into a symbol of solitary, productive, and regenerative imagination.

"Roast Possum" (*SP* 167–168) offers a different kind of mental expansion, as Thomas turns into an imaginative storyteller for his grandchildren. In presenting a possum in his tale, he clearly sets a counterpoint to Werner's encyclopedic white world of learning: the (o)possum as well as the monkey, rabbit, or raccoon are popular animals in African-American folklore.[35] Yet, according to Werner's encyclopedia, *"The possum's a greasy critter / that lives on persimmons and what, / the Bible calls carrion."* Thomas bought the "Standard Work / of Reference in the Arts, / Science, History, Discovery, and Invention" . . . "*Complete in Twenty-Five Volumes* / minus one—"at a rummage sale" . . . "for five bucks / no zebras, no Virginia, no wars," that is, no black and white dichotomy or coexistence, no former British Colony, and, therefore, no war ("One Volume Missing," *SP* 163). To protect his family—as Rita's father did (cf. "Elevator Man, 1949")—Thomas knew how to undermine biased or complement missing information. "A granddaughter / propped on each knee, / Thomas went on with his tale— // but it was for Malcolm, little / Red Delicious [his only grandson], that he invented / embellishments." . . . "When the girls [among them most likely Rita Dove] / got restless, Thomas talked horses."

> They liked that part.
> He could have gone on to tell them
> that the Werner admitted Negro children
> to be intelligent, though briskness
> clouded over at puberty, bringing
> indirection and laziness. Instead,
> he added: *You got to be careful*
> *with a possum when he's on the ground;*
> *he'll turn on his back and play dead*
> *till you give up looking. That's*
> *what you'd call sullin'.*

The salvation implicit in one's generation's nurturing another by gathering and making palpaple history and myth, fact and fiction, is the greatest defense and preservation against the cruelties we force on one another. Not only does Thomas rectify and amplify Werner's derogatory description of a possum as just *"a critter"* ("creature") by putting it both into a neutral context—the possum plays dead when stared at—and one of African-American folklore, he also withholds from his grandchildren the devastating white suprematists' stereotyping of "Negro children" as indirected and lazy. The highpoint of the storyteller and educator's guiding spirit however, shows in the final stanza. Malcolm's material curiosity in questions like "who **owned** Strolling Jim [a horse], / and who **paid** for the tombstone" deliberately remain open. Thomas, who values mind-expanding tall tales more than facts from judgmental and biased encyclopedias, offers a morsel of thought-provoking soul food from man to man instead: "*Yessir, / we enjoyed that possum. We ate him real slow, with sweet potatoes*[36] Dove writes on "Roast Possum" in *UVA Alumni News*:

> Now, while my grandmother dished out concise, if sometimes cryptic, advice, my grandfather had his own sly way of dispensing wisdom: he told stories. And in these stories, it was often in what wasn't said where the life lessons lay that would strike home 15 years down the road. In the following poem, my grandfather decided against telling his grandchildren what is really on his mind: his rage after stumbling across a racist bit of misinformation in an old encyclopedia; instead he renders his warning as a parable about survival in his childhood town in south-central Tennessee. (Jan. / Feb. 1994: 24)

"Anti-Father" (*SP* 112–13), a sequence of thirteen short couplets with a single closing line, witnesses a female speaker's detachment from her father and a decisive step from the past into her own future: "Contrary to / tales you told us // summer nights when / the air conditioner // broke—the stars / are not far // apart. Rather / they draw / closer together / with years. // And houses / shrivel, un-lost, // and porches sag; / neighbors phone // to report cracks / in the cellar floor, // roots of the willow / coming up. Stars // speak to a child. / the past // is silent. . . . / Just between // me and you, / woman to man, // outer space is / inconceivably/ / intimate." Poems like "Geometry" (*SP* 17), "Sic itur ad astra" (*Washington Post Magazine* 7 May 1995: 29), or "Anti-Father" are mind-expanding explorations of new spaces of perception, visualized in a broken air conditioner—hot temperature out of control—shrivelling houses, sagging porches, "cracks / in the cellar floor, // roots of the willow / coming up." While the old structures called home break up or are outgrown, the process of the speaker's individuation proves her father's tales inaccurate against her own ob-servaticns: "the stars/are not far / apart. Rather/they draw / closer together / with years." The final couplets of "Anti-Father" perfectly illuminate Bachelard's notion of "intimate immensity" where "Just between / me and you, / woman to man, / " a new alliance opens the skies and

> outer space is
> inconceivably
>
> intimate.

"Immensity is within ourselves. It is attached to a sort of expansion of being that life curbs and caution arrests, but which starts again when we are alone" (Bachelard 1994: 184). The multifarious contrasts and conflicts between past and present, houses and outer space, hot summer nights and (broken) air con-ditioning indoors—a sign that hot temperature can no longer be controlled—father's tales and daughter's scrutiny, father and beloved, are formally mirrored in couplets that consist of two to three words only. The tight-knit spare poem develops from resenting the superego to the essence of intimate space linked to the universe, a trajectory further developed in a group of ecstatic "zero-point" poems that focus on private moments. "Zero-point" squares the paradox of "no space and time at all" with an "immensity with no other setting than itself." Bachelard, referring to Baudelaire, declares this ecstatic mind, body, and soul expanding experience "a conquest of intimacy" (1994: 195). Ecstatic moments—falling in love, knowing the right answer, listening to music, watching a lover, breastfeeding a daughter—shine through these titles: "Happenstance" (*SP* 7)—"When you appeared it was as if / magnets cleared the air"—; "Flirtation" (*SP* 128)—"There are ways / to make of the moment / a topiary / so the pleasure's in // walking through"—; "Flash Cards" (*GN* 12)—"The faster / I answered, the faster they came"—; "Exeunt the Viols" (*SP* 129)—"Magnificence spoke up briefly"—; "His Shirt" (*SP* 59)—"it's / a sail surprised / by boundless joy"—; and "Pastoral" (*GN* 38), an extraordinary poem on motherhood. It evokes "a physical and spiritual intimacy, celebrating the ethos of the child, without sentimentality" (Costello 1991: 436). The second of two stanzas of equal length reads:

> I liked afterwards best, lying
> outside on a quilt, her new skin
> spread out like meringue. I felt then
> what a young man must feel
> with his first love asleep on his breast:
> desire, and the freedom to imagine it

A remarkable shift of attention from mother love to erotic intimacy—the speaker imagines a male lover's delight in the baby's position—turns the final line into an ecstatic moment of androgynous consciousness: "desire, and the freedom to imagine it" indeed fuses female and male fantasies, erotic desire, and altruistic nourishment.

"Medusa" (*GN* 55) shall close our discussion on mental expansion and / through renegotiated social space and at the same time lead to *transcultural enspacement*, as the intertextual references of the poem are rich and varied. Medusa is one of the mythical three Gorgons; she was slain by Perseus. Her name also denotes the tentacled, usually bell-shaped, free-swimming sexual stage in the life cycle of a coelenterate, such as a jellyfish (Latin "medusa," from Medusa's snaky locks). In Dove's fusion of Greek myth with the Germanic tradition, Medusa resembles the naiad-like existence of Melusine, Undine, or Hans Christian Andersen's Little Mermaid,[37] all symbols of a hybrid existence, half-animal, half-human. Between the elements of water and air, they are longing to be absolved and to become fully human through strong unconditional love. The snaky locks and the decapitated head of the Greek Gorgon, however, led Sigmund Freud to equate her attraction and decapitation with castration. In "Medusa's Head"[38] he elaborates his theory:

> The hair upon Medusa's head is frequently represented in works of arts in the form of snakes, and these once again are derived from the castration complex. It is a remarkable fact that, however frightening they may be in themselves, they nevertheless serve actually as a mitigation of the horror, for they replace

the penis, the absence of which is the cause of the horror. This is a confirmation of the technical rule according to which a multiplication of penis symbols signifies castration. The sight of Medusa's head makes the spectator stiff with terror, turns him into stone. . . . If Medusa's head takes the lace of a representation of the female genitals, or rather if it isolates their horrifying effects from the pleasure-giving ones, it may be recalled that displaying the genitals is familiar in other connections as an apotropaic act.

In her comment on Freud, Elisabeth Bronfen sees him aligning "a fear of death with the radical Otherness of Woman not only explicitly (in his notes on the Medusa figure . . .), but also implicitly in his late writings, given that writing on both subjects involves speculation and incompletion" (*Over Her Dead Body*, 1992: 255). Freud calls femininity a "dark continent" but, close to his death, lacks the time for analytic research to prove his findings. Nonetheless, beheaded Medusa has become an emblem for castration as well as the talking womb or talking body, that is, hysteria. The horror man experiences at the sight of the devouring snake-like hairs that surround female genitals and her castrating stiff body under scrutiny must be compensated by maiming and disempowering her flesh. A petrified Medusa, however, is able to return the look of those who gaze on her. Here is "Medusa's" inner monologue in Dove's reinterpretation.

> I've got to go
> down where my eye
> can't reach
> hairy star
> who forgets to shiver
> forgets the cool suck
> inside
>
> Someday long
> off someone will
> see me
> fling me up
> until I hook
> into sky
>
> drop his memory
>
> My hair
> dry water

No punctuation, unique in Dove's poetry, impedes the visual and verbal flow of her interlocking hair imagery. In the darkest watery depths, Medusa must seek to forget the shiver, "the cool suck / inside" of sexual passion, procreation, and earthbound pleasure her eye, an other "hairy star," "can't reach" to see. This reading, of course, privileges Medusa as an unmaimed water nymph longing for absolution and annihiliation of desire in the arms of the all encompassing Mother Earth, the Sea.

Yet the descent in the first stanza does not yet feature water and could be read without any mythical dimension. In this case a woman's eye, or I, two "hairy star[s]," must go down and bend in an attempt to square the circle: that is to unite the upper body hairy stars with the lower hidden one, the female genitals, her eye / I can't reach. Rearranged along these lines, the first stanza reads: "I've got to go down / where my eye / hairy star / who forgets the cool suck inside / can't reach. In this interpretation closest to the text, the poet seeks to bring together animus and anima, the life principles of the mind and the body, her spiritual and physical selves.

The second stanza predicts transformation "Someday long / off." Yet it is not necessarily a knight in shining armor that triggers this metamorphosis, though, for a second, the reader is beguiled to believe that "someone will / see me / fling me up" only to find out that this "someone" could as well be witnessing the persona's own change from tentacled, free-swimming jellyfish into airy star: "fling me up / until I look / into the sky." At this point the image of the eye as hairy star looking "into the sky" and the dried jellyfish-star flung into heaven fuse in an extraordinary way. One line singled out, "drop his memory," offers the only clue of a male presence—to be dropped from memory. Thus the paradox is solved in the final couplet. Seldom has complex metamorphosis been expressed in such a precise and spare way: "My hair / dry water." No snaky locks symbolize her knowledge, only the watery flow of dry hair in the astral cold, art's eerie passion.

In this sense Dove lifts Medusa from object to subject position. No longer victim but agent, she writes her own story. "Drop his memory" and it will work. Dove's sense of transition recalls both Adrienne Rich's poem "Diving into the Wreck" and her epigraph "In the Old Neighborhood": *"To pull yourself up by your own roots; to eat the last meal in your own neighborhood"* from *"Shooting Script" (SP* xxii). Is "Medusa" a "mythological tale of the redemption of blackness" as Helen Vendler suggests ("Rita Dove: Identity Markers," 1995: 87)? Dove's "black identity" certainly lives "without being constricted by it to a single manner" (87–88). But "Medusa" cannot and should not be reduced to one reading. After all—and Dove loves puzzles—the anagram of MEDUSA is AMUSED. This trajectory ties in with Hélène Cixous's[39] reorientation of the myth in "The Laugh of the Medusa" (1976), and "Castration or Decapitation?" (1981). Here she argues for a feminine unconscious that allows women to seize loss and live it by the oblivion of *acceptance*: by "leaping" (1981: 54). "Women have wept a great deal, but once the tears are shed, there will be endless laughter instead" (55). Thus the laugh of the Medusa shatters any placid surface constituted by the petrifying gaze of a single hermeneutic decoding. Dove's "Medusa" always remains one leap or one dive ahead of the pack.

On her corkboard the poet keeps an observation of "clear-headed, no-nonsense wisdom" by the Talmudic scholar Hillel the Elder that has guided her "through many difficult moments" (*UVA Alumni News* Jan./Feb. 1994: 27): "If I am not for myself, / Who will be for me? / If I am for myself only, / What am I? // And if not now, / When?" This is the spiritual and artistic point of departure, the leap of the Medusa, for Dove's astounding range of *transcultural enspacements.*

An early example is "Ö," the final poem of her first book, *YH* (*SP* 64). It answers her key question, "Where's a word, a talisman, to hold against the world?"[40] and reflects her profound concern with language: Poetry is the best words in the best order; to say most with least, or as she expressed in her conversation with Rubin and Kitchen:

> Language is everything. As Mallarmé said, "A poem is made of words." It's by language that I enter the poem, and that also leads me forward. That doesn't exclude perceptions and experience and emotions or anything like that. But emotion is useless if there's no way to express it. Language is just the clay we use to make our poems. (1986: 237)

"Ö"

Shape the lips to an *o*, say *a*.
That's *island.*

One word of Swedish has changed the whole neighborhood.
When I look up, the yellow house on the corner
is a galleon stranded in flowers. Around it

the wind. Even the high roar of a leaf-mulcher
could be the horn-blast from a ship
as it skirts the misty shoals.

We don't need much more to keep things going.
Families complete themselves
and refuse to budge from the present,
the present extends its glass forehead to sea
(backyard breezes, scattered cardinals)

and if, one evening, the house on the corner
took off over the marshland,
neither I nor my neighbor
would be amazed. Sometimes

a word is found so right it trembles
at the slightest explanation.
You start out with one thing, end
up with another, and nothing's
like it used to be, not even the future.

In producing the exotic Swedish sound "Ö"—island-like within English—the lips mimic the very shape of the umlaut. This "sensual awareness of the Other transforms and intoxicates the speaker" (Stein 1995: 59). Between alpha and omega a new sound emerges to denote "island" and to connote "a word . . . so right it trembles at the slightest explanation." Freed and empowered by language, the speaker embraces "Ö" as a poetic program, the breaking of new ground that liquefies the mainland and sets afloat an entire neighborhood.[41]

No longer bound to a place, imagination evokes a ship to board and an un-known space to conquer. "We don't need much more to keep things going." In this instance, a Swedish sound within English territory demonstrates how a double tongue introduces a double, stereotopic vision, and an incomparable strategy for depth perception. Dove's "Ö" indeed functions as a chronotope, a timespace, in Bakhtin's sense (Clark, and Holquist 1984: 280). It materializes time in space, concretizes representation, and lends body to the entire poem.

Dove fleshes out the skeleton of her artistic program with factual detail. A Swedish family has moved into "the yellow house on the corner," and it has be-come a yellow "galleon stranded in flowers." The yellow amidst the flowers' blue may suggest the Swedish flag. "Around it the wind. Even the high roar of a leaf-mulcher could be the horn-blast from a ship as it skirts the misted shoals." . . . "and if, one evening, the house on the corner / took off over the marshland, / neither I nor my neighbor / would be amazed." What is the effect of this imagi-nary flight aboard the one right word? Whereas the house—usually stable, em-bodying space—begins to move, even to float away, families—usually unstable, embodying time—"complete themselves and refuse to budge from the present." In its perfect circular shape, Dove's talisman "Ö" redefines both space and time; "the present" itself is aboard the house turned ship and "extends its glass fore-head to sea (backyard breezes, scattered cardinals) . . . and nothing's like it used to be, not even the future." Past ("used to be"), present, and future are imaginatively expanded and moved by "wind" and ironic romantic "backyard breezes," together with the "scattered cardinals," bright-red crested American songbirds, one of the poet's emblems. To Dove "Ö" felt like a different kind of poem, as she told William Walsh, "one that signaled the end of an apprentice-ship." She recognized the liberating power of language as that you work with and through it, both "your tool and your clay" (1994: 150).

"Ö" is a telling example of what "minority constructs within a major lan-guage" (Deleuze and Guattari 1986: 16). Dove breaks new ground and fills these transcultural enspacements with new dimensions and identities of how art pro-vides a home away from home. I say "home," because for Dove a house is never a home. It is a receptacle for memory, a secure life, and yet at the same time an en-closure to overcome and to be expanded as poems like "Geometry" (*SP* 17) and "In the Old Neighborhood" (*SP* xxii–xxvi) indicate. "Ö" is Dove's prolific "Eiland" that playfully twists the commonly dreaded coloring of a so far all-white neigh-borhood. Not that one single word literally changed the neighborhood, but it changed "in the eyes of the speaker and how the speaker now understands the neighborhood, the future, and the value of language" (Walsh 1994: 149–50).

"Reading Hölderlin on the Patio with the Aid of a Dictionary" (*SP* 88) visu-alizes a similar process, yet in the opposite direction. Here the speaker has to match signifier and signified in a difficult deciphering of verse by the German poet Friedrich Hölderlin. Only "One by one, the words / give themselves / up white flags dispatched / from a silent camp." This courageous step-by-step-journey into a language foreign to the speaker starts from the liminal space of the patio where words, "white flags" in the opening stanza, emerge like dark silhouettes against the sunset. They release the skeleton of a tree, the poem's structure, into the vast realm of meaning between two cultures. Yet the speaker "whose shyness returned" in front of one of the most complex and musical texts, nonetheless experiences a Medusa-like transformation, though in the reverse direction "word for word, until I am."

> The meaning that surfaces
>
> comes to me aslant and
> I go to meet it, stepping
> out of my body
> word for word, until I am
>
> everything at once: the perfume
> of the world in which
> I go under,
> a skindiver
> remembering air.

It becomes clear how the encoding speaker-poet of "Medusa" leaps up from water into eerie spirituality, while the decoding speaker of this poem dives down, "remembering air," to reach for deeper meaning, not unlike "The Fish in the Stone." Transcultural enspacements in Dove, however, are always multifaceted. Hölderlin, also from Tübingen, where Dove studied, was confronted with a similar experience when he became absorbed by Greek (before he went back to the sources of German). In his poem "Mnemosyne" he "dramatically expressed the anesthesia of the person that is snatched up by a foreign language: 'A sign, such are we, and of no meaning / Dead to all suffering, and we have almost / Lost our language in a foreign land.'"[42]

Dove explores not only the contact zones of languages but also the spatialization of time in European landscapes. The poem whose title heads the first section of *M* reads "The Hill Has Something to Say" (*SP* 74–75). In her interview with Kitchen, Rubin, and Ingersoll the poet explains how:

A narrow way of looking at that title would be simply that every hill contains things which make it a hill, speaking specifically of Europe where practically every hill has ruins underneath it. So it has its history, if we would just listen, if we could look at what is very obvious—a hill—and imagine the layers of time. There's an archaeological sense and a magic that I was trying to get at in that title. But also I was trying to get at the inability of that hill to say anything. It's an inarticulate object. We have to dig into it, which is why at the end of that section, there are lots of characters, individuals from history who can't speak to us anymore. (1986: 233)

The skeleton of the poem reads as an artistic exhortation, enforced by the fact that "The hill has a right / to stand here." As if to visualize the compact ties of the surface with all layers below the title connects with the beginning of each stanza.

"The Hill Has Something to Say"

but isn't talking.
Instead the valley groans as the wind,
amphoric,
hoots its one bad note.
Halfway up, we stop to peek
through smudged pine: this is Europe
and its green terraces.

and takes its time.
what's left
to climb's inside us,
earth rising, stupified.

: it's not all in the books
(but maps don't lie).
The hill has a right
to stand here, one knob
in the coiled spine of a peasant
who, forgetting to flee, simply
lay down forever.

bootstrap and spur
harrow and pitchfork
a bugle a sandal
clay head of a pipe

(For all we know
the wind's inside us, pacing
our lungs. For all we know
it's spring and the ground

moistens as raped maids break
to blossom. What's invisible
sings, and we bear witness.)

if we would listen! Underfoot
slow weight, Scavenger Time,
and the little old woman
who lives there still. (emphasis mine)

In Dove's enspacement of time, the silent hill represents a wilderness above the busy "valley [that] groans as the wind, amphoric, hoots its one bad note." Hers is clearly a rewriting of Wallace Stevens's "Anecdote of the Jar." While Stevens's sovereign gesture places a symbolic artifact right at the top of a hill in Tennessee and makes the wilderness rise up to it—this is "Art in America" emplaced—Dove's European hill is bare, if not empty, but art in itself; it "has a right / to stand here." Her poet is an archaeologist who must come to realize that "What's left / to climb's inside us." . . . ("What's invisible / sings, and we bear witness)." In this spatialization of time, books may lie "but maps don't." The hill's layers ready to be unearthed and revised, "earth rising, stupified," also recall the shape and function of a womb: "spring and the ground moistens as raped maids break to blossom." Scavenger Time may be outwitted if the poet lends a voice to the raped maids and to "the little old woman who lives there still" to bear witness. While the females are linked with the remembrance of passing time, the male peasant's "coiled spine"—he forgot to flee, and "simply lay down forever"—visualizes the spatiality of the hilly landscape.

"Delft" (*SP* 96), however, envisions the plains of the Netherlands: "Flat, with variations. Not / the table but the cloth. / As if a continent / raging westward, staggered / at the sight of / so much water, sky / on curdling sky." The Dutch in particular as well as the European in general "*may be standing / on a porch / open to the world / but the house behind us / is sinking.*

Dove, however, presents not only a range of protagonists who cross borders, thresholds, and gates but also liminal or, rather, marginalized characters who gain their presence, cultural significance, and influence precisely through the poet's transcultural enspacement: women who turn from objects into subjects; revised myths and legends of female saints that reveal heretofore unheard, unnoticed voices; displaced persons, artists, writers, dyers, migrants through world and time who enrich and revive the stale stasis of those seemingly at home. The following poems illustrate the extraordinary power of threshold figures, migrants, exiles, visitors in different cultural contexts who not only gain a home in art through Dove's lyrical enspacement but who also fuse various cultural backgrounds or cut out their own pluricultural identity and niche in an unprecedented way.

Section II of *Museum*, entitled "In the Bulrush," contains poems that break new transcultural ground out of the seemingly well defined and fixed European "museum." "Robert Schumann, Or: Musical Genius Begins with Affliction" (*SP* 6) is a striking example of Dove's homemaking in art that transcends geographical and cultural boundaries. Here she undermines the myth of a well-known white composer by presenting his relationships with women, often the source of his artistic compositions, in an unromantic and unheroic manner: "It began with A—years before in a room / with a white piano and lyre-back chairs, / Schumann panted on a whore on a coverlet / and the oboe got its chance." Schumann's compositions, his "Cello Concerto in A minor," his "Symphony in A, Phantasiestücke, Concerto . . . in A minor," all grow out of "a thicket of its own making," out of a primeval room with "no wretched sounds," where "He was Adam naked in creation, starting over as the sky rained apples." Like apples out of an Eden furnished with delicate "lyre-back chairs," the apple-like notes, often returning to A, "stack themselves onto the score-sheets like unfamiliar furniture."

Woman as sexual object or as a sacrificial offering to the male artistic imagination has been a recurrent theme in women's poetry, including Dove's work. In addition to the whore in "Robert Schumann . . . " Dove presents women treated as sexual objects in "The Boast" (*SP* 45), "For Kazuko" (*SP* 57), "Beauty and the Beast" (*SP* 58), "Shakespeare Say" (*SP* 89), "The Sailor in Africa" (*SP* 119), "Uncle Millet" (*GN* 18), and in "Genie's Prayer under the Kitchen Sink" (*GN* 60). Nonetheless, "Robert Schumann . . ." is not merely

Dove's critique of a man using, if not abusing, a woman for his creative and recreative purposes. In using spatial metaphors (room, piano, lyre-back chairs, notes that stack themselves like unfamiliar furniture), she conducts the way of music out of the private composer's paradise into the public space of the concert hall; and she spatializes music, an essentially linear art, into the architectural frame of unfamiliar furniture, thus lending the composition a room of her own creation.

Dove's synthesis of a historical consciousness with her poignant analysis of everyday life provokes a series of humorous revisions of myths. Though the chosen characters' lives have been the stuff of legend, the beginning of "Nestor's Bathtub" (*SP* 72–73)—"As usual, legend got it all wrong," . . . "Legend, as usual, doesn't say," . . . "For the sake of legend only the tub stands"—announces a deep dissatisfaction with the conventional ordering of events and an intention to rejuvenate history by coming up with new ways of telling it. In "Nestor's Bathtub," a pivotal poem in this respect, the title already undermines the public name of this wise old Greek counselor by juxtaposing it with a bathtub. This satirical tale of the tub truly shows the underside of heroism not in terms of historical facts, but in terms of imagined female activity while a husband is absent "counting the jars of oil in storeroom 34, or on the move at the Trojan wars." The wife's private amorous fire—"her white hands scraped the dirt from a lover's back" in the meantime—grows into exploding pots of olive oil "spreading in flames to the lady's throne." "Look how they fell," . . . "look at the pattern left in stucco from the wooden columns," . . . "look at the shards scattered in the hall" invites the reader to look anew and to privilege the process over the surviving result in the shape of a monolithical bathtub, a legendary "heap of limestone [that] blocks" our view. Whereas the tub as receptacle stands for a solid male legend (with its owner mostly absent), Nestor's wife is linked to its liquid content, twisting the trite symbol of woman as vessel to be filled by man. She is the bearer of "fragrant water poured until the small room steamed," and she is also associated with the pot breaking hot oil ultimately turning into growing olive trees "into the hill." His is a world of counting his assets, hers is a world of internal provisions. Nestor's nameless wife, however, is no saint, only the witness of the overlooked, the forgotten, and the untold. Traces of his past grandeur and her secretly undermining betrayal conjoin in Dove's historical remake.

In a combination of fact and fiction, language writes and rewrites history as art: no longer are frozen legends like Nestor's bathtub in demand. The single monolithical "spot of time" (Wordsworth) finds itself replaced by those shards we as readers have to rearrange in order to recreate history out of the overlooked, the untold, or the simply forgotten. In her interview with Rubin and Kitchen, Dove confirms that

> There are some things which in fact are ideal museum objects—the fish in the stone, for instance, the fossil that we observe; but there are also people who become frozen or lifted out and set on a pedestal, a mental pedestal. (1986: 232)

Among her portraits of female historical figures, Dove includes women who chose sainthood over conventional social roles (*SP* 80, 81; *GN* 59). Yet factual accuracy is not so much Dove's concern as is the rewriting of legends.[43] She depicts "Catherine of Alexandria" (*SP* 79), historically a beautiful, young, and well-educated noblewoman, as "deprived of learning and the chance to travel." This enables Dove to lend Catherine her own voice so that sainthood is no longer the only voice and choice. The poet is even vying with Jesus for confessions of nightly joys ("and what went on each night was fit for nobody's ears but Jesus'"). The undergrowth of Catherine's story shows the saint may be pregnant: "a kept promise, a ring of milk."

The historical Catherine of Alexandria rebuked the Roman emperor Galerius Valerius Maximinus, who then condemned her to be broken on the wheel. Catherine indeed seems empowered through sainthood, which enables her to confront the Emperor's violence. In Dove's poem, however, the emperor is not mentioned at all. Sainthood appears not as a free choice but as the only alternative to a woman "deprived of learning and the chance to travel." The significance of Catherine of Alexandria for Dove is not in the mannes of her martyrdom, but in her invention of the notion of a mystical "marriage" to Jesus, a notion that is paradoxically also conveyed through erotic imagery. We may wonder whether Dove presents the Savior as a deified man like the Roman Emperor, which would turn sainthood into another version of female submission to male authority.

"Fiammetta Breaks Her Peace" (*SP* 83) sets Boccaccio's idealized love, Fiammetta, against the reality of the plague: "I've watched them, mother, and I know the signs. The first day, rigor, [. . .] Day two is fever [. . .] Then, at least, there is certainty, an odd kind of relief; a cross comes on the door." Fiammetta's viewpoint, so far unknown, has been given a voice not only to describe the symptoms of the disease but also to relate the mourners' reaction to a painful death. Yet Fiammetta's realistic dirge contrasts with Boccaccio's belief that ideal love and art may conquer time and physical decay. But his "little flame," Fiammetta, is left to tell the tale. She "who isn't anybody really because she's not treated as real" (Rubin and Kitchen 1986: 233) has been installed by Dove next to "Boccaccio: The Plague Years" (*SP* 82). These two companion poems, which present his and her stories, illustrate how Dove unites viewpoints that reconstruct forgotten events or people. In adding once more the excluded female side, Dove clearly focuses on the undergrowth of history, on the margin within the heart of European culture. Her shedding light on these blind spots is a gesture by an African-American poet who pays attention to human beings no one will ever remember but who are just as important in shaping our concept of ourselves. Out of her empathy with those neglected or excluded through history, often women, children, or men in minor positions, Dove—like Lorde, Rich, among others—adopts a retrospective and reconstructive method. By including what History has excluded, she further "expresses her distate for conventional hierarchies and interpretations" (Georgoudaki "Rita Dove: Crossing Boundaries," 1991: 421).

Many of the figures in Dove's poems are displaced, or between different worlds: *TB* (*SP* 141f), "Banneker" (*SP* 93), "David Walker" (*SP* 30), "The Bird Frau" (*SP* 5), "The Island Women of Paris" (*GN* 65), and "Zabriah" (*FS* 55f). The experience of "living in two worlds, seeing with a double vision" consistently compels Dove's imagination. Yet her identification with a historical, mysterious, and artistic male-female consciousness is most complete in the poem picture, or picture poem in the making entitled "Agosta the Winged Man and Rasha the Black Dove" (*SP* 98–100). In a moment of empowerment, the American Black Dove recreates the genesis of an existing painting in turning directly to the German painter Christian Schad, who is in need of artistic inspiration. Whereas Katja, the Russian aristocratic model mentioned in the poem, serves as mere remembrance of things past, a traveling road show consisting of a Black snake woman from Madagascar and her deformed Caucasian partner, literally a winged man—one socially marginal, the other medically so—form a vital pair of true inspiration and pluricultural representation in this iconic painting of the *Neue Sachlichkeit*. The label *Neue Sachlichkeit* seems to acquire suggestive power not only in conjunction with the medical arena of the Charité, where Agosta's crests and fins—like a colony of birds—are exposed to the not overly rational scrutinizing eyes of medical students. It also applies to this pluricultural tableau vivant, where creativity and inspirational power renegotiated beyond the boundaries of race and gender might lead to a *Neue Sachlichkeit* in transcultural understanding. In the end it is the stigmatized figures, heroically posed, and so often gawked at in sideshows and hospitals, who stare fixedly and somehow disdainfully at the beholder. Painting and poem thus intertextually recreate a minority discourse within a dominant Germanic / Anglo-American culture. Yet the most astounding twist lies in the doubling of painter / poet and the models. The poem complements the ubiquitous male gaze using a female model with a female co-artist and a male model. Rasha the Black Dove is no longer a merely gazed-at object. She is accompanied by an equally inspiring man whereas Schad, the painter, is accompanied by an equally creative woman. As Rita the Black Dove, she not only lends her voice to the painter but controls the creative process as an omniscient narrator who develops a range of intertwining images "coiled counterwise" as the boa constrictor around Rasha's body: The "blank space" of the canvas is linked and likened to Schad's skin, which "he could not leave" though "he'd painted himself in a new one, silk green, worn like a shirt." Rasha's boa constrictor, however, may cast its slough: Identity, the skin or robes we put on, art, the blank space we fill in, and skin, put on or cast away, Dove virtually represents as open canvases to be inscribed according to inspiration and artistic needs. Color thus is treated as artistic creation rather than in terms of racial segregation. From the outset, "The canvas, not his eye was merciless," to "Not the canvas but their gaze . . . was merciless," in the end art has taken on wings, and Agosta's malformation, "a colony of birds, trying to get out" has led to the formation of art. In English the Winged Man's deformity, a pigeon breast, figuratively ties him to the Black Dove, whereas her plucking "a chicken for dinner" or bringing "eggs into the studio" only gains full meaning in view of Agosta's "Hühnerbrust." Dove's subtle use of German beside the clear cut "Hardenbergstrasse" reveals a web of intercultural exchange, an exchange not only nurtured artistically but also by the life-sustaining efforts of Rasha.

Yet, what appears to be a harmonizing picture in the making, the barebreasted white male enthroned above the black female at his feet, remains deterritorialized. The protagonists, though united in artistic inspiration, remain individuals; they arrive separately, live and work apart. Whereas Rasha right from the beginning initiates movement into the stasis of Schad's imagination, and even suggests motion in potentiality with the artistic act Schad remembers as "turning slowly in place as the boa constrictor coiled counterwise its heavy love," with her moving "slowly, as if she carried the snake around her body always." Agosta's is a static presence throughout. Yet both models, artists themselves, are icons of the scopic satisfaction (Lacan 1991: 76), used to being gawked at, she at kermesses, he at the hospital grand rounds of the Charité. They are by no means passive objects but emerge empowered by the gaze they attract and are aware of it. Seeing, as the most rational of the senses, calls for a distance from the observed object and frees the observer from a feeling of disarmed passivity. The observer, however, is not entirely freed, because the observing subject finds him- or herself mirrored and objectified in the gaze of the models. And despite or rather due to their physical difference, Rasha and Agosta also emanate and inspire desire: she as a black Eve[44] whose boa constrictor "coiled counterwise its heavy love," he as "he spoke in wonder of women trailing backstage to offer him the consummate bloom of their lust." Their being monstrously and vitally uncanny, the Other personified, turns them into Jacques Lacan's "objet petit a," a source of jouissance, that is, abundant artistic vitality for the painterly eye / I. Whereas Schad's vision is clearly associated with his eye—he is "staring at the blank space," "His eyes traveled to the plaster scrollwork on the ceiling"—Agosta and Rasha are linked with each other by being looked at: "their gaze, so calm, was merciless." In spite of Rasha, Agosta, and Schad's communion in art, each person remains distinct in this economy of "the eye and the gaze." As Lacan points out, "this is for us the split in which the drive is manifested at the level of the scopic field." "I see only from one point, but in my existence I am looked at from all sides" (1991: 72). In spite of Agosta and Rasha's independence and the success with which they turn their difference into assets, they are not harmonized under the motto "'all the colors of the world,' none of the oppression" (Gates 1992: 186). Rather, at stake in this poem is a critique of the myth of "universalist humanism." There, *différance* is integrated and leveled into a homogeneous world picture. Dove's poetic netting and working, however, combine aspects of displacement, fragmentation, and isolation within her search for artistic plenitude. It is precisely out of this double consciousness and tension, I argue, that she creates those spots that underlie and undercut her universalizing discourse. This pair of circus performers, an inscrutable deformed man and an equally inscrutable black woman who dances with snakes—the lines' endings meander like a snake —are performers, who like the poet, look at the world in unique ways. This is probably the only unifying principle: a moment of artistic performance.

Without passion. Not
the canvas
but their gaze
so calm,
was merciless.

In the ultimate poem of our discussion, "At the German Writers Conference in Munich" (*SP* 101–2), Dove examines and exploits this preoccupation from a different angle. Here another art—another way of performing—is described. The calm, stiff characters of a tapestry are not outwardly grotesque as are the characters in the preceding poem. Nevertheless, they appear to be out of step with their woven environment, existing as they do in a world of flowers. The two poems, together, illustrate a brilliant shifting of focus, a looking out of the eyes of characters, then a merciless looking into them.

The large hall of the Munich Hofbräuhaus, center of Bavarian and tourist merrymaking, hosts the German Writers Conference. Instead of speeches, the non-white participant visualizes the interaction of three texts, one of them written, two woven. Superimposed but not congruent, these texts reenact the process of writing poetry in its textual grid and underlying imagery. The writer/poet finds an intertextual frame, a context, and out of it creates a whole. With its ladies-in-waiting, soufflé-like crown, and ash-blonde crinklets allowed exposure to smoke, the medieval tapestry also offers an obliquely ironic comment on the "royal [writers'] party" going on underneath.

above the heads of the members
of the board, taut and white
as skin (not mine),
tacked across a tapestry
this banner:
Association of German
Writers in the Union of Printers
and Paper Manufacturers
Below it some flowers (. . .)
The tapestry pokes out
all over: (. . .)
At the bottom strip of needlework
four flat bread loaves.
Far in the eaves
two doves signify
a union endorsed
by God and the Church. (. . .)
Above them all a banner
unfurled and inscribed
in Latin. Maybe it says
Association of Tapestrers
in the Union of Wives
and Jewish Dyers.

Dove contrasts a one-dimensional, text-oriented "Association of German Writers in the Union of Printers and Paper Manufacturers" with a Latin banner of her own pluricultural translation. It refers to the visual art of weaving as well as to the usually forgotten hands involved in the making: Wives and Jewish Dyers. Imaginatively completed from the fragments poking out, the medieval tapestry shows a royal party's full personnel: "A king with a scepter and crown puffed like a soufflé; an ash-blonde princess by birthright permitted her to bare her crinklets to sun and smoke." A white horse, two doves, and dainty shoes next to a "grotesquely bent fetlock-to-ivory hoof," all embedded in flowers, supplement the tableau. Any tapestry is an ubiquituous symbol for a well-woven written text.

With this poem, however, Dove's netting and working reaches further dimensions. Her exquisite chronotope—that is, the primary means for materializing time in space—grasps and visualizes the reality of a single event as a multilayered expansion, both in its temporal depth as well as in its spatial width. Her spatialization of time includes a zooming of history (from medieval motifs to the present) and geography (from Munich to Jewish, and most likely African-American grounds). With Dove's poem, the Hofbräuhaus, well-grounded in the Bavarian tradition of ash-blonde maidens and fetlock-to-ivory hoofs, grows into an international home for artistic endeavor beyond boundaries. And beyond topicality: Neither the Hofbräuhaus nor other Munich breweries display a tapestry of Dove's description.

The issues raised so far lead to a redefinition of space in terms of a virtual new self as Dove is both the systematizer and spontaneous crosser.

Her micro-poetics of space draws a quickened attention to the very status of space and time as a complicity of strategies. Yet strategies and categories serve as angles of perception rather than reified boundaries and should not press poetry that successfully attempts to cross borders back into moulds. Mindful of these premonitions, Dove's worldmaking was explored under three aspects: first, *borders*, *boundaries*, second, *movements;* and third, *transcultural enspacements*. Outer and inner boundaries appeared as *dividing line, area of contact or unilateral division*, or *brink, edge*, and *threshold*. A variety of border crossings opened the horizon to movements such as *travelogues* and *sightseeing, flights into freedom, quests, metamorphoses*, and *imaginary voyages*, journeys that led into the psychotopology of *dreamscapes*, and further into samples of *mental expansion* through imagination and renegotiated *social space*, and into the particular experience of *transcultural enspacement* that, as a result of its exemplary richness and variety, lends its name to the study *Crossing Color* as a whole. In concentrating on a range of poems, Dove's concern with transcultural space, with the magic of language, her visual imagery, and multivocality provide a syncretic vision of the world beyond traditional confinements as she honors and fuses her own with foreign backgrounds. Her roommaking and roomtaking work in the present, in the past, and into the future. "Upon Meeting Don L. Lee, in a Dream" carves a niche for a fresh female voice that will be able to expand a neighborhood ("Ö"), an artist's studio ("Robert Schumann . . ."; "Agosta the

Winged Man and Rasha the Black Dove"), a private patio ("Reading Hölderlin . . . "), even a "German Writers Conference in Munich."

The one right word will not only expand the world but also may kill people ("Parsley"). While lending a voice to silent, forgotten, or unnamed figures in the past (Nestor's wife, "Catherine of Alexandria," "Fiammetta . . . "), thus unearthing hidden truths, Dove also reaches into the future with groundbreaking poetic statements of her own ("The Hill Has Something to Say"). Next to "Parsley," "The Sailor in Africa" proves an immensely political poem: harking back to the past, this postcolonial rehearsal of colonialization reveals a perennial danger and a perennial consolation. Art may reterritorialize any historic deterritorialization with a sense of its own. Imagined communities that share "tales of strange lands" emerge.

Though not hermetic, Dove's poetry falls within the scope of Roland Barthes's *texte scriptible*. A "writerly text" requests a reader's full participation through a plurality of connotations, as distinguished from a *texte lisible* or, "readerly text" that allows a sequential reading and passive, easy consumption (Barthes 1985: 17): "Lire cependant n'est pas un geste parasite, le complément réactif d'une écriture que nous parons de tous les prestiges de la création et de l'antériorité. C'est un travail" [Reading, however, is not a parasitic gesture, the reactive complement of a writing which we pare from the prestige of creation and anteriority. It is labor]. Dove's need to think beyond boundaries and easy identifications is indeed an innovative and crucial labor, with aesthetic and ethical rewards. Yet despite her inclusive view, Dove resists all labels. Her search for wholeness, balance, and reconciliation with the self and the world keeps vying with an unmitigated sense of displacement, fragmentation, and isolation. The result is a cosmopolitan realm with its undergrowth alive—a point of view that by its breadth and force stands apart, her lending a voice to many positions and many characters central, liminal, and marginal, her determination to be a citizen of the world.

T H R E E

MOVEMENTS OF A MARRIAGE;
OR, LOOKING AWRY AT U.S. HISTORY

Rita Dove's *Thomas and Beulah*

I think that all poetry is political. Poetry fires the soul.
That can easily turn into something political.
> Rita Dove in conversation with Susan Stamberg
> (Library of Congress video production, 1993)

Ever since black people were taken out of Africa they have had to be on
the run, in flight from injustice, in search of wholeness, of community, of
home. . . . The pieces themselves, the fragments of hope, have been
their destination.
> Calvin Hernton

Time has two aspects. There is the arrow, the running river, without
which there is no change, no progress, or direction, or creation. And there
is the circle or the cycle, without which there is chaos, meaningless
succession of instants, a world without clocks or seasons or promises.
> Ursula K. LeGuin

"Family" in an African-American historical and literary perspective is still an encumbered social concept rooted in the trauma of slavery, which deprived black people of the hallmarks of identity: a birth date, a name, a family structure, and legal rights. While the poet Haki Madhubuti, the critic Houston A. Baker, Jr., or the historian Andrew Billingsley try to redeem the image of the black male and the black family,[1] a league of literary voices testifies to the disruption of marital and familial ties. In the "peculiar institution" and its aftermath, rape, incest, exploitation, and separation abound, most notably in Toni Morrison's interpretation.

Rita Dove, with *Thomas and Beulah* (1986), counteracts this stereotype of black family failure. The Pulitzer Prize–winning double-sequence of forty-four poems (twenty-three for Thomas, twenty-one for Beulah) is a story twice-told, symbolizing a mysterious third element, a lifelong bond. Albeit lived in color, it is not marked by race, class, and gender. I shall not only trace Thomas and Beulah's development through their signature poems but also Dove's rethinking of the poet's relation to the history of color and of the United States. Dove allows the successive facts of life to become pieces in a jigsaw puzzle for a reader to assemble toward a series of his and her stories that depict and illuminate History from a marginalized perspective. Text meets countertext. To Dove:

> History with a small *h* consists of a billion stories. History with a capital *H* is a construct, a grid you have to fit over the significant events in ordinary lives. Great historians, those who can make history "come alive," realize that all the battles lost or won are only a kind of net, and we are caught in that net. Because there are other interstices in that large web. Whereas History is a chart of decisions and alternatives, history is like larding the roast: you stick in a little garlic and add some fat, and the meat tastes better. (Bellin 1995: 19)

Thomas and Beulah's time, as the added chronology demonstrates, spans from 1900 to 1969. All poems are linked through a coherent place: Akron, Ohio. Yet the "two sides" also suggest the claims of history and literature, fact and fiction. Such "a contradictory conjunction of the self-reflexive and the documentary is precisely what characterizes the postmodern return to story in poetry," as the cultural critic Linda Hutcheon (1993: 64) observes from a larger perspective. In her illuminating chapter on "Re-presenting the past" Hutcheon acknowledges the fact that postmodern poetry opens up material once excluded from the genre as impure: things political, ethical, historical, philosophical.

TB (1986) is a couple's journey that brings to life Dove's maternal grandparents, Thomas and Georgianna Hurd, not as a historical account but as the poet imagines it could have been. A multilayered framing relates their cover photo(s), posing as Thomas and Beulah in front of a new car, to their granddaughter's portrait of an artist as a young woman on the book's back cover. Dove's use of photographs instantly initiates an ingenious dialogue between documentary fact and historic metafiction. To Linda Hutcheon this "typically postmodern border tension between inscription and subversion, construction and deconstruction—within the art itself—" (1993: 119) presents photography in its apparent transparency. Hutcheon, however, keeps warning that "the photographic semblance of eternal, universal Truth and innocent, uncomplicated pleasure . . . always potentially links the medium to institutional power" (123), a power Dove challenges in her text. Within this outer visual parenthesis, the poetic essence of forty-four lyrical snapshots is again bracketed by a linearity-enhancing epigraph, *"These poems tell two sides of a story and are meant to be read in sequence,"* and a chronology. A carefully wrapped center thus holds the author's own recreated sense of family and history.

When Bill Moyers asked her to comment on *TB* Dove related the private and public spheres as follows:

> I think we understand history through the family around the table, and those
> who aren't there anymore but who are called in through the past. For exam-
> ple, in *Thomas and Beulah* I call my grandparents in to show how grand histori-
> cal events can be happening around us but we remember them only in relation
> to what was happening to us as individuals at that particular moment. How
> we act in our lives is how we memorize ourselves in the past. (1995: 124)

Family history, an ongoing process of how we felt and will feel in a certain way,
allows Dove to resonate between past, present, and future and to trace "eternity
in a grain of sand" (Moyers 1995: 124). If we adhere to the general observation
that history is a collection of narratives we tell ourselves in order to create a
past from which we would like to be descended, we can say that Dove is not only
fictionalizing her past but forging her own history.

Dove's reclamation of her ancestors' lives represents both an aesthetic and
an eth(n)ic act of historical recovery. "The 'confrontation' might be described as
a 'daughter's story and the father's law,' (Christine Froula)" to borrow from Deborah E. McDowell (1989: 78). Only the granddaughter no longer needs to return
to the slave narratives, the inaugural texts of the African-American literary tradition at the crossroads of history and literature, but—as *TB's* appended
chronology testifies—to the Great Migration of southern blacks northward
to find work and a modicum of peace in the postslavery United States. The
mass movement of "30,000 workers [who] migrate to Akron" in 1916 punctuates the individual journeys of "Beulah's family" from Rockmart, Georgia, in
1906, and Thomas's riverboat life between his leaving Wartrace, Tennessee, in
1919, and his arrival in Akron in 1921, a boomtown at that time. The occupa-
tions of the 2 million blacks who migrated from the South to the North between
1890 and 1920 were, according to Houston A. Baker, Jr. (1991: 115), labeled as
twofold. "In the North, the Afro-American world of works splits into '[black
women] domestics' and '[black men] laborers.'" Thomas and Beulah's lives reflect not only this particular division but also the couple's varying backgrounds:
her slavery past in Georgia and his free Tennessee traveling musician's path.

Nonetheless, the second displacement after the "peculiar institution,"
which went largely unrecorded though it compared to European immigration,
for the first time offered black people a chance of pursuing "the American
dream" (Schneider 1989: 116–17). The black migration northward—counter to
the white infiltration of the antebellum South—also enacts, in Henry Louis
Gates, Jr.'s words, a "tropological revision": "The vertical 'ascent' from South to
North, . . . and especially double consciousness" recur "with surprising fre-
quency in the Afro-American literary tradition" (1989: xxv). Had Thomas and
Lem lived in the days of slavery, they might have been going *down* the river, as in
Mark Twain's *Pudd'nhead Wilson* or *Huckleberry Finn*, and Lem might have made
his dive in an effort to escape a grim fate. *TB's* initial reversal of direction[2] with
"1916: 30,000 workers migrate to Akron" (after three personal entries) finds its
parallel toward the end (before three personal entries) in "1963: August: The
March on Washington." The chronology recurrently juxtaposes the individual

and the collective, often by means of a suggestively ironic "double conscious-ness": In "1922: Completion of viaduct spanning the Little Cuyahoga River" [and] "1924: December wedding" the couple's marriage will viaduct-like span a lifetime of hope. Only, in "1928: New car bought for the trip to Tennessee" and "1930: Lose car due to the Depression. Second child born" (Agnes), the journey back to Tennessee in a sky blue Chandler, the American dream fulfilled and ready to be shown off, comes to a sudden end. The car was even repossessed. At least the birth of a daughter makes up for the loss. Private and public grand designs are, however, equally destroyed. In "1929: The Goodyear Zeppelin Airdock is built—the largest building in the world without interior supports." But hope and glory end in "1931–[33]: The airship Akron disaster." "Largest building . . . without interior support": What a perfect symbol for the booming yet financially unsubstantiated 1920s shattered in the crash of the stock market in 1929. While official entries mark the first part of their marriage, their absence in the second signifies Thomas and Beulah's resigned retreat into their private sphere.

Within this larger historical context, the narrative poems string imagina-tive moments of history as beads on a necklace, as if a strict sequence could re-construct the sweep of time. Dove told Steven Schneider (117) that she indeed tried to construct *TB* in the dimensions both of lyric (discrete moments) and narrative (unfolding line). However, the subjection of story time to historical time lends also "a tragic linearity, a growing sense that what is done cannot be undone and that what is not done but only regretted or deferred cannot be re-deemed by telling" (Shoptaw 1990: 374).

The sequence with its opening and closing events, the Great Migration and the March on Washington, visualizes the tension between two time schemes: a narrational linearity competes with an individual and collective circularity. Life's cyclic principle that punctuates the sequential movement of history is pal-pable not only in the chronology's span of three generations, reflected in the verbs "born, move, migrate, leave, arrive, marry, take up, quit, marry off, born, die," but also in the gripping symbolism of the circle. Hourglass-like and with equal textual weight, Thomas and Beulah's life stories are rounded from birth to death. Following each other, they form two separate circles that intersect only at the threshold of his death and her childhood, linked by an "and." An ampersand, that small figure eight at his life's closure and her life's beginning, mirrors but the big eight of their double circle, that, lying, suggests infinity. Finiteness resides in eternity.[3]

In fact, the figure of the circle permeates not only both sequences but also the opening and closing poem of each section: Thomas begins and ends "at the wheel"[4] ("The Event," "Thomas at the Wheel" [*SP* 141, 172]); Beulah starts out as her father's "Pearl" ("Taking in Wash" [*SP* 175]) and dies in the company of a paltry angel of death, a mechanical "Oriental Ballerina" (*SP* 201–2) whose pirouettes are drilling through the globe "a tunnel straight to America."

In his study of the same title (1986: 79), Jacques Derrida poignantly pic-tures the "Schibboleth," the mystery of the creative act, as a circle, a wedding band:

Elle a la forme de l'anneau. . . . la date commémorante et la date commé-
morée tendent à se rejoindre ou à se conjoindre dans un anniversaire secret. Le
poème est cet anniversaire secret.

[It has the form of a ring. . . . the date of commemoration and the date com-
memorized tend to rejoin or to join each other in a secret anniversary. The
poem is this secret anniversary.]

What is the circular shibboleth-turned-wedlock-poem to denote and to connote
if not a mystery? A poetic password to innermost feelings, or lack of feelings,
hypostasized in varied circumscriptions? A loss whose devastating presence
even governs in absence? "A lost / child," Dove writes in "Missing" (*ML* 62), "is a
fact hardening around its absence." As Cathy Caruth argues, "the impact of the
traumatic event lies precisely in its belatedness, in its refusal to be simply located, in its insistent appearance outside the boundaries of any single place or
time" (1995: 9). "To be traumatized is precisely to be possessed by an image or
an event" (5), but an event "that is itself constituted in part, by its lack of integration into consciousness" (152). Dove's brilliant achievement as a granddaughter turned poet lies in her artistic inscription of the repressed, deferred,
and unknown. Hence, the figure of the circle in *Thomas and Beulah* is highly
ambivalent: it denotes an infinite union but also connotes a world impenetrable
for the partner. Because a death of the other cannot be known in itself, it is a difference, a lack known only in its effects and sustained by constant displacement
as the titles "Variation on Pain," "Variation on Guilt," "Variation on Gaining a
Son," and "Refrain" (*SP* 143, 150, 162, 148) suggest.

   TB's marriage cycle is indeed framed by a double loss and a double lyric commemoration: "The Event" (*SP* 141–42) and "Variation on Pain" (*SP* 143) mark
Lem's fatal dive, "Company" (*SP* 200) and "The Oriental Ballerina" (*SP* 201–2)
Thomas and Beulah's exit. Death, the great leveler, doubly brackets his and her
stories. A prosodic parenthesis, however, counterbalances loss and decay: Both
the first and final poem in *Thomas and Beulah* are singled out by barely punctuated
cadences of tercets (with a single closing line), as if to formally mirror and hold a
third element that determines their union: his love for Lem and his mandolin;
hers for dreams deferred and referred to a caged singing canary. Thomas and Beulah speak *about* each other rather than *to* each other, as Kevin Stein notices (1995:
65), and their stories told in the third person refuse the intimacy of a first person
or a dialogic "you." Nevertheless, even their symbols for ersatz-music complement each other: his "half-shell mandolin" and her "canary's cage" bring two orphic hemispheres to full circle. Like a mandolin's four or five pairs of strings,
Thomas's life reverberates both gleeful and melancholic at the same time.

   "The Event" and "Variation on Pain," which drove the other poems into existence, are Thomas' signature poems:

> Ever since they'd left the Tennessee ridge
> with nothing to boast of
> but good looks and a mandolin,

> the two Negroes leaning
> on the rail of a riverboat
> were inseparable: Lem plucked
> to Thomas' silver falsetto. . . .

Already the first stanza thwarts the reader's expectations: Tercets, not couplets, open a sequence of marriage poems, and "they" does not refer to husband and wife. Inseparable were two riverboat musicians. Lem played the mandolin to "Thomas' silver falsetto," until he took a dare and, drunk, "Dove / quick as a gasp" upon Thomas's request:

> *You're so fine and mighty; let's see*
> *what you can do,* said Thomas, pointing
> to a tree-capped island.
>
> Lem stripped, spoke easy: *Them's chestnuts,*
> I believe. **Dove** . . . (Emphasis mine)

Why diving for chestnuts? Lem and Thomas, on their way to Ohio, the Buckeye State, are ready to become "buckeyes," that is, horse-chestnuts, as the natives or inhabitants of Ohio are nicknamed. Dove, who inscribes herself as "Diving into the Wreck" (Adrienne Rich), salvages a story her grandmother told her:

> . . . my grandfather had said to his friend whose name was Lem, "Why don't you swim across the river and see if you can get some chestnuts?" There was an island there, and his friend took the dare, dove in the river and drowned. (Cavalieri 1995: 12)

The island, however, proved to be a treacherous pseudo patch of tree capped mangroves. Dove renders the dramatic turn as a sequence of increasingly void circles:

> . . . Thomas, dry
> on deck, saw the **green crown** shake
> as the **island** slipped
>
> under, dissolved
> into the thickening stream.
> At his feet
>
> a **stinking circle of rags**,
> the **half-shell mandolin**.
> Where the **wheel turned** the water
> gently shirred. (emphasis mine)

Thomas sees "the green crown" of the chestnut tree on "the island" drowning. Two solid bodies (a third one unmentioned) liquefy before his drunken eye whereas an empty "stinking circle of rags" and"the half-shell mandolin" mark the gap of a lifetime at his feet somehow signifying what it never quite sees, the loss of Lem. "Where the wheel turned the water / gently shirred." The water, contracted object of the penultimate and subject of the final line, linguistically corroborates the maelstrom in which Lem disappeared. On and off the boat, the circular gap is marked and from now on will protean-like draw memorial circles in Thomas's imagination. Lem's drowning, for which Thomas feels responsible for the rest of his life, creates psychic chasms closed to Beulah.

> Two strings, one pierced cry,
> So many ways to imitate
> The ringing in his ears.

Thomas bewails Lem's fate in "Variation on Pain" while learning to play his mandolin and performing a sacrifice. His pierced ears mark him no longer as innocent. Following the primordial "Event," "Variation on Pain" commemorates Thomas's decision to survive and carry on and to transform loss, guilt, sorrow, and loneliness by means of music.

> He lay on the bunk, mandolin
> In his arms. Two strings
> For each note and seventeen
> Frets; ridged sound
> Humming beneath calloused
> Fingertips.

The first part of the poem, one tercet and this sestet, is formally mirrored across a symmetrical axis containing the most powerful imagery for Thomas's pain and its artistic remedy:

> There was a needle
> In his head but nothing
> Fit through it. Sound quivered
> Like a rope stretched clear
> To land, tensed and brimming,
> A man gurgling air.

The final line confirms Lem's disappearance, whereas Thomas's mandolin sound seems to tie and rescue ropelike both the dead and the surviving members of the team. Only the needle in his head—echoing the globe drilled through in Beulah's final poem "The Oriental Ballerina"—remains without a fitting thread. The final tercet resonates in the poem's pervasive piercing [i] sounds of "strings, pierced, imitate, ringing in his ears, ridged, Fingertips, needle . . . Fit through it, quivered, clear, brimming":

> Two greased strings
> For **each pierced** lobe:
> So is the past forgiven. (emphasis mine)

Thomas's initial pain, "Two strings [for Lem's mandolin], one pierced cry [for Thomas's pain]," is balanced in the end—on the surface at least—by two pierced earlobes. "The past is forgiven" but not forgotten until the final poem, "Thomas at the Wheel" (*SP* 172), confronts him again with "the river he had to swim," when "his chest was filling with water" due to congestive heart failure. His own "drowning" reminds him of "the writing on the water," of Lem's death. Thomas in fact becomes Lem, when he sees "the drugstore" . . . "lit up like a casino," like the Mississippi riverboat Lem must have perceived while drowning. Thomas's cycle, however, closes not on Lem but with his imagining "his wife as she awoke missing, / cracking a window."

In Beulah's life there is no loss equal to Lem's death. Her canary's music seems insignificant compared to Thomas's mandolin. However, as John Shoptaw points out, "the gap in Beulah's side is not an unrecovered loss but an unfulfilled promise. Beulah misses what she never knew" (1990: 378). She enlivens her routine, which is marked by poverty and hopelessness, with bittersweet daydreams of a better life. Poems like "Magic," "Dusting," and "The Great Palaces of Versailles" (*SP* 176, 179–80, 190–91) depict a sanctuary of feelings Thomas cannot penetrate. Yet her artful inventing of a "second world" keeps her alive. Early on "she rehearsed deception / until ice cubes / dangled willingly / from a plain white string." (. . .) "Like all art / useless and beautiful, like / sailing in air, / things happened / *to* her." And when "the Sunday paper / showed the Eiffel Tower / soaring through clouds. / It was a sign / she would make it to Paris one day" ("Magic"). "Extravagance redeems," remarks Beulah as a milliner in "Headdress" (*SP* 194). Dove conceived

> Beulah as being a very strong woman who still has no way of showing how strong she could be. She is the one who really wants to travel, to see the world. She is curious; she is intelligent; and her situation in life does not allow her to pursue her curiosity. If there is anything I want to honor in her, it is that spirit. (Schneider 1989: 120)

Only in her final poem, "The Oriental Ballerina," the dying Beulah knows: "*There is no China*" beyond.

Their respective sequences present the couple as capable in their own right and united in coping with pain and despair but beyond a symbiotic equation. Beulah's section II, "Canary in Bloom," recalls the bird's various functions: "Canaries . . . have a beautiful song; it's also a term that musicians use for the female vocalist. And the canary is the type of bird that miners take down to the mines to test for poison gas leaks" (Cavalieri 1995: 15). The canary's singing as well as testing and probing abilities in vital matters seem to be essential in any companionship.

Beulah's signature poem, "Dusting," not only links her to the Tuskegee tradition of cleanliness advocated by Booker T. Washington, who literally dusted and swept his way into college.[5] "Dusting" also testifies to her ability to fuse good memories into her daily drudgery presented as a "wilderness" bathed in raging light:

> Every day a wilderness—no
> shade in sight. Beulah
> patient among knicknacks,

the solarium a rage
of light, a grainstorm
as her gray cloth brings
dark wood to life.

Each gesture of dusting among "knicknacks" unearths layers of remembrances, as if Beulah's "gray cloth"—gray contains all colors—could produce a "grainstorm," a fruitful nonce-transformation of dust into grains of hope. In the first stanza, blinding and hiding forces, evoked by one vowel sound (day, shade, patient, solarium, rage, grainstorm, gray), are gently but forcefully cleared *away* by another sound, found in words that conclude syntactic units and that deftly add an almost scriptural finish to Beulah's dusting (sight, light, life). Between the extremes of "a rage of light" and the "dark wood" . . . "gleaming darker still" under her hand bringing into relief wood pattern and ornaments, a range of wavery memories are unlocked. They bear a young man's name:

Not Michael—
something finer. Each dust
stroke a deep breath and
the canary in bloom.
Wavery memory: home
from a dance, the front door
blown open and the parlor
in snow, she rushed
the bowl to the stove, watched
as the locket of ice
dissolved and he
swam free.

Dusting in the first stanza, "diving" in the second (into "the clear bowl with one bright / fish"), and "thawing out memories" in the third "as the locket of ice dissolved" are three states of remembering that gradually revive deep layers of buried emotions. "But how can housework be made into a creative activity?" Gaston Bachelard asks in *The Poetics of Space*:

> The minute we apply a glimmer of consciousness to a mechanical gesture, or practice phenomenology while polishing a piece of old furniture, we sense new impressions come into being beneath this familiar domestic duty. For consciousness rejuvenates everything, giving a quality of beginning to the most everyday actions. It even dominates memory. How wonderful it is to really become once more the inventor of a mechanical action! And so, when a poet rubs a piece of furniture—even vicariously—when he puts a little fragrant wax on his table with the woolen cloth that lends warmth to everything it touches, he creates a new object; he increases the object's human dignity; he registers this object officially as a member of the human household.(1994: 67)

Yet, whereas Thomas's watery circle of longing revolves around the absence of his drowned friend, Beulah's is a well contained "clear bowl with one bright fish," a bowl "she rushed / . . . to the stove, watched / as the locket of ice / dissolved and he / swam free." At this point the embodiment of her dreams also changes the element and turns from "bright fish" to "canary in bloom." Yet Beulah's longing in the beginning of her cycle ties in with the "China" of her final poem, "The Oriental Ballerina": "Bright fish," most likely carps in a bowl, a pond, or a lake, are typical Chinese mascots Beulah sets free to swim until she finally realizes *"There is no China,"* no daydreaming beyond dying. Yet the pure reality or real (according to Lacan) in life is destructive. Beulah's dreamwork, her imagining and imagination, which bridges the gap of her split situation, provides precisely those useful representations of a better life she needs to overcome. In her youthful years the unfettered dream answered a name:

> That was years before
> Father gave her up
> with her name, years before
> her name grew to mean
> Promise, then
> Desert-in-Peace.
> Long before the shadow and
> sun's accomplice, the tree.
>
> Maurice.

Maurice, the "chevalier servant" memorized—who materializes later as Thomas in "Straw Hat" (*SP* 145)—recalls "Paris" in Beulah's "Magic" and surfaces earlier in the assonances of "ice," "Promise," "Peace," "accomplice." Beulah's intense [i] sound of longing echoes Thomas's "Variation on Pain" with its "pierced cry" and "greased strings." This is the hidden beauty and musical truth of their seemingly separate cycles. Maurice emerges as a cipher for memory, "Not Michael— / something finer," as if her pursed lips would try out various shades of Mnemosyne.

Dove's "signifyin(g)" on the myths of such perennial characters as Aunt Jemima[6] and Uncle Tom[7] lends *TB* additional historical dimensions. Dove, however, twists the stereotypes of a trustworthy but sexless Tom, who at the dropping of his title "Uncle" could turn into a violent, sullen, and crafty menace to any white woman, and a Jemima who was forbearing, strong, pious, wise, and loyal yet at the same time weak, faithless, and immoral. Nonetheless, as James Baldwin emphasizes the stock traits of Tom and Jemima in "Many Thousands Gone":

> They prepared our feast tables and our burial clothes; and, if we could boast that we understood them, it was far more to the point and far more true that they understood us. . . . Aunt Jemima and Uncle Tom, our creations, at last evaded us; they had a life—their own, perhaps a better life than ours—and they would never tell us what it was. (*Notes of a Native Son* 1984: 28)

Dove not only refashions her grandparents' lives but presents us with a virile, guilt-ridden Tom and a subdued, daydreaming Beulah. Her name oscillates between hope and renunciation, between the African-American stereotype of the enduring slave-servant—the first television series to feature a black female actress, *Beulah* (1950–1953), had a housemaid as the central character—and the biblical persona: In *Isaiah* 62.4, in John Bunyan's *Pilgrim's Progress*, and in Audre Lorde's *The Black Unicorn* ("Dream / Songs from the Moon of Beulah Land") Beulah is the name for the Promised Land, and in Hebrew it means "married" (Shoptaw 1990: 380). But Beulah gradually grows into "Desert-in-Peace." In its figurative lighting, the beginning of the poem, with a secretly blooming grey between "a rage of light" and "dark wood" brought forth by means of dusting, finds itself mirrored in the end where "the tree" is "the shadow and / sun's accomplice." Imagination, connoting "love" and "fantasy," turns a grain of dust, a dead piece of dark furniture, back into a living tree.

Thomas's realm of longing is art ("Jiving" [*SP* 144]; "Straw Hat"); hers has not yet been discovered. Besides the desire for names of equal length, it was this longing open sound and biblical as well as popular ring that prompted Dove to turn the factual Georgianna, which "seemed too male based," into the fictitious Beulah (Cavalieri 1995: 12).

The penultimate poem, "Company," the only sonnet in the sequence, stands as the couple's signature poem of Beulah's telling. As Thomas heads the entire sequence, he heads the octave, followed by her sestet:

> **No one** can help him anymore.
> **Not** the young thing next door
> in the red pedal pushers,
> **not** the canary he drove distracted
>
> with his mandolin. There'll be
> **no more** trees to wake him in moonlight,
> **nor** a single dry spring morning
> when the fish are lonely for company.
>
> She's standing there telling him: give it up.
> She is weary of sirens and his face
> worn with salt. *If this is code,*
>
> she tells him, *listen: we were good,*
> *though we never believed it.*
> And now he can't even touch her feet. (emphasis mine)

Reiterated negative particles ("No one," "not," "no more") enhance Thomas's fatal impasse. Neither human beings or animals in the first stanza, nor nature in the second, can prevent him from dying. Hostilities and disaffection, represented by the couple's ersatz-music at war—Thomas's mandolin distracts the canary—are not glossed over. Despite dissonances, the half-shell of his mandolin and the caged singing bird keep the potential to come full circle. Ultimately she, whose canary was driven distracted by his mandolin, finds her own voice in "telling him: give it up." Both parts feature music as a cornerstone. Though no joyous love song was at stake, frictions and tensions are forgiven in her telling him: "*listen: we were good, / though we never believed it.*" Perhaps this detached respect and fondness is at the core of their communion, devoid of suspense, passion, rape, murder, or incest. Sensitive and strong, they remained capable of enjoying moments of joy in the face of adversity.

TB is unified, if not in time, in its action and location: Akron, Ohio,[8] in Greek, "the highest point." The spirit of place represents both the ground and vanishing point as the couple's hometown and the embodiment of a collective dream: the Goodyear zeppelin USS *Akron*, built to scout naval movements from the air, acquires traits of an omniscient narrator and develops into a complex artistic symbol. In *IG* the heroine Virginia King would close her eyes and imagine she was in the Goodyear blimp.

> Three steps below the landing she could feel the silver of the moon on her eyelids; if she went slow enough and if Mom didn't snap on the light at the bottom yelling "What's gotten into you, child?" she would keep on rising, through the window and toward the moon, cool and buoyant. Leveling out far above the city, she'd open her eyes and find out just how high Akron was. (*IG* 72)

It was also at the 1851 Akron convention that the black abolitionist and freed slave Sojourner Truth spoke out her refrain, "Ar'n't I a woman?" and named her own toughness in a famous peroration against the notion of women's disqualifying frailty.[9]

TB is not a place, Dove writes (*PW* 1995: 15), but "the two names establish a condition—these two protagonists are to be regarded as a unit . . . that becomes irrevocably wedded to a defined and also *confined* place, Akron, Ohio—much in the same way other famous moniker-teams evoke specific milieus—Barnum and Bailey . . . Adam and Eve," or Uncle Tom and Aunt Jemima revisited.

Initially planned as a third part, Akron, the city, is indeed present throughout, conspicuously in the airship USS *Akron* featured in both sections: Whereas Thomas's "The Zeppelin Factory" (*SP* 154–55) links a public disaster to his private loss and death—the airship turns into Lem's grave—Beulah's "Weathering Out" (*SP* 183–84) compares the gas-filled body with her pregnant belly and life, mirrored in far-reaching lines. *Akron* to him is a tomb, to her a womb.

"The Zeppelin Factory"	"Weathering Out"
. . .	. . .
That spring the third large airship was dubbed the biggest joke in town, though they all turned out for the launch. Wind caught, "The Akron" floated out of control. three men in tow— one dropped to safety, one	Last week they had taken a bus at dawn to the new airdock. The hangar slid open in segments and the zeppelin nosed forward in its silver envelope. The men walked it out gingerly, like a poodle, then tied it to a mast and went back inside. Beulah felt just that large and placid, a lake;

hung on but the third,
muscles and adrenalin
failing, fell
clawing
six hundred feet.

. . .

Thomas . . . eying
the Goodyear blimp overhead:

> *Big boy I know*
> *you're in there.*

In spite of the USS *Akron*'s disasters—in 1932 and 1933—her cross section marks yet another empty circle to be filled according to the couple's psychic needs, or rather to the poet's artistic crafting. "Poetry communicates to the silences in all of us," Dove states (Ethelbert Miller 1994: 33). In her high floating yet ambivalent and fragile state, the airship grows into a symbol of the American dream, only temporally deferred as a result of to the Great Depression. The zeppelin's rigid aluminum structure filled with gas, might as well represent the art of poetry, the shaping and framing of dreams and disasters, the rising above Akron in the *Akron*, in the name of art. Fluctuating between materiality and spirituality, between presence and sudden absence, the zeppelin indeed marks the precarious borderline between grandiosity and ridicule, between the elements of water, earth, air, and fire, and between the male and female principle. Stored in her airdock, known as the largest self-supportive structure at that time, the womb-like zeppelin grows into a phallic symbol as well. With its multifarious semantic layers, the town and the airship in her shed, symbol of social, erotic, and artistic aspirations, perfectly represents Thomas and Beulah's postepithalamium. Yet Akron / *Akron* reflects as well the Bakhtinian notion of the *chronotope* (literally, "time space") that determines certain conditions of experience, changing visions of distance and proximity, in an "intrinsic connectedness of temporal and spatial relationships" (Bakhtin 1992: 84): public and private, roots and routes, high hopes and disillusions.

As to the "genius loci" of her hometown Dove does not hesitate to testify that she is safely moored in her native ground:

> All of my beginning memories come out of my experiences in Akron . . . It's
> not true to write about some place that doesn't have that emotional resonance
> for you. I'm not going to write about Paris and try to make it my own. Akron is
> my own. (Brazaitis 1995: 14)

These roots ultimately allow her to rise above ground, to step out in order to explore the uncanny in-between spaces in "one's storehouse of memories," as Dove explains her poetic expansion in *PW* (1995: 24):

> I am in two places at once and yet, curiously, not there at all. It is the moment
> of ultimate possibility, and of ultimate irresponsibility. Of course there is no
> absolute demarcation of the moment when *in* becomes *out*; indeed, one passes

> through a delicious sliding moment when one is *neither* in nor out but *floating*, suspended above in the interior and exterior ground.

If places are no longer the clear and only creators and supports of an identity, they nonetheless play a crucial role in the symbolic and psychical dimension of the identification process. It is not spaces that ground identifications, but places.

Dove's *TB* encodes the conscious recorded as well as the unwritten or under-written text of history and culture. Still, if History and history—German distinguishes between "Geschichte" (History) and "Historie" (history)—are present in all of her works, in *TB* the recorded past becomes the object of reinterpretation and reconstruction. Dove shows how underneath the old-fashioned, white-generated markers, Aunt Jemima / Jezebel and Uncle Tom, individuals are struggling with History while creating their own. Theirs is a story to pass on.[10]

As Thomas is separated from Lem and music, Beulah is separated from herself: "things happened / *to* her" ("Magic"). Though both spouses revolve around their respective worlds, his is an empty space, a gap he knows defined by loss, pain, and variations of guilt, symbolized by the ship and car's wheel: a spirituality revolving around absence. Hers, as the initial symbol Pearl ("Taking in Wash") and the final "drilled tunnel to the other side of the world" ("The Oriental Ballerina") make believe, is a solid unexplored planet on whose surface she travels in her daydreams: to Paris ("Magic," "Dusting"), to some "Turkish minarets against / a sky wrenched blue" until "She feels / herself slowly rolling down the sides of the earth" ("Pomade" [*SP* 192–93]). The sequence comes full circle in harking back to the outset of the journey: The fatal treasure hunting for chestnuts that symbolizes the shining and well-rounded promise of the Buckeye state ("The Event") falls equally flat in the "cracked imitation walnut veneer" of Beulah's deathchamber. Yet only now Beulah comes to realize that there is no Promised Land:

> . . . *There is no China;*
> no cross, just the papery kiss
> of a kleenex above the stink of camphor,
> the walls exploding with shabby tutus.

"No China, no cross": no religious answer, but no escapist one either. Dove refuses to do for the imaginative Beulah what Beulah offers Thomas, absolution at the grave: *We were good, though we never believed it.* No myth, no symbol will survive Beulah's death, except the very poem that performs this final refusal.[11] All we can do at this point, according to Elisabeth Bronfen (1996: 38), is "heroically assume the loss by converting its traumatic impact into protective fictions that oscillate between the horrific return of the phantasmatic body of discarded plenitude [Lem and the dream of upward mobility], and the protective fiction of a family romance" [*TB*]. Paul Celan's "singbarer Rest" (singable rest) and Jacques Derrida's prophesy of the shibboleth (1986: 79) the mystery of the creative act as a circle, a wedding band, are fulfilled: art is the ultimate homeplace for the displaced.

Dove's 1995 sonnet cycle *ML* (76) concludes with a comparable "telos," the Greek term denoting "rounding out, fulfillment, completion, ending, and successfully passing through an ordeal." Here she equates life and poetry in the symbol of a racetrack surrounding the lake that marks Persephone's abduction by Hades's chariot:

> To make a sport of death
> it must be endless: round and round
> till you feel everything you've trained for—
> precision, speed, endurance—reduced to this
> godawful roar, this vale of sound.

Though Beulah's individual struggle for a better life has come round in sound as well, the public hope lives on in the linearity of the March on Washington. With *TB* fusing myth and historical facts, Dove moves beyond the apparent "ahistorical" dimension of a lyric sequence. History's lesson, private and public, teaches "that we must be each other's allies, even when we most disagree" (Gates 1987: 353). This holds true for a couple as well as for a nation.

FOUR

TRANSCULTURAL
SPACE, PLACE, AND MOVEMENT
IN THE BILDUNGS- AND KÜNSTLERROMAN

Through the Ivory Gate

> *When you exit through the front door of your family home, you are*
> *saying goodbye to a womb, you are about to sell yourself to the world.*
> *The wind that meets you is chilly.*
>
> Rita Dove

> *I was fascinated by occupied space; I was tempted and then pushed . . .*
> *to go where I had been too frightened to go before.*
>
> Rita Dove

> *The houses that were lost forever continue to live on in us.*
>
> Gaston Bachelard,
> *The Poetics of Space*

Dove's collection of eight short stories, titled *Fifth Sunday* (1985),[1] lays the foundation for her first novel, *Through the Ivory Gate* (1992). The topics of *FS*—that rare fifth Sunday in a month—are autobiographically colored like many of the poems and passages in this novel. They address growing up in middle America and coming to terms with a range of life's twists and tests, first loves and betrayals, forgiveness, dark memories of marginalization, and exposure to as well as gleeful encounters with the arts. In short, *FS* is a journey from Valerie's loss of innocence in the first story to Aunt Carrie's intense level of experience in the final piece. Included and expanded in *IG* are *FS*'s "Second-Hand Man" (*IG* chapter 4) and "Aunt Carrie" (*IG* chapter 13). In the former, a wife of six months discovers that her husband has been married before and grimly waits three days for him to fall asleep so that she can shoot him. In the latter, Aunt Carrie entrusts her life's secret, an incestuous teenage liaison between siblings, to her maturing niece.

Shared themes in both prose texts are the passion and complexity of homo-

and heteroerotic triangles ("Damon and Vandalia," *IG* chapter 10), the power of music ("The Vibraphone," *IG* chapters 6, 10), or the transcultural experience reflected in the heroine's art lessons by Kadinski and Nathan Mannheim, who introduce her to the secrets of playing Bach and miming (*IG* chapter 6). Particularly poignant in crosscultural terms is "The Spray Paint King," a tale about a mulatto youth of black and German origin who spray paints the walls of ancient buildings in Cologne. He turns into an international star but also recalls the names of three construction workers who died as a result of his father's negligence. Although marginal, the independent women "Aunt Carrie" and "Zabriah" ultimately provide companionship and culture outside the current norms. Zabriah, a passionate and incorruptible bag lady "with lint in her nappy hair and one shoe in her hand" (*FS* 55), storms a poetry meeting in a sterile shopping mall and refuses to be thrown out. The assertion of individual pride, even if it involves an act of despair, is the thrust of these episodes, an assertion that follows in the wake of shattered innocence. Surviving in the American Midwest, with its landlocked dreams or coming-of-age within a world grown past dreaming, Dove's characters insist on being acknowledged as individuals, such as Carrie and Zabriah, who become spokeswomen for anyone on his or her way out of fixity and barrenness. In both *FS* and *IG*, it is the old outsiders, like Carrie and Zabriah, who out of their anger or innocence span the bridge back to youth.

In the fall 1986 issue of *Black American Literature Forum* the short story "The First Suite" (a complex tale about a traveling puppeteer who performs for elementary students), from the novel *IG* in progress, was published.

This chapter's purpose is twofold: In recasting *IG*'s protagonist Virginia King's voyage into selfhood—she is the omniscient third person narrator, a rarity in Dove but not in the genre of the Bildungsroman—I will not only portray the (trans)cultural movements involved in her search for identity. I will also examine key episodes of her individuation in terms of growing selfhood and artistic enspacement, for example, dolls, puppets, music, and acting. Conclusively, Dove's novel will be situated within the tradition of the Bildungs- and Künstlerroman.

"My novel *Through the Ivory Gate* connotes a place that exists in order to be moved through; it is a passage, transient space," Dove writes (*PW* 16). One could pluralize "transient space," since Virginia King's peregrinations from Akron, Ohio, to Phoenix, Madison, back to her hometown Akron, through Oberlin, and finally to New York, off Broadway essentially define moodscapes as well as transitory conditions of coming-of-age.

The delicate story[2] that entails a prelude and sixteen chapters interweaves past and present associatively yet in a controlled and symmetrically structured way. Triggered by present events, flashbacks of varying length and depth lead the heroine back into her childhood, where puppets, family, schoolmates, friends, children, and love vie with a growing compassion for the arts.

In a nutshell: *IG* focuses on the puppeteer Virginia King. She was a drama major at the University of Wisconsin (courageously insisting on her right to study mime), but when she had difficulty finding roles for black women, she briefly worked as a stenographer, then joined the recently disbanded theater group "Puppets & People" and a bohemian commune close to her alma mater. Meanwhile, she accepts a position as artist-in-residence at Booker T. Washington Elementary School in Akron, Ohio, where she grew up until her family's sudden and hasty move to Phoenix. It is her new work with schoolchildren that brings to the surface memories long forgotten or cast away. As she guides her students in creating their own puppets—cutting, stitching, and sewing their faces and bodies together, then bringing them to life with their own fantasy— she struggles in the opposite direction, against memories of her own childhood that threaten to undo her carefully equilibrated self. Slowly they come back to her—questions about her dark skin, the racial epithet "nigger" hurled by the envious playmate Karen to denigrate her outstanding school record, her falling down into white snow (*IG* 70)—and she rejoices and despairs as each layer of pain is peeled away, both terrified and curious about what she might find at her center. Outwardly her professional and private lives maintain their smooth surface. She joyfully and successfully engages students and parents to join forces toward a final puppet show and lectures on the universal art of puppetry (*IG* 101). She embraces the children yet recoils when their small pains begin to echo her own. However, the agonizing recollection of her first love for music and for the cellist Clayton Everett, who turns out to favor men, as well as her dedication to the arts keep her from tumbling into a new, outwardly more promising relationship with Terry Murray, the divorced father of one of her students.

Yet her life, after all, is still ruled by music, acting like a suite (*IG* 90), as the novel's structure mirrors this "instrumental composition consisting of a series of dances in the same related keys" (*Webster's New World Dictionary*). Indeed, Virginia plays her life carefully and in stages, imaginatively and self-reflectively moving forward and backward, as if she were performing or, rather, practicing a demanding piece of music. This structural motion eases the discovery of something deeper than her occasional distress at having been unable to act and play professionally: her aunt Carrie's revelation of a brief premarital incestuous relationship with her brother, Virginia's father. The family's sudden move to Arizona in order to save the marriage seems to threaten her perception of home and family, but only briefly. Unlike her mother, Belle, who becomes fixated on the incident, Virginia takes the early episode in her father and aunt's lives easily and naturally, as if to recollect and at the same time neutralize "unspeakable things unspoken." She just doesn't know what to do with the story at this point.[3] This is but a narrative to her, "a passage, transient space," or, as her wise grandmother Evans puts it, "Old bones, dead and buried" (*IG* 248).

Also in tune with the symmetrical structure is the motto *Through the Ivory Gate*. The quote from Homer's *Odyssey* states that those dreams that pass through the gates of honest horn are the true dreams, and those that pass through the ivory gate are glimmering illusions and fantasies. Any threshold is a space to move through daringly and judgingly, but as a puppeteer Virginia is familiar with the notion of illusion, that is, the proscenium as well as the shifting between imagination and reality. This test of the gate is brought up in chapter 9 by Virginia's acting colleague Parker and indeed divides the novel into two halves as if the reader him- or herself had to pass the textual threshold midway (*IG* 153). Gates and thresholds, of course, are ubiquitous in rite-of-passage narratives. In *The Dream and the Underworld* James Hillman maintains:

> Doors and gates are the places of "going through," of "passing over." . . . They are the structures that make possible a rite of passage . . . entry signifies initiation. At the beginning, one must move into the Janus-faced double nature of the gate, so that everything within is able to be understood in a double sense, hermetically, metaphorically. The gates make possible the underworld perspective.
>
> We meet the gates less in dreams than at the moment of awakening from them. Then we experience the wrestling at the threshold. Awareness struggles between nightworld images and dayworld plans. (1979: 181)

Symmetrical arrangement around the gate's central axis also characterizes chapters 4 and 13. They both portray second-hand men and the way their wives—Virginia's grandmother and mother—come to terms with their hand-me-down loves. The symmetry is drawn even further as Virginia's first love, Clayton Everett, appears at the novel's beginning and is followed by her own second-hand man Terry Murray toward the end.

By that time Virginia must not only deal with her lover's growing needs but with a student's affection as well. Out of jealousy and despair, Renee jumps down the stairs to take her own young life. This incident in the penultimate chapter 15 (*IG* 270) mirrors Virginia's own hurling of a despised black puppet down the stairs in the Prelude (*IG* 7).

The true test, however, awaits Virginia in the final chapter, when she chooses to play the role of a black militant in an off Broadway production instead of settling down to homey respectability in Akron, Ohio. Before moving on to New York the considerate and caring heroine will, of course, meet her obligation as artist-in-residence in Oberlin, her next station.

In *PW* Dove tellingly illuminates the predicament Virginia faces in terms of Bachelard's "dialectics of outside and inside" (1994: 211ff.).

> As with a screen door, the opening is effortless—in fact, the barrier between exterior and interior is nearly illusory, a gray space: already one can see the outdoors, darkened and vague through the checkered wire-hatching, and smell the smells of freshly mown grass . . . the exterior sensations filter into the interior space, taking up residence in one's storehouse of memories, becoming *recollections* of the outside. This sets up in me a peculiar state, one in which I am in two places at once and yet, curiously, not there at all. It is the moment of ultimate possibility, and of ultimate irresponsibility. Of course there is no absolute demarcation of the moment when *in* becomes *out*; indeed, one passes through a delicious sliding moment when one is *neither* in nor out but *floating*, suspended above the interior and exterior ground. (*PW* 24)

Virginia's passing through the ivory gate reflects her inner progress from love's disappointment and pain to a new hopefulness and state of independence. Hers will be a place in the professional world and in her mind where she can delight in being herself. Like Grandma Evans, Virginia knows how to put to use what she learns. And what an intriguing woman she is: a student of Bach and Brecht who also cares about her family and friends and the children to whom she brings the magic of theater; who even grows close to her white roommate Kelly in college but reserves Saturday afternoons for visiting with her black girl-friends, "scattered like raisins among the white swirls of coeds during the week" (IG 186–88; Foreman 1993: 12). Like any other woman of just about any race, she falls in love for the first time with a man who cannot help but break her heart. The happiest and truest moments, however, are in her encounters with old ladies, children, and art.

Dove uses this narrative of migration to explore the way a personal and cultural identity develops within the dialectics of home as mainstream United States and a sense of strangeness for a young African-American artist within this very home. Can this sense of belonging and not-belonging be appropriated or straddled within her experience of dislocation and professional self-determination? Will Virginia King eventually become her own "transcendental self'" fusing, with nature and culture in Zora Neale Hurston's sense,[4] a boundless self not to be tied down by any definition and restriction, with an internal drive to make a self out of herself?

The key episode in terms of identity and ethnicity, a form of ivory gate and a recurring trauma in Virginia's life, is an incident I choose to call WHITE SNOW-SNOW WHITE. A temporary setback in her emancipation by means of excellence is thrust upon her when she shows her brilliant report card to her white schoolmate Karen. The girl cannot stand the towering superiority and pushes "her in the chest so that she sprawled against a speckled mound of bull-dozed snow and ice, when Karen flung Virginia's starry report card to the ground and stomped it once, twice, with her boot as yellow as her viciously swinging hair" so that "Virginia felt like a glass jar had lowered around her, closing her off from the world that she could still see, out of reach, on the other side of her fingertips. . . . Now she knew how those crickets felt; pinned to the hard side of the snow mound, she could feel snow melting under her head as the word floated between her and the paling sky, clearly visible long after Karen had spat out her revenge and run off: *Nigger*" (IG 70).

Being imprisoned under a "glass jar" recalls the glass coffin of another sleeping beauty. Grimm's fairytale "Snow White and the Seven Dwarfs" also exposes a beautiful untouchable young girl who is cast in glass out of jealousy. Incidentally, the episode with Karen takes place close to where Virginia had thrown "that hard plastic baby doll out into the street" (IG 71) in order to get rid of preconceived notions of identity and to strive for excellence instead. Now her face is doubly marked: by its darkness, that is, by the proverbial drop of black blood it represents that renders white even whiter (as Ralph Ellison maintains in *Invisible Man*), and by the white mask of ice and snow forced on her by a white person precisely when she is aglow with the light and color of her excellence. This painful experience haunts her for years, even as she continues to follow her extraordinary way through educational empowerment.

At this point, we should be aware that ethnicity still plays a major role in the process of self-fashioning, yet, and paradoxically so, it is notoriously deficient in terms of formulating identity.[5] Identity is never a matter of common culture; identity is a matter of identification and ascription (that is, how people shape their own identity and how they respond to their ascribed identity). How does Dove create a multiple self for Virginia King, that is, the possibility to axt upon all of her personalities in a culture still imbued with race, class, and gender divisions? This issue helps to explain Dove and Virginia's consistent urge to go beyond regressive patterns of ascribing labels with an inherited racial essence.

American social distinctions indeed cannot be understood in terms of the concept of race: the only human race to K. Anthony Appiah is *the* human race. Moreover, to his mind, it is not helpful to replace the notion of race with the notion of culture, because American social distinctions that use racial vocabulary do not correspond to cultural groups. If we are to move beyond racism, Appiah urges, we must move beyond current racial identities. The aim is a process of identification in which no label or group identity will shape the intentional acts of those who fall under it. This is exactly what Dove aims at through the role-playing of her heroine, Virginia King.

Only the ethics of authenticity, other things being equal, will allow people to become publicly what they already are. This then includes notions of individual and collective identity as each person's notion of self consists of both personal and collective elements. Yet only, and more often than not, collective properties act as social categories that overpower individual traits. For Virginia this means synthesizing both her personal ethics and her personification of a collective character: the black militant. Unfortunately, Appiah concludes, there is "no social category of the witty, or the clever, or the charming or the greedy."

In terms of identity formation Dove, like Anthony Appiah, consistently privileges individual over social categories. Painfully aware of their constraining potential, Dove seeks to expand the social part by consciously increasing her personal latitude. In this respect, her heroine Virginia King is—among many other things—an extension of her creator. Coming successfully to terms with both marginalization and mainstream is a constant preoccupation in the novel. Yet a "minor" literature, the French philosophers Deleuze/Guattari maintain:

> doesn't come from a minor language; it is rather that which a minority constructs within a major language. . . . It is literature that produces an active solidarity in spite of skepticism; and if the writer is in the margins or completely outside his or her fragile community, this situation allows the writer all the more the possibility to express another possible community and to forge the means for another consciousness and another sensibility. (1986: 16, 17)

One operational strategy of acculturation for Dove and Virginia King is to move into the mainstream or, "whitestream"—through the ivory gate—and refashion and expand it from within. Count us in, Dove and her protagonist in *IG* seem to demand, and they share a less restrained, more diverse, and increasingly humane self in the future. This is not to suggest that the author fails to address important issues of race, for race is still central to Virginia King's predicament.

Yet the heroine who hates "to fall into stereotyping" (*IG* 25) is not an African-American prototype but a type of friend for the author. Like Dove, Virginia King belongs to those women who went to college in the 1970s, a time in the history of the United States—just after the Civil Rights Movement—that promised a brief flair of possibility that was somehow sidetracked through Richard Nixon's Watergate scandal. Virginia for Dove is "an exploration of all those women who were concerned with trying the best individually and really remain true to whatever they thought it was they were."[6]

I will now trace Virginia's growing authenticity along the key episodes that involve dolls, puppets, and acting, in other words, artistic enspacements and issues of growing identity.

In terms of selfhood and authenticity the Prelude is the key text for Virginia's development and her declaration of independence from racial constraints. When Grandma Evans offers the nine-year-old girl one of the first commercially produced black dolls in the country, an infant without movable limbs and, crucial, no hair to groom, the girl rejects what is supposed to be her mirror image. Even worse: the doll is cheaply made and does not look like any kind of real person, black or white. What was intended to be a positive reinforcement of Virginia's heritage strikes her as a slap in the face. "I don't look like that—why she say it's supposed to be me?" (*IG* 4). Virginia's experience with image and self-image is something with which all young girls and boys struggle throughout childhood and adolescence, as children are remarkably adept at picking up the subtle judgments and ascriptions of identity patterns that society passes on. And for generations black dolls as role models simply did not exist. Their long overdue mass-production in the 1960s is one of the reasons why in Toni Morrison's *The Bluest Eye* and in *IG* the central experience revolves around dolls. Yet already as a young girl—and this is revolutionary in the African-American literary tradition—Virginia, the future actress, the dedicated enthusiastic teacher, a woman with dreams and an absolute sense of quality, objects to mediocrity rather than race. "It had brown skin. It looked like an overturned crab. And the eyes didn't close" (*IG* 7). "The new doll . . . in its flimsy, striped sunsuit . . . felt cheap" (*IG* 9). In rejecting a black doll that lacks beauty and flexibility she steps out of her metaphorically colonized self and distances herself from her forebears (mother and grandmother), who try to sell her a shoddy image she cannot identify with. This is why she not only hangs on to her light-skinned doll Penelope—a gift from Aunt Carrie whom she meets in the end—but also hurls the Negro baby "down the stairs" (*IG* 7).

Virginia is more impressed by the Sambo puppet shows her grandmother watched as a child. Sambo "is wearing red jacket blue trousers purple shoes with crimson soles and linings and a green umbrella. Oh what a friendly boy he looks to be! Too bad he is so silly" (*IG* 5–6). Though she cannot identify with this funny but silly stereotype, Sambo's comic masks—"minstrel shows . . . for the grown-ups and puppet shows for the children" (*IG* 6)—seemed one way to refashion one's identity in the face of an audience. In his limited and limiting manner Sambo unconsciously became a role model for Virginia's puppetry.[7]

Her quest for a flexible, beautiful, unrestrained self finds its deepest expression in a recurrent dream:

> in it she was wearing white shorts and a yellow T-shirt, and she was running through all the streets in the old neighborhood. Though the sun bore down fiercely and the cobbled bricks were precarious, she ran without the least effort. Her hair streamed behind her, long and shining, red as the tulip shedding and the cardinal flashing. *Isn't she lovely,* they whispered as she ran past, *a wild deer, an antelope.* And in the dream her skin was still dark. *(IG 9)*

Her imaginary youthful longing, like any other girl's, revolves around grooming—"hair," "movement," and "beauty"—a multiracial identity not defined by old neighborhoods and skin color, though she wears yellow and white as the colors of success in white worlds.

With her family's sudden move to Arizona, music becomes the landscape in which she feels at ease. She chooses the cello, "the philospher's instrument . . . as the sound is one that invites meditation and contemplation."[8] Most important, she plays the cello and not the violin because she wants to be different, literally outstanding. To her "the back of the cello was rounded like a belly, the belly of a tiger she had to bring close to her, taming it before she was torn limb from limb. She had to love and not be scared" *(IG 23)*.

She wanted to *"do things right"* *(IG 23)*. "Efficiency was her salvation" *(IG 39)*. "Even before the day she'd brought home her first straight-A report card, she'd felt the unspoken pressure to be The Best" *(IG 93)*. The very pressure to reach beyond mediocrity is expressed in this recurring vision: "For years she'd had dreams of falling. She would stand on the landing, considering the trajectory, and when she finally jumped, her only fear was that she had not leapt far enough and wouldn't clear the last stair. If it was a good night, she landed as soft and insubstantial as a feather. If it was a bad night, she woke up in the darkness, flat on her aching back" *(IG 125)*.

"Far Hills Kachina wasn't the name of the figure on the shelf. It was what they used to call their father" *(IG 52)*. His and Virginia's sympathetic inspiration and salvation in Arizona is the wide and wild landscape full of Indian cultures. In their transcultural presence the Hopi and Pima mesas provide a home away from Akron, Ohio, for the displaced family, as well as an opportunity for the author to introduce the Native American heritage. Father Ernie is thorough in his interest and takes the children out on excursions. Above all, he treats them to long speeches on Kachina dolls and religion. "Hopi parents hang kachinas up on the walls so that their children learn to recognize their gods," Virginia learns *(IG 138)*. "When a Hopi man puts on a kachina mask . . . his troubles disappear. He forgets his name" *(IG 138)*.

This has a profound impact on Virginia because she remembers everything. Talking about the Hopi culture, her father says something powerfully influential in terms of his daughter's way into selfhood: the Hopi Indians believe that when you are cut off from your culture you whither. You need to keep in touch with your roots. Virginia thinks about this in terms of her father, who seems to be lost in Arizona for all his erudition, for all of his obvious enthusiasm. For Virginia, then, her own return to Akron is an opportunity to find out why he feels cut off and what made him move.

When she gets involved with a colorful group of students and ex-actors at the "Puppets & People Repertory Theater" outside Madison, her way into the world begins. An actor, a puppeteer, creates his or her own masks, a conscious choice rather than white molding of dark skin. As Virginia runs across this puppet troupe, she finds herself magically relieved. "This is theater where it doesn't matter whether you are black or white," (*IG* 138), she thinks. From there she moves into Washington's elementary school in Akron, Ohio, and sparks the fourth graders' imagination to choose and shape their own puppet identities. When the students would not listen to their teacher she invents the puppet Gina who proudly declares, "I like being myself" (*IG* 33).

Virginia is most appealing in relation to her arts and crafts, her puppet chest full of "creatures whose magical powers were inversely proportional to the probability that they could really exist: an apple tree with a hundred red eyes, a talking bush, a blue-eyed dragon, a ballerina bewitched in the hide of a hippopotamus, a cross-eyed peacock" (*IG* 34). When a student wants to know what her favorite color is, she ingeniously answers: "I have two: black and white. My best friend's a zebra" (*IG* 34). Her suggestive mailing address reads "123 Transformation Drive, Lockerbox, USA" (*IG* 85), as her identity and her home are constantly in motion, yet safely moored in her "remembrance of things past" as well as in her art.

"The Puppet Lady" also lectures to the parents: "Puppets are universal. There are puppet shows in Japan as well as New York, in Turkey and Mozambique, in Spain and Indonesia. And 'dolls' are nothing more than puppets without a means of movement" (*IG* 101), she reflects on her immobile childhood doll. When she evokes Cortez, who had a puppeteer among his soldiers; the Egyptian marionettes; Javanese shadow puppets; and the Japanese *Joruri*, the concerned parents also get to know those new worlds that their children explore instinctively. Under Virginia's inspiring guidance and in the best tradition of "prodesse et delectare," learn and enjoy, both adults and youngsters move beyond dry lessons in political correctness.

Acting out, "to perform in or as if in a play; to express (unconscious impulses, for example) in an overt manner without awareness or understanding" (*The American Dictionary III*), describes what happens to Virginia when she decides "to stop off at Oberlin and get a sneak preview of the next station assigned by the Arts Council; she'd move there in less than two weeks" (*IG* 144). When asked on Oberlin campus where she came from, Virginia represses her past and lies: "I'm from the East . . . Upstate New York" (*IG* 145). However, her "imagined home" that replaces reality turns into intuitive foreknowledge: she will indeed move to New York.

Her unconscious longing to use her own body finds itself nourished and visualized in Oberlin's amphitheater. A young African-American singer is on stage, "her caramel-colored skin glowing against the emerald green of her dress" (*IG* 147). When she sings Schubert's *Ihr lieben Mauern hold und traut, / Die ihr mich kühl umschliesst*, Virginia feels the power of music. This is her home.

In these artistic surroundings, musing on what is to become of her, she drifts back to her days with "Puppet & People." At this point, in chapter 9, Parker reveals the secret of the ivory gate, the gate of glimmering illusions or honest horn. By calling on her hopes and plans he already causes her to move on.

When Nigel, a colleague from "Puppets & People," offers her "a tasty little part for a person of your caliber" (*IG* 257), she is more than ready to accept, although she assumes the part to be "not my color." Yet Nigel offers her a role "positively *drenched* in blackness" (*IG* 257). She will play a dashikied and spouting Marcuse, a black militant, off Broadway. Interpreting a black personality, to play one's own part but freely so, is Virginia's final step into her own self. She accepts her heritage and her skin color and literally moves into her body and mind as a black person. Moreover, a part off Broadway will gratify her sense of achievement (*IG* 264).

Her work in Akron and Oberlin, the strong attachments of her lover Terry Murray, and her student Renee Butler are her ultimate tests toward freedom. Torn between the girl's mother's reproof *"You think you can start something, then put it on hold while you go dabble somewhere else"* (*IG* 274) and her own misgivings—isn't she just always running away?—she must take her chance and muses: *"But when everything you've dreamed of suddenly comes together, how can you not drop everything else?"* (*IG* 274). Letting go is difficult for Virginia, but necessary. On Halloween, among children asking for tricks or treats, she leaves their world of innocence and glimmering illusions and moves through the gate of honest horn to partake in a play of experience that deals with Nixon's Watergate.

Virginia King's voyage into selfhood—her development from little Sambo's sweet black stereotypical innocence in the Prelude to the tiger's experience of a black militant challenging white government in the final chapter—has passed successful stages of individuation. In this light her latest dislocation is not a form of leaving but rather of going to a destined future. She has to embrace risk and transformation to keep the trajectory of dislocation open and alive. Yet, in one and the same gesture she accepts her fate as an internal difference and empowerment: woman, artist, teacher, musician, actress, multitalent, lover, African American, keeper of family secrets. She just has to trust her innate resilience.

Unlike *Thomas and Beulah*, who moved vertically from the South up North, Virginia, two generations later, traverses the United States horizontally: from the Midwest to the Southwest and back East, into the center for artistic achievement: New York City. In a nutshell and as the title suggests, *IG* is devoted to rites-of-passage that correlate the needs of a young girl's growing up with her student's need for substitute mothering.

Her search for identity, which is linked to her ethnicity, follows the key episodes of her process of individuation: from dolls to puppetry and into her own role as an African American who plays a black militant off Broadway. In fact, the heroine's growing sense of mirroring and refashioning her self can be observed in three stages: first, as a child with her dolls; second, as a puppeteer with her masks; and third, as an actress in her role(s).

Whereas the novel's theme of growth mirrors Virginia King's circular external moves, the text's structure stresses a strong symmetry invoked by the symbol of the ivory gate. Placed centrally and halfway through the narrative (chapter 9), the gate serves as the touchstone as well as the axis around which major experiences revolve. Spatiotemporally well balanced between before and after, left and right, the storyline develops.

The textual strategies also make use of a particular circular form of development: life's journey through different stages and spaces, the devices of education and art, and a strong oral and matrilinear way of storytelling—from grandmother to granddaughter, from aunt to niece, from female tutor to female tyro. Though the narrative flow seems disrupted by flashbacks and detours, the chapters and paragraphs are associatively linked and juxtaposed like strong visual imagery in poetry. On a thematic level this enables Virginia to recapitulate, control, and narrate her own story of becoming, the key sign of sophisticated self-understanding. Dove is interested in showing how a character like Virginia King carries her emotional and cultural baggage through her life, through her dreams, deceptions, and decisionmaking. On the broadest level *IG* depicts the quest for knowledge, excellence, and artistic achievement. It is shaped in small, short story–like sections as Dove confirms in her interview with Wayne Ude:

> I think short stories are much closer to poetry, so the transition was easier. Stories seem to have the same concentration of energy, the same sense of radiating from one event or one moment. The images that are used in stories, especially the images that really serve the story, tend to be compact and all of a piece in the same way that most lyric poetry is. (1993: 1)

It is neither a plotted novel nor a thriller in that sense, but its lyrical vignettes are linked like beads on a string.

Doors and gates are important in Dove's poetic worldmaking,[9] particularly in the liminal transient spaces of the Bildungs- and Künstlerroman. Within this genre[10] Dove's *IG* grasps the ethnic ethic, and artistic dimension and diversity of a young female African-American mind in its double-consciousness and transcultural facets. Her sovereignty and her sense of an artistically aspiring unified self are even coterminous with Wilhelm Dilthey's definition of the classical Bildungsroman. *IG* is a novel in which a "regulated development within the life of the individual is observed, each of its stages has its own intrinsic value and is at the same time the basis for a higher stage. The dissonances and conflicts of life appear as the necessary growth points through which the individual must pass on his [or her] way to maturity and harmony" (in Kester 1995: 7). Indeed, until the rise of feminist criticism the Bildungsroman was traditionally regarded as the novel of the development of a young man or artist. Johann Wolfgang Goethe's *Wilhelm Meister* became the prototypical hero of the Bildungsroman, "a seeker for some whole, some community outside himself in which the individual existence will be meaningful and productive" (Kester, 1995: 7).

The continuing struggle for the right to define and develop one's own ethnic, ethic, and gendered cultural identity has created within African-American literature an unprecedented awareness of the power of textuality in shaping identities in the present and past, most notably in the slave narratives—the classical Bildungsroman of African Americans—or in the biographies of community leaders like Frederick Douglass (*Narrative of the Life of Frederick Douglass, an American Slave. Written by Himself,* 1845), Booker T. Washington (*Up from Slavery,* 1901), or the black ex-slave Isabella, who created the emblem of female strength, Sojourner Truth (*Ar'n't I a Woman?* 1850). Incidentally, this public figure who reinvented herself and redefined gender identity delivered her most influential speech in Akron, Ohio, in 1851.

In spite of these examples of self-fashioning, the notion that an unwritten reality remains invisible has left its deep and lasting traces far too long in the African-American cultural memory, as in Ralph Ellison's *Invisible Man,* Toni Morrison's *The Bluest Eye,* Charles Johnson's *Oxherding Tale,* or Sherley Anne Williams's *Dessa Rose* (Kester 1995: 6)[11]

Rita Dove continues to write within Sojourner Truth's tradition, yet her late twentieth-century heroine Virginia King embodies lineage, perspective, versatility, and meaning. She is the moving locus of self-engendering power and determination, and her talent and uncompromising sense of quality are the cores of her artistic aspiration and achievement. Dove, I argue—and this is revolutionary within the African-American Bildungs- and Künstlerroman— writes against the grain, against the Zeitgeist. Everyone talks and writes about love[12] or the terrible fragmentation of the African-American family.[13] But *IG* is a hymn to life and growth through education. Artistic not erotic initiation is at stake.

When Virginia becomes a puppeteer, she calls her puppet self Gina Prince (Gina Lynn Augusta von Claybourne-Prince, *IG* 84), which means that the puppet is like her little child, the prince and heir to the crown. How does a prince become a king? That is Virginia's journey. How does she become her own ruler of her own artistic universe?

What happens, we asked initially, when the strategies of literary spacing are appropriated by a female writer creating a heroine? The answer is this: Dove's strengths come alive most vividly when she describes, or when the narrative is in the mouths of, its younger and older female protagonists.

FIVE

MYTHS' REMAKES

THE DARKER FACE OF THE EARTH

> *You'd think the question raised by Oedipus —fate versus free will, mother love and blind power—would have faded by now, but they haven't. Those are the questions posed by great literature: unanswerable, yet forever asked.*
>
> Rita Dove

> *In den Mythen wird nicht verdrängt, sondern werden uns die Verdräng-ungsprozesse selbst vorgeführt. [Myths do not repress but present these very repressive processes.]*
>
> Sigrid Weigel

In her 1995 conversation with Steven Bellin, Dove maintains:

> Myth begins in anecdote—telling a story in order to entertain—but it also con-structs a narrative as a way of explaining our place and our progress in the world . . . A myth or a legend becomes indispensable through the retelling. Why do we still repeat these tales and listen to them with such pleasure? Be-cause they touch the yearning inside us; they explain our impulses on a level deeper than logic but do not require blind faith, because they are allegorical. They explain some of the mysteries of our own existence and our relationships with each other. . . . For me, to work with myths is a way of getting at the in-effable. (1995: 20f)

The Oedipal conflict of incest and patricide in the context of slavery and miscegenation in *DF*, and the Demeter-Persephone cycle of death and renewal in *ML*, indeed prove their perpetuity in a contemporary setting. While *ML* cen-ters on mothers and daughters, *DF* focuses on mother-son relations, yet in both cases a promising young African American faces the controversies of white worlds.

In terms of space, "*The Darker Face of the Earth*, . . . locates us in the beyond, since to see the face of the earth implies a distance, an estrangement, from our world," Dove maintains in *PW* (1995: 15–16). The greater the distance, the more alike, or global, diversities appear to be. Yet, *The Darker Face of the Earth* refers not only to a vantage point far above or beyond, but also to that half of the Earth always in the shadow, invisible but present: darker skin tones, darker truths, darker joys and sorrows, the night side of daylight. It is a voyage back into the darker phase of slave history where—despite close human contact— the alienation between oppressor and oppressed reaches cosmic dimensions.

At the center of our discussion is the "completely revised second edition" of the verse drama. *DF*'s prologue and two acts had their world premiere at the Oregon Shakespeare Festival (OSF) in Ashland, on 27 July 1996, yet they are the product of a long gestation. Dove's first full-length play[1] began as *Oedipus Rex: A Black Tragedy* in 1980[2] and led to the 1994 first edition of *DF*, a free-verse tragedy in fourteen scenes. Visions and revisions turned the first edition into the Ashland stage success.[3]

Set in South Carolina before the Civil War, an Oedipal tragedy develops between the white plantation owner Amalia and her mulatto son Augustus, whom she had with her slave Hector. In an adroit inversion of roles, Dove connects black slave history with elements of the Judeo-Christian, Greek, and Roman traditions. The prologue reveals the complexities surrounding the hero's birth. Quickly and economically, Dove leads us into the plot's crisis, provides the essential details about the past, and presents the chief protagonists in action.

The storyline spans some twenty years, featuring a motley cast of six female slaves, among them the conjure-woman Scylla; the every(slave)woman Phoebe; Ticey, a house slave; Diana, a young girl; Psyche; and a slave woman / narrator.[4] Four black conspirators, three of them free (an anonymous leader, Benjamin Skeene, and Henry Blake) and the slave Augustus Newcastle, encounter four white adversaries: the plantation's master and mistress, Louis LaFarge and Amalia Jennings LaFarge, the doctor, and Jones, the overseer. A chorus of unnamed slaves accompanies, counterpoints, and comments on the action on stage throughout the play.[5]

The prologue opens in the slave quarters, where the imminent birth of a child to Amalia Jennings LaFarge is being discussed. When, after a sharp cut, the lights are up on Amalia's bedroom, the doctor replies: "This is serious, Amalia! / If the niggers get wind of this—" (*DF* 15). "Get rid of it! Kill the bastard," the duped Louis LaFarge demands (*DF* 18). Indeed, family honor and the rules of the "Peculiar institution" compel Amalia to cut all ties with her newborn dark-skinned son whom she has conceived in love as well as in retaliation for her husband's infidelities in the slave quarters. Yet, it is her reacting to her husband's betrayal—the "master" plan requires that she appear as the wronged wife —not her acting in love for a slave that must govern public policy. Taking one last look at her son, Amalia bids him farewell in order to save his life: "I dreamed you before you came; / now I must remember you before you go" (*DF* 30). She does not, however, divulge the name of Hector, Augustus's father, and the slaves retain the belief that the child died at birth, though Ticey heard it cry and Scylla knows "That baby weren't born dead" (*DF* 35). Abandoned in a sewing basket into which Louis LaFarge has slipped spurs that should kill the boy, he is brought to Charleston and eventually develops into a redeeming Moses figure.[6] While Hector, apparently going mad over the loss of his son, seeks to kill all the snakes[7] (those symbols of temptation) he can find in the swamp into which he has retreated, Amalia's husband Louis shamefacedly turns his back on humanity and devotes himself to the stars, which promise him wisdom and guidance, at least until the final denouement.

From the prologue the time leaps twenty years ahead to the drama's present, when the boy, like Oedipus, having survived the attempted infanticide, returns to the Jennings plantation as a new slave. In the interim, Psyche has died, and her daughter Diana, the slave Scipio, and the white overseer, Jones, have joined the staff. Occupied with the day-by-day operation of the plantation in acts I and II is Amalia, a strong father's daughter, who learned from him "to calculate inventory" all the morning (*DF* 20). It is she who buys her son back from the auction block, "the most talked-about nigger / along the southern seaboard!" (*DF* 42), "an educated nigger" known for his "Twenty-two / acts of aggression and rebellion" (*DF* 43). Yet Amalia is no stupid, cruel beauty. The stage direction portrays her as "*an attractive white woman . . . who exhibits more intelligence and backbone than is generally credited to a southern belle*" (*DF* 15). Both Hector and Augustus praise her cool, sweet look (*DF* 117, 160). As a fine example of how racialization is not a ready-made but a class and age generated phenomenon, she grows up playing with slave children, as was customary in the antebellum South. "How many times / did he [your father] have to haul you back from the fields, / kicking and scratching like a she-cat?" the doctor recalls (*DF* 20). So close has she been with Hector since childhood that he offers the bride of Louis LaFarge one red rose (*DF* 21) instead of the "awkward bunches of wildflowers" other slaves would toss. After all, he once covered the girl's body with "rose petals, / then blew them off, one by one" (*DF* 22). Only later, as the unhappily married "missy" of the place who has lost her son, Amalia earns a reputation for cruelty.

As if to prove her own strength and superiority, Amalia sets out to break the newly purchased Augustus but finds herself irresistibly drawn to him. Having been raised by a sea captain, he can read, write, and count and is familiar with Greek mythology, the Bible, Milton, and the world. Most important, he has witnessed the Haitian revolution and quickly joins the planned slaves' insurrection meeting. In I.7 he goes so far as to tell the conspirators how the Haitians "chopped white men down / like sugar cane. For three weeks / the flames raged; then the sun / broke through the smoke and shone / upon a new nation, a black nation— / Haiti!" (*DF* 79). Yet Amalia, who enters the secret scene accidentally, "punishes" Augustus, but with an invitation to the big house: "A lovely speech / . . . I see you're a poet / as well as a rebel" (*DF* 79). Soon Augustus begins to fulfill Scylla's prophecies not only by unwittingly falling in love with his mother but also by slaying his father, the mad slave Hector, in a blaze of anger at and fear of being exposed in his plans for insurrection. Though Augustus feels unsettled by his murder of a man who lived as an outcast at the plantation's edges trying to rid his world, the swamp, of snakes, he is unaware of his crime's atrocity: patricide. It will take Louis and Augustus's lover / mother Amalia to reveal the superstructure of their entanglement. In addition, he must choose between true love and freedom: "Everything was so simple before! / Hate and be hated. / But this—love or freedom— / is the devil's choice" (*DF* 146). The brutal system of slavery traps both Amalia and Augustus as they play out their fateful love against a vast, bloody slave uprising. The gist of acts I and II involves falling in love and deceiving the old order, and falling from grace and dreaming a new one. Augustus only imagines his origins, and wrongly so, literally between acts I and II (*DF* 92–93).

The plot unravels according to its doomed and bloody plan: Amalia and Augustus's love in act II is discovered by his fellow conspirators, who fear betrayal and death, and force him to act. The rebellion takes its course; Augustus storms Louis's study, kills his supposed "white father," enters Amalia's rooms, and learns the truth of his origins. In an intense moment of grief he is torn between love and hate, between his dedication to a woman and to a task. At this very moment Amalia stabs herself, and the incoming slaves erroneously credit Augustus with the deed.

Dove's masterstroke is her reinterpretation of Greek myth in terms of her own forgotten and undervalued African-American history with towering and courageous figures like Augustus Newcastle fighting for freedom and human dignity.

The play's historical antebellum South Carolina setting—"the Jennings Plantation and its environments. Prologue: about 1820. Acts I and II: twenty years later" (*DF* 10)—recalls landmark events toward the abolition of slavery. While Toussaint L'Ouverture's revolution in Haiti and Joseph Cinque's "Amistad" incident are explicitly mentioned (*DF* 87–88), two other principal events are implicitly present: Denmark Vesey's conspiracy in South Carolina in 1822 and the publication of David Walker's *Appeal, in Four Articles; Together with a Preamble to the Colored Citizens of the World, but in Particular, and Very Expressly to Those of the United States of America.* Published privately in Boston in 1829, Walker's *Appeal* (republished in 1978) was "lamentably violent and provocative" even in the eyes of the antislavery leader William Lloyd Garrison.[8] Walker's master stroke, a direct reference to the Declaration of Independence—"we hold these truths to be self-evident, that all men are created equal" (Walker 1978: 75)—made the *Appeal* unpardonable to white Americans, so that the American Colonization Society, among them Henry Clay, Daniel Webster, and Andrew Jackson, advocated the resettling of free and light-skinned mulattoes outside the United States, since they served as incitement for insurrection. With its strong appeal for freedom and adequate education, Walker's manifesto to "Men of color, who are also of sense" (28) left indelible traces in *DF*'s main character, Augustus, as well as in Dove's poem "David Walker (1785–1830)" (*SP* 30): "A month— / his person (is that all?) found face-down / in the doorway at Brattle Street [Cambridge, Mass.], / his frame slighter than friends remembered."

David Walker and Denmark Vesey, like Augustus Newcastle, demonstrated a certainty and sophistication not thought possible for a black person at that time.[9] Denmark is reported to have proved a most faithful slave and to have traveled all over the world with his master, learning to speak various languages. Without falling into the trap of documentary fallacy, that is, replacing fiction with fact, I would like to quote the account of the intended insurrection published by the authority of the Corporation of Charleston for its firsthand historical information:

As Denmark Vesey has occupied so large a place in the conspiracy, a brief notice of him will, perhaps, be not devoid of interest. The following anecdote will show how near he was to the chance of being distinguished in the bloody events of San Domingo. During the revolutionary war, Captain Vesey, now an old resident of this city, commanded a ship that traded between St. Thomas' and Cape Francais (San Domingo). He was engaged in supplying the French of that island with slaves. In the year 1781, he took on board at St. Thomas' 390 slaves and sailed for the Cape; on the passage, he and his officers were struck with the beauty, alertness and intelligence of a boy about 14 years of age, whom they made a pet of, by taking him into the cabin, changing his apparel, and calling him by way of distinction Telemaque,[10] (which appellation has since, by gradual corruption, among the negroes, been changed to Denmark,[11] or sometimes Telmak). On the arrival, however, of the ship at the cape, Captain Vesey, having no use for the boy, sold him among his other slaves, and returned to St. Thomas'. On his next voyage to the Cape, he was surprised to learn from his consignee that Telemaque would be returned on his hands, as the planter, who had purchased him, represented him unsound, and subject, to epileptic fits. According to the custom of trade in that place, the boy was placed in the hands of the king's physician, who decided that he was unsound, and Captain Vesey was compelled to take him back, of which he had no occasion to repent, as Denmark proved, for 20 years his faithful slave. In 1800, Denmark drew a prize of $ 1500 in the East-Bay-Street Lottery, with which he purchased his freedom from his master, at six hundred dollars, much less than his real value. From that period to the day of his apprehension he has been working as a carpenter in this city, distinguished for great strength and activity. Among his color he was always looked up to with awe and respect. His temper was impetuous and domineering in the extreme, qualifying him for the despotic rule, of which he was ambitious. All his passions were ungovernable and savage; and, to his numerous wives and children, he displayed the haughty and capricious cruelty of an Eastern Bashaw. He had nearly effected his escape, after information had been lodged against him. For three days the town was searched for him without success. As early as Monday, the 17th, he had concealed himself. It was not until the night of the 22d of June, during a perfect tempest, that he was found secreted in the house of one of his wives. It is to the uncommon efforts and vigilance of Mr. Wesner, and Capt. Dove, of the City Guard, (the latter of whom seized him)[12] that public justice received its necessary tribute, in the execution of this man. If the party had been one moment later, he would, in all probability, have effected his escape the next day in some outward bound vessel. (Kennedy and Parker 1822: 42–43)

"All of the leaders, with the exception of Monday Gell and Rolla Bennett, who confessed under coercion, met their death with calm and dignity. . . . Vesey defended himself ably in court, challenging witnesses and disputing the charges against him, and faced his execution with complete composure" (Starobin 1970: 5). Although Augustus Newcastle, sharing the fate of Denmark Vesey and David Walker, will most likely be executed after the play's catastrophe, the courage and dignity of these fictional and factual freedom fighters presage in historical terms the conflagration that will soon befall the South and its "peculiar institution." Scylla was right in her poetic prophecy: "Four people touched by the curse: / but the curse is not complete" (*DF* 39).

Structurally, Dove's two versions of *DF* have more in common with Sophocles's *Oedipus* than we might glean from the plot's analogies.[13] Of interest beyond issues of incest, patricide, and politics are the differing versions and endings of both plays. Some twenty years after *Oedipus Tyrannus*, Sophocles wrote *Oedipus at Colonus*.[14] While the hero of Sophocles's first play—trapped by incest and patricide—blinds himself at the sight / site of failed matricide and promises to impart his troubles to the world, the mature protagonist of the second work emerges as a wise man who accepts his fate. Oedipus's transition from someone whose wounded hubris dominates his tale to someone capable of dealing with guilt, a wicked criminal turned wondrous savior, touches Dove's Augustus as well.[15] Not unlike *Oedipus at Colonus*, Augustus is both horrified by his deeds yet innocent and might well grow into a powerful hero whose grave comes to promise victory and freedom. In both versions, 1994 and 1996, *DF* reenacts Sophocles's *Oedipus Tyrannus* and its sequel *Oedipus at Colonus*—the first has the hero ending in unspeakable grief, guilt, and horror, the second shows him marked out for distinction.[16] Despite its mother-son dilemma, *DF* is also and foremost a play about power, freedom, and love.[17]

Were "the Greeks / . . . a bit too predictable" (*DF* 84)? Is it enough to "have a purpose. / Something bigger than anything / they can do to you" (*DF* 59) to overcome dark doom as Augustus puts it? The playwright's elucidations in the final interview offer interesting insights.

As a result of the "peculiar institution," all protagonists in *DF* are symbolically castrated. Slavery denies black people their primary rights of freedom, a name, legal protection, and the pursuit of happiness and turns their oppressors and proprietors into monsters, curtailed of their humanity and caught in the ersatz-world of power, leisure, and boredom. To maintain such an island of luxury in the big house surrounded by sorrow and deprivation in the fields, boundaries must be effective unilaterally. Slaveholders have access to, or control, the living space of the other group, but not vice versa, a situation that invites acts of aggression and transgression such as Amalia and Augustus's quadruple border crossing in terms of race, class, gender, and incest taboo. Both "dramatis personae" remain violent figures to the very end, the source of maledictions as well as of blessings and promise. Augustus is both a cursed outcast and a bearer of hope. Like Oedipus he will eventually turn into a ritual scapegoat, a "pharmakos," the figure who is symbolically laden with all the evils and impurities of the community and then expelled, that is, executed, to purify it.

Yet Augustus's personality and integrity beyond bloody deeds and his struggle for knowledge and self-knowledge set him apart for a special destiny. The irony of Dove's play is in the role reversals of the main characters, for it is the white woman who has deliberately produced a child by a black slave, in defiance of convention. That son will later prove the classic nemesis of his mother, her husband, and himself, because he so firmly believes—as the stereotype would predict—that he is the product of a white man's rape of his black slave mother. Yet, despite the inherent twists of slavery and human oppression, truth triumphs in the end. There is no escape from dark truths, the existence of hidden facts and their causes, neither now nor then. The seer / conjurer Scylla stands taller in her fulfilled prophecies.

Dove's message in *DF* is different. To her, the greatest dangers and temptations lie not in what we can create with the human mind, but in what we choose not to see through the veil of human denial. Truth, the darker face of the earth, will always be revealed, but, not without a sacrifice. The longer we hold out against it, the greater the price we will pay in the battle of self-will against the intervention of fate or politics. In the end, the slaves cry, "We're free! We're free!" How dark this passage can be.

MOTHER LOVE

> *The freedom of fine cages!*
> Rita Dove (1989)

> *This will sound masochistic: I like cages,*
> *I like working under that kind of pressure.*
> Rita Dove (1996)

Loss and pain contained in the fine cage of a sonnet has a tradition in writing as a survival strategy. With his 1840 sonnet "Thirty Years," the Cuban slave Juan Francisco Manzaño initiated the movement of abolition in his country.[18] And from Phillis Wheatley's exquisite handling of the form,[19] in 1772, which convinced eighteen of Boston's most notable citizens of the poetic abilities of a slave girl, to Gwendolyn Brooks's breakthrough in 1950 (Pulitzer Prize), the sonnet has marked momentous personal and public turning points in African-American careers. Countee Cullen uses the Shakespearean sonnet after the breakdown of his marriage, and Langston Hughes fights isolation and despair with a blues version of the form.[20] Yet it was Claude McKay's "If We Must Die," first published in *The Liberator* (1919), that enshrined a new idea of resistance, racial consciousness, and aesthetic rendering. McKay's sonnet, motivated by the black blood that flowed in the race riots of the "Red Summer" of 1919, came to express the dignity of the New Negro (Alain Locke) at the outset of the Harlem

Renaissance. As a Petrarchan sonnet, "If We Must Die" fuses a romantically inspired poetic structure with a theme that appears to cover revolutionary ground.

The highly emotional dichotomy of love and war, ideally housed in the sonnet, overshadows the fact that the structure is also an important form of aesthetic transfer. Introduced by Petrarch in the fourteenth century, the sonnet lent itself to a new consciousness, a wider horizon of thought reaching its apogee in the Renaissance. At this crucial moment in history, sonnets and sonnet writers came to embody the lifestyle of lyrical subjects who asserted themselves as self-contained and autonomous. Dove is aware of the inherent power structure of the sonnet and the criticism waged against it. When she was told that "some modern poets, women particularly, have rejected the sonnet form, calling it outdated, false, patriarchal, even fascist," her reply was clear: "I think that it is bogus to talk about patriarchal form in art. . . . I became . . . interested in the early stages with how I could make the sonnet fresh again" (Kirkpatrick 1995: 36). In her foreword to *ML*, she calls the sonnet "an intact world where everything is in sync, . . . any variation from the Petrarchan or Shakespearean forms represents a world gone awry." Its charmed structure nonetheless acts like a talisman against the vicissitudes of fortune and serves as a sanctuary while chaos is lurking outside.

"The Demeter-Persephone mythic cycle of betrayal and regeneration, is ideally suited for this form since all three—mother-goddess, daughter-consort and poet—are struggling to sing in their chains," Dove writes in her foreword to *ML*. Wrestling with fate, life through death, is indeed inseparable from wrestling with composure and form. Myth, the oldest and most widespread form of "speaking about gods" in the ancient world of oral tradition, is above all determined, even overdetermined, material whose narrative inscribes itself into history with "blood and fire" (Treusch-Dieter 1984: 176–77). [It is a holy scripture that allows for an unlimited number of reinterpretations but whose essence remains inviolable.]

The gist of the myth is Kore (the girl) / Persephone's abduction by Hades, the god of the underworld, while she is gathering narcissi in Sicily. This date rape within the Olympian family is sanctioned by the bride's father, Hades's brother Zeus,[21] but occurs against her mother Demeter's will. Her grief over the loss of her daughter and subsequent neglect of her duties as goddess of agriculture is finally appeased by Persephone's semiannual return to earth. The plot is handed down in variations through the *Homeric Hymn to Demeter*,[22] to Ovid's *Metamorphoses* (V), and more recently by Margaret Atwood (b. 1939) and Jorie Graham (b. 1951).[23] The secret of this particular cycle lies hidden in the seeds of a pomegranate. Pomegranates as apples of love are well known. Less familiar is what Artemidor von Daldis notes in his *Book of Dreams*: "The pomegranate's color suggests wounds, its spine torture, and due to the Eleusinian mystery, bondage and submission" (lib. I, c. 73; Treusch-Dieter: 199). One line in the second poem of Part III (*ML* 25) subsumes the myth's essence and inscribes the poet-mother-daughter in her own name:[24] "*my dove my snail.*" While the pomegranate links the realms of life and death, "snail" and "dove" acquire meaning beyond the animalistic male and female principle. "Like a bird

soaring over land and sea, / looking and looking" the Lady Mother "sped off,"
the *Homeric Hymn to Demeter* reports (l. 43). Beyond Demeter's search from a
bird's-eye view, Persephone's abduction is linked to birds in several ways: In the
fifth book of the *Metamorphoses*, Ovid recounts the muses' pledge of secrecy
when they sing of her erotic initiation. They compete to perform the song but
disunite over the task: while the "good" muses, the peace-loving doves, render
death as an orgasmic "little death," the "bad" muses, the talkative magpies,
foreground a violent act of rape by Death personified (Treusch-Dieter: 192f). Is
Rita, the muse, a dove or a magpie? She is all in one, withholding the secret yet
telling the story.

Let us return to the main plot. Having tasted the mortal seven seeds of the
pomegranate upon her goodbye to Hades—Part III, "Persephone in Hell," and
ML comprise seven parts each—Persephone remains caught in the signifying
chain of deferred desire, a revenant between the realms of life-in-death with
Hades and death-in-life with Demeter. The only German title in the sequence,
"*Wiederkehr*" ("Return," *ML* 38), foregrounds this liminal state between a
mother and a lover who ultimately rejects her: "He only wanted me for happiness
/ to walk in air / and not think so much . . . . Which is why, / when the choice
appeared, / I reached for it." Persephone is ready for "Wiring Home" (*ML* 39).

The site of Persephone's abduction, I argue, is also a decisive mythopoetic
spot at the intersection of life and death. The *omphalos*, the cult object in the
temple of Apollo in Delphi, the navel of the world, or the navel of life, is indeed
"a symbol for the connection between child and mother, between human and
earth, and as such for ideas about being centred, about a site of origin and ter-
mination of being," as Elisabeth Bronfen maintains. ("From Omphalos to Phallus," 1992: 151). Life, we are forced to perceive, is always tainted with death.
Myth and regeneration, we might recall at this point, inevitably begin with
death through sacrifice.[25] It is the poet / narrator's task to reinitiate and config-
ure extreme feelings of pain, loss, and joy that surround the blind spot of initiation and to render them not only durable in words but also endurable through
artistic enspacement.[26]

Beyond Dove's passion and expertise at experimenting with form and
theme stands her experience as daughter and mother:

> I hadn't anticipated the vulnerability of being a mother; the vulnerability of
> accepting that there are things you can't do anything about in life; that you
> can't protect another person completely; that in fact when you were the
> daughter, you didn't want to be protected. The feeling of exposure and help-
> lessness is something I was trying to explore in this book. But I learned that the
> mother can still be strong through all this conflict as well, that she can still
> turn around and stare Hades down, so to speak, and say, You didn't think
> about the consequences. (Kirkpatrick 1995: 37)

Dove's poetical concerns—the magic of words, the polyphony of voices, and an
artistic third space growing out of a revised tradition—are as finely tuned in
Mother Love (*ML* 1995) as in her Pulitzer Prize-winning *Thomas and Beulah*
(1987). No longer writing directly about her family the way she did in that

work, she bases her lyric sequence on myth and at the same time transforms overdetermined source material into something deeply personal. The result is a Demeter-Kore/Persephone plot in a contemporary setting and idiom in which Dove as a daughter-mother-poet remembers and deploys all the voices and stages of sacrifice and metamorphoses she can imagine: protagonists, a chorus of witnesses and bystanders, wiggling tongues, the Olympians. Whereas the mythical abduction is played out on a vertical axis of "upper- and underworld," this worldly modern version develops horizontally between the stereotypes of an innocent America and a Paris of erotic experience. While the Greek model features a white girl in a dark world, *ML* highlights a dark girl in a white world.

Dove drives us along a maze of thirty-five poems in seven parts, mirroring the seven seeds of the pomegranate. Seven times two equals the sonnet's magic number of fourteen lines. Yet in giving her audience but half of the whole, she keeps the cycles of both sonnets and myth open to re-creation. Except for Part III, counted as one poem, and "Lost Brilliance," which closes Part IV, most of them can loosely be termed sonnets. They gesture at rhyme, then pull back off meter and constantly regroup the fourteen lines to dovetail form with theme. Thus comforted and held in place are ambiguities already palpable in the title. *Mother Love*, the German "Mutterliebe"—or should we rather read *Mother and/or Love?*—oscillates between gain and loss, fertility and barrenness, innocence and erotic initiation. The cyclical reiteration between Eros and Thanatos, death and rebirth, opens with a short introductory fable, "Heroes," followed by Part II, a series of mother-daughter pieces that drift between myth and autobiography. Part III is the seven-section piece "Persephone in Hell," a memory of the poet's, her daughter's, or any teenager's descent into Paris's erotic "underworld." There are no sonnets in hell, as a dramatic monologue with a latter-day Hades from the city's artistic "bohème" reveals. Yet the form still lingers on the margins of the underworld, for two times seven equals fourteen. Dove loves number puzzles, as John Greening notes. (1995: 41–42). Part IV prepares the ground for an anxious mother meeting her dizzily damned daughter in "The Bystro Styx." Parts V and VI concentrate on Demeter's sense of loss, the inescapable hell of watching a daughter sacrifice her innocence, and her finally coming to terms with her own narcissistic fixation. Part VII consists of an exquisite cycle of eleven sonnets titled "Her Island." The tourist-visit of Dove's family to Sicily, one of the classical sites of Persephone's abduction,[27] develops into a true "ars poetica." Dove equates life and poetry in the symbol of a racetrack surrounding the lake that marks Persephone's abduction[28] by Hades's chariot: "To make a sport of death / it must be endless: round and round / till you feel everything you've trained for— / precision, speed, endurance— reduced to this / godawful roar, this vale of sound" (*ML* 76). Of course, the structure of this closing section is circular with sonnets whose first and last lines overlap into one big round around the abyss.

Crucial to our discussion of "the dialectic between artistic freedom and formal constraint," is the redefinition of myth within the sonnet form and the interaction of theme and form. In a few signature poems we will discuss to what extent and to what result form interacts with theme.

Dove introduces and summarizes *ML* on non-personal absolute grounds. Her prologue "Heroes" could be the conclusion, her final poem (*ML* 77), as well the opening piece, with one distinction: while the first poem focuses on heroes and plot, the last one, which follows, presents site and poetic enspacement.

> Through sunlight into flowers
> she walked, and was pulled down.
> A simple story, a mother's deepest
> dread—that her child could drown
> in sweetness.
>   Where the chariot went under
> no one can fathom. Water keeps its horrors
> while Sky proclaims his, hangs them
> in stars. Only Earth—wild
> mother we can never leave (even now
> we've leaned against her, heads bowed
> against the heat)—knows
> no story's ever finished; it just goes
> on, unnoticed in the dark that's all
> around us: blazed stones, the ground closed.

Two parts rotate around an axis of two half-lines that connect and sever the sonnet into a factual upper world and an "underworld" of elemental powers. "Water," "Sky," "Earth," and "blazed stones" (fire) join the poet to recreate a story never finished. Though Earth, "wild / mother" to whose ground we are bound, is the only stable, tied-down element, she "knows" with a poetic vision what is going "on, unnoticed in the dark that's all / around us."

Now, I will return to the book's beginning. The first poem thwarts the reader's expectations: not a sonnet, "Heroes" features nine tercets (and one extra line), as if to represent the three protagonists involved: a hero / thief / killer / poet figure, a plucked poppy, a woman losing flower and life. In twenty-eight lines—two times fourteen—[29] innocent details keep snowballing into an inevitably tragic flow: the flower is plucked, the woman's only joy destroyed. Because she refuses to accept "a juicy spot in the written history" as consolation prize for the loss of her flower, the angry stranger kills her and turns into fate's victim, mirrored in a fugitive, explanatory single line in the end: "O why / did you pick / that idiot flower? / Because it was the last one / and you knew // it was going to die." Only, the poppy would have died had it not been plucked, as Lotta Lofgren points out: "The flower's near-miraculous task is to form new roots; this is its only chance at sustained life. Disintegration, separation, alienation, all are essential ingredients for growth" (1996: 140). Yet why would *ML*, whose central image is plucked narcissi, open with a picked poppy? According to Ovid (*Metamorphoses* V.392), Kore was gathering "violets or white lilies," symbols of death and resurrection. Poppies, however, together with the ears of grain, are constant attributes of Demeter,[30] and the Eleusinian mysteries use drugs in her honor (Burkert 1987: 108). The poppies' soporific and soothing qualities are also associated with the narcotic essence of *narcissi* (Graves 1960:

96, 288). Poppy further foreshadows decisive features of the pomegranate whose addictive seeds keep Persephone under Hades's spell. The flower recalls Hades's anti-hero Orpheus as well. Rainer Maria Rilke's sonnet IX to Orpheus reads: "Only he who has eaten / poppies with the dead / will not lose ever again / the gentlest chord."[31] This is how Dove accentuates various sources and begins to unfold a constant dialogue between "the given and the made."[32]

The Demeter-Kore / Persephone myth, the absolute myth of womanhood, discloses the dramaturgy of an abduction that pairs rape with enrapture. Sanctioned by Zeus who fathered Persephone, the deed bereaved Demeter in favor of Zeus's brother Hades, whose queen his daughter was destined to be. As a goddess, daughter of Rhea, Mother Earth, Demeter should know how to conform to the dynastic Olympian law whose stability rests on two imperatives: never abdicate, always procreate. Demeter's narcissistic grief and neglect of duty, which interrupts the regenerative-procreative cycle, affect the welfare of the community and illustrates the conflict between personal and official obligations. In questioning the hierarchy of these duties Demeter may win the sympathy of mortals but doubtless the contempt of immortals: "Grief: The Council" (*ML* 15–16) frames a double demand for compliance and composure by the Olympians and a chorus of well-meaning neighbors and friends. No single voice in a sonnet but various strands of speech in stanzas of changing size and typography furnish advice.

> I told her: enough is enough.
> Get a hold on yourself, take a lover,
> help some other unfortunate child.
>
> > *to abdicate*
> > *to let the garden go to seed*
>
> Yes it's a tragedy, a low-down shame,
> but you still got your own life to live. Meanwhile,
> **ain't nothing** we can do but be discreet
> and wait
>
> . . .
> I say we **gotta** see her through.
>
> . . .
> > *at last the earth cleared to the sea*
> > *at last composure* (emphasis mine)

Form, poise, and self-control result in a downpour of recreative rain, an oxymoron of abundance in containment. This effective Olympian council is strikingly African-American in its speech (double negations, colloquialisms) and references to self-help, maybe a subtle hint that form and composure as sources for creation and recreation might well be of non-white ancestry. In this praisesong for the spirit of black sisterhood, Sister Jeffries could drop in with one of her Mason jars of soul food, "something / sweetish, tomatoes or bell peppers" or "Miz Earl can fetch her later to the movies— / a complicated plot should distract her." Inner-city poise and neighborhood help equal Olympian strategies. What the well-meaning sisters cannot perceive at this point is: there is no escape route from fate. Every detour, like the one they suggest, a "car chase through Manhattan, / loud horns melting to a strings-and-sax ending," points back to the very center of the despair they want Demeter to forget: Hades's pursuit of Persephone.

In the title poem, "Mother Love" (*ML* 17), form and theme interact to expound the ambivalence of love and duty from the archetypal mother Demeter's perspective. The first part depicts a mortal mother's call to duty in casual language.

> Who can forget the attitude of mothering?
>   Toss me a baby and without bothering
> to blink I'll catch her, sling him on a hip.
>   Any woman knows the remedy for grief
> is being needed: duty bugles and we'll
>   climb out of exhaustion every time,
> bare the nipple or tuck in the sheet,
>   heat milk and hum at bedside until
> they can dress themselves and rise, primed
>   for Love or Glory—those one-way mirrors
> girls peer into as their fledgling heroes slip
>   through, storming the smoky battlefield.

"Mothering" rhyming with "bothering" is indeed duty's bugle call until "those one-way mirrors / girls peer into as their fledgling heroes slip / through" appear. Then the primary narcisstic identification of a child with his or her mother is replaced by a teenager's narcisstic identification with a "fledgling hero." The image of the mirror and its function as idealizing exaltation brings the poem back to Persephone's abduction and mirrors a mortal mother's sense of duty against Demeter's mythic or, rather grotesque, dimension of coping. Hers is a more elaborate speech, garnished with heavenly mockery:

> So when this kind woman approached at the urging
>   of her bouquet of daughters,
> (one for each of the world's corners,
>   one for each of the winds to scatter!)
> and offered up her only male child for nursing
>   (a smattering of flesh, noisy and ordinary),
> I put aside the trousseau of the mourner
>   for the daintier comfort of pity:
> I decided to save him. Each night
>   I laid him on the smoldering embers,
> sealing his juices in slowly so he might
>   be cured to perfection. Oh, I know it
> looked damning: at the hearth a muttering crone
>   bent over a baby sizzling on a spit
> as neat as a Virginia ham. Poor human—
>   to scream like that, to make me remember.

The goddess presents herself by three anaphoric decisions: "I put aside the trousseau of the mourner . . . / I decided to save him . . . / I laid him on the smoldering embers." Mother-love leads Demeter to try to preserve her ersatz-child by searing him in immortalizing fire. Thus she wanted to thank Metaneira, who had offered her late-born son for her to nurse, as the Greek sources reveal. Despite the best intentions, mother-love may develop grotesque, even cruel and deadly traits of overprotection. Form reflects theme: We could read the poem as two single sonnets slightly gone awry. The first part, marking Persephone's absence, lacks two lines; the second one, featuring the ersatz-child, exceeds in two. We could as well read the two parts as one epic sonnet of long split lines. The sestet, dedicated to the mortal mother, is lighter and collo-quial in tone. The goddess's octave is statelier, more formal. Yet, in tune with the content, division and fragmentation persist in form, either vertically (sestet before octave) or horizontally (split lines).

Part III is the archetypal Persephone's seven-part descent into the hell of Paris, "the stone chasms of the City of Lights" (*ML* 23). Dove renders this jour-ney into life-in-death not only from the perspective of the girl, who is less a naive victim than one curious about life. Except for the final poem, where two parallel columns of fourteen lines each signal a return to poetic shape, hope, and light, this is no sonnet world but rather the most realistic part of the se-quence, a prosaic realm, if not a hell of prose. "Lost Brilliance" (*ML* 51) at the end of Part V, which depicts Persephone's return to Hades, is no sonnet either. Part III features various voices: the lyrical self's, the party small talk of Ameri-can expatriates, a mother's "super-ego": "*are you having a good time / are you having a time at all*" (*ML* 27).

Visiting "a former schoolmate who'd married / onto the *Ile*"— the Seine is the river Styx—the girl reaches the bottom pit of the underworld. In one of Dove's witty anticlimactic reversals, this is "a two-room attic walk-up / crammed with mahogany heirlooms," an "offensive tin sink," and "gargoyles," props of a stale past world full of artifice and "bad sculpture" like "upright coffins"—containers for dead material—and worse, neither form nor theme for language but small talk centering on "dog shit." "Crudités, peanuts" all over. The poet's message is clear as light in darkness: Death resides wherever artifice and make-believe have replaced art and life, good sculpture, and "meaningful conversation."

Poem V presents a self-revealing interior monologue,[33] in which Hades, a French gallery owner and a stage villain by Dove's standards, exposes his inner racist, rightist, undiscerning self. Absence of artistic enspacement—this is but "an incomprehensible no-act play"—signals an atmosphere of death and decay. Hades's voice, longing for change, is typographically distinguished (*ML* 30).

> I need a divertissement:
> The next one through that gate,
> woman or boy, will get
> the full-court press of my ennui.

> Merde,
> too many at once! Africans,
> spilling up the escalator
> like oil from lucky soil—

Distilled in a tercet ushered in by Hades's comment, *"Merde,"* Dove commemorates the collective abduction of African victims into American slavery, "spilling
up the escalator" like human leftovers from the "Middle Passage," "like oil from
lucky soil," drifting on the waters of a growing diaspora.

Section IV still plays in Paris. Yet the four poems in sonnet form signal the
daughter's increasing composure and willingness to meet with her mother.
"Wiederkehr," "Wiring Home" (*ML* 38–39), and the meal of Demeter and Persephone in "The Bistro Styx" (*ML* 40–42) counteract the opening of "Hades'
Pitch." At this decisive moment in the sequence axes turn and the poet-
daughter becomes the poet-mother or, rather, the true blood artist who notices
the mannerisms of her daughter's dark uniform. Her "gray," "graphite," and
"brushed steel" are Hades's non-color imprints grafted on to her personality,
beside the "blues and carmine," half-American, half-French, in which he
drapes her in private. "Are you content to conduct your life / as a cliché and
what's worse, // an anachronism, the brooding artist's demimonde?" the artist-
mother asks. How sad for her to see her daughter regress into the state of passive muse, the object of a male gaze, instead of a subject with a voice and style
of her own. The third sonnet, however, offers consolation in the form of real
soul food shared, a "Chateaubriand," "smug and absolute / in its fragrant crust,
a black plug steaming / like the heart plucked from the chest of a worthy
enemy." This is real meat set against the daughter's "posing nude for his ap-
palling canvases, / faintly futuristic landscapes strewn / with carwrecks and
bodies being chewed / by rabid cocker spaniels." Hades remains a flat and banal
figure. "And he never thinks of food. I wish / I didn't have to plead with him to
eat," the daughter complains in the fourth sonnet. In "The Bystro Styx,"
though the primordial fusion with Persephone has been broken, and union
with Hades has engendered consciousness and separation, Demeter is at least
able to provide nourishment for her starving daughter. By the time they reach
dessert, however, she realizes how far she is removed. This is the last of the five
strung sonnets:

> I stuck with café crème. "This Camembert's
> so ripe," she joked, "it's practically grown hair,"
> mucking a golden glob complete with parsley sprig
> onto a heel of bread. Nothing seemed to fill
>
> her up: She swallowed, sliced into a pear,
> speared each tear-shaped lavaliere
> and popped the dripping mess into her pretty mouth.
> Nowhere the bright tufted fields, weighted
>
> vines and sun poured down out of the south.
> "But are you happy?" Fearing, I whispered it

quickly. "What? You know, Mother"—
she bit into the starry rose of a fig—
"one really should try the fruit here."
I've lost her, I thought, and called for the bill.

Instead of having her "cream child" (*GN* 41) back, the mother is "stuck with [ersatz] café crème." After the girl "bit into the starry rose of a fig"[34] full of seeds, Demeter / poet knew she was gone for good and graciously asks "for the bill" for this last meal, not the check, since this is Paris.

Section V still shows "Demeter Mourning" (*ML* 48) but poised: "I'll not ask for the impossible; / one learns to walk by walking. . . . but it will not be happiness, / for I have known that." Freed from her task of mothering and bothering, as "Nature's Itinerary" (*ML* 46) suggests—"Irene says it's the altitude / that makes my period late; / this time, though, it's eluded / me entirely. I shouldn't worry (I'm medically regulated)" (*ML* 46)—Dove's lyric self explodes and rises above the dichotomy between the inexperienced American and the experienced European, which has enjoyed currency since the time of Henry James and James Baldwin. A third world, Mexico, with its open skies, becomes the artistic new ground where the poet is "prepared / for more than metaphorical bloodletting among the glad rags / of the Festival Internacional de Poesía." The cycle of art and nature, however, is still threatened by temptation, "a beer— / a man's invention to numb us so we / can't tell which way the next wind's blowing."

Blood plays an important role in rites of passage, be it in the apparent menstrual death of a young girl, in Mark 5.23–42 (*The Holy Bible*), in Apuleius's *Amor and Psyche,* or in Dove's short story *Fifth Sunday.*[35] In all cases "dying" refers to a sexual initiation that sees no end in death but a transformation: the girl dies and becomes a woman. These metamorphoses and ritual cleansings or stoppings of blood—in Dove's *ML* a halt in "Nature's Itinerary" (46)—finally make room for a moment of true art. The only sonnet in the cycle that bears the name of the form in its title is "Sonnet in Primary Colors" (47). No longer in sultry Paris but in the high altitude of Mexico,[36] poetry is again possible and dedicated to the painter Frida Kahlo (1907–1954).

> This is for the woman with one black wing
> perched over her eyes: lovely Frida, erect
> among parrots, in the stern petticoats of the peasant,
> who painted herself a present—
> wildflowers entwining the plaster corset
> her spine resides in, that flaming pillar—
> this priestess in the romance of mirrors.
>
> Each night she lay down in pain and rose
> to the celluloid butterflies of her Beloved Dead,
> Lenin and Marx and Stalin arrayed at the footstead.
> And rose to her easel, the hundred dogs panting
> like children along the graveled walks of the garden, Diego's
> love a skull in the circular window
> of the thumbprint searing her immutable brow.

"One black wing" and "parrots" immediately link Frida Kahlo with the birds of Demeter. Yet, as a *mater dolorosa*, who suffers in her supporting corset but continues to paint, she conquers her excruciating physical and mental pain by shaping it into art. Thus her creative but maimed body symbolizes another third space or common ground where "suffering woman" and "artist" meet and at the same time overcome their barren grief. Frida Kahlo, married twice to the philandering Diego Rivera (1886–1957), who comes and goes like Persephone, masters anger and loss through her brush. The thin air; the stark primary colors, her signature blue, yellow, and red; and the mental strength of Frida Kahlo maintain a high, clear counterpoint to the decadent underworld of Hades's Paris. Cultural space, not the fixation of a beloved person, is the ultimate homeplace for the displaced and deprived.

Part VI finds Demeter in her second, more sedate cycle of mourning and coping with a fate ancient and modern. With Persephone pregnant in "History" and "Rusks" (*ML* 58, 59, 61), Demeter is able to perceive her fate as one she shares with others. From Hades ("Demeter's Prayer to Hades," *ML* 63) she seeks but knowledge and understanding. "There are no curses—only mirrors," and mirrors reveal without judging.

ML ends with section VII, a cycle of eleven sonnets titled "Her Island," depicting a tourist visit to Sicily (Persephone's island) by Dove, her German husband, and their daughter. Two concentric circles mark the final sequence. As if to unwind the past, the family drives "counterclockwise" (*ML* 73) around Sicily, and then watches a race around the site of Persephone's abduction, the lake of Pergusa in the center of Sicily.[37] The increasingly circular movement is enhanced by eleven strung sonnets in which the last line of each poem becomes the first in the next. The section also opens and closes with a slight but significant variation of the same line: "Around us: blazed stones, closed ground" (*ML* 67) and "around us: blazed stones, the ground closed" (*ML* 77). Whereas myth, symbolized in the archeological remnants of a "closed ground"—"These monstrous broken sticks, . . . Sicily's most exalted litter" (*ML* 74)—first invites to be unearthed, the "ground" may be "closed" after myth's revision and reevaluation. The final sonnet, however, is the poignant realization that "no story's ever finished," including this one.

In *ML* Dove uses and recharges the sovereignty of two significant structures: the theme of myth and the form of the sonnet. Both are particularly suitable carriers for variety within repetition, an interplay of freedom and form. Dove, who otherwise resists and rejects limiting demarcations, explicitly welcomes these artistic borders whose inclusions and exclusions she renegotiates at will. What renders the rewriting of myth so attractive is the absence of a single canonized original. Given the variants, what should be enhanced? In *ML* a mother mourns her daughter, not her sons, and Demeter has sons, according to various sources from one to three: Jachos, Plutos, and the holy horse Arios. Though including a range of voices and perspectives, Dove chose to enhance the mother's perspective: how to let loose, how to come to terms with loss, grief, humiliation, and prostration in the face of Olympian power. Yet, she does so without subordinating Hades's love to the love of mother and daughter timewise. Remember, in the *Homeric Hymn to Demeter,* Hades has Persephone only for a third of the year. A compromise with never healing wounds is reached. Mother and Lover share the young woman equally—"half a happiness is better / than none at goddam all" (*ML* 61)—and "death and life continue to take each others' toll." Two metamorphoses, however, are crucial to the myth's solution: Demeter's reconciliation with loss and pain and Hades's transformation from uncle / rapist to power-sharing and loving consort. The fruit of this resolution is not only the happy family life present in the poet's visit to Sicily (*ML* VII), but also the mystery revealed at Eleusis: the recognition of identity in difference, the fulfillment of the individual through communion.

SIX

THE VOYAGE OUT

On the Bus with Rosa Parks

For the problem of the Twentieth Century is the problem of the color line.

W. E. B. Du Bois

History must restore what slavery took away.

Arthur A. Schomburg

To change life . . . we must first change space.

Henri Lefebvre

[Cultural identity] is not something which already exists, transcending place, time, history and culture. . . . Far from being eternally fixed in some essentialized past, [it is] subject to the continual play of history, culture and power.

Stuart Hall

Poetry as well as criticism have attempted to separate the personal from the politically engaged poem. For that reason Seamus Heaney and Rita Dove have drawn criticism and admiration: they use both modes.[1] Dove's 1999 poetry collection *On the Bus with Rosa Parks* offers critical and political introspection as well as a poetic celebration of the complexities of black life and of desegregation and its effects, particularly in the 1950s. Crossing color, getting on (the bus) poetically and politically, and paying homage to black women's stamina are the five-part sequence's pivotal aims. Never before has Dove's sense of time rendered as space covered and shaped African-American History and histories[2] throughout the twentieth century. *DF* reincarnates the Oedipal conflict within the institution of slavery from 1820 to 1840, *TB* deals with the lives of a couple from the Great Migration to the March on Washington, and *IG* presents a Bildungsroman in the 1970s. Rosa Parks, the activist heroine of 1955, however, not only rides her bus halfway through the twentieth century looking back, through the poet's eye, on the very beginning of what W. E. B. Du Bois in 1903 termed the century's problem, "the color line," but she is still with us by the end of the millennium, either "In the Lobby of the Warner Theatre, Washington, D.C." (*RP* 86–87) witnessing the premiere of Steven Spielberg's film *Amistad* in December 1997 or riding on the bus with Dove and her family. The poet's "Notes" (*RP* 91) recount how in 1995 her daughter, Aviva Dove-Viebahn, as the conferees at a convention in Williamsburg, Virginia, were boarding buses to be driven to another site, . . . leaned over and whispered, "Hey, we're on the bus with Rosa Parks!" Three generations of activists as poets or poets as activists carry the torch of black liberation beyond the color line. The future reminds the present of the past.

The History of the color line was indeed rewritten on 1 December 1955,[3] with the arrest of Parks, a black seamstress born in Tuskegee, Alabama, in 1913 who refused to give up her bus seat to a white man and gave birth to the civil rights movement. Parks subsequently lost her job, but History continues to reward her courage, for her act of defiance prompted two young black ministers of Montgomery, Alabama, Dr. Martin Luther King, Jr., and the Reverend Ralph D. Abernathy, to organize a boycott against the segregating Jim Crow laws on the bus system. To coordinate this massive protest, King formed the Montgomery Improvement Association (MIA). After 381 days of walking or using car pools arranged by the MIA, citizens of Montgomery were able to return to a nonsegregated transport system. With the successful ending of the boycott, the MIA also came to an end, but by then Martin Luther King, Jr., was established as an emerging black leader. He made African Americans not only more aware of the effectiveness of unified action, but his work also produced the leaders of the Southern Christian Leadership Conference (SCLC). Together they were to organize the Great March on Washington, D.C., that gathered momentum in 1963. Only after Martin Luther King, Jr.'s assassination in Memphis in 1968 did he become the sole hero of the civil rights movement, while its female initiators, including Claudette Colvin, a fifteen-year-old pregnant high school student who had refused to give up her bus seat to a white passenger in March 1955, and the indomitable Parks, remained in the shadow of the great leader.

Dove's *On the Bus with Rosa Parks*, both as a book and as the last chapter of the five-part sequence,[4] pays a complex tribute to the writing of linear History through circular histories that led up to these emancipatory acts. The women ready to prevail and provoke for the sake of freedom are portrayed through their inner voices, preoccupations, observations, and actions. Obvious from the beginning of the book, which explores the intersection of individual fates with the grand arc of History, is the double-track emancipatory effort of poetic action paired with political activism.

Yet, four sections precede the final chapter, "On the Bus with Rosa Parks," which enhances the emblematic grace of a living legend. The opening sequence, "Cameos," probes the private griefs and dreams of a working-class family, from the birth of a baby to educating the kids, while "Freedom: Bird's Eye View" depicts the lyrical self's spiritual growth through childhood and adolescence. "Black on a Saturday Night" visualizes physical black experiences, while "Revenant" explores the supernal shades, mysteries, and wounds that mark the *"Journey to the Frontiers of Art"* (RP 57). What appears to be a series of miscellania leading almost unwittingly to Parks's culminating passive activism and its liberating consequences emerges from a shell like a strand of five exquisitely crafted and luminescent pearls. Moreover, the succession of these five chapters, replete with a baroque pearl's coatings, skinnings, and implosions, is mirrored on a small(er) scale right from the start.

CAMEOS

A cameo is either a "carving in relief on certain stratified gems or shells so that the raised design, often a head in profile," appears sculpted; "a minor, but well-defined role in a play, movie, etc., especially when performed by a notable actor," or "a fine bit of descriptive writing" (*Webster's New World Dictionary*). Dove's "Cameos" enact these denotations in every part. But beware, carved profiles are traditionally of a lighter hue rising from a darker backdrop. Dove however, reverses the color in her "Cameos," which emerge as a series of black acts (of love and giving birth) and actions (of growth and resistance) highlighted against a white foil. "Depression Years" ("Cameos," RP 18–20) echoes the gem or string-of-pearls hypothesis as clear-cut black silhouettes not only in the heroine's given name, Pearl, but in its baroque iconicity, a device that characterizes the entire first section. Of vast importance, for instance to W. J. T. Mitchell,[5] is the consideration of the image as an ideologically informed and informing entity, one whose impact relies on its social context for its force, even as it shapes that context. Dove's visualization of lack reversed into excess during the Great Depression proves the point.

> Pearl
> can't stop eating;
> she wants to live!
> Those professors
> have it all backwards:
> after fat came merriment,
> simply because she was afraid to
> face the world, its lukewarm
> nonchalance
> that generationwise had set
> her people in a stupor of
> religion and
> gambling debts. (Sure, her
> mother was an angel
> but her daddy was
> her man.)
>
> Pearl laughs
> a wet red laugh.
> Pearl oozes

everywhere. When she was
young, she licked the walls free of chalk; she
ate dust for the minerals.
Now she just
enjoys, and excess
hardens on her like
a shell.
She sheens.

But oh, what
tiny feet! She tipples
down the stairs. She cracks a chair.
The largest baby shoe
is neat. Pearl laughs
when Papa jokes: *Why don't*
you grow yourself some feet?
Her mother calls them
devil's hooves.
Her brother
doesn't

care.
He has
A Brain; he doesn't notice.
She gives him of her own
ham hock, plies him with
sweetened yams. Unravels
ratted sweaters, reworks them
into socks. In the lean years
lines his shoes
with newspaper. *(Main*
thing is, you don't
miss school.)

She tells him
it's the latest style.
He never laughs.
He reads. He
shuts her out.
Pearl thinks
she'll never marry—
though she'd
like to have
a child.

Pearl, Papa's girl,[6] not yet on her own feet, caught and lost in the patriarchal
quandary between a joking father, "those professors," and her brother's capitalized "Brain" is a person as well as a type. Rounded to obesity and in sharp contrast to the lean 1930s, she has encased her self behind walls of protective body
fat[7] so as to keep at bay the world's "lukewarm / nonchalance / that genera-
tionwise had set / her people in a stupor of / religion and / gambling debts." Reit-

erated stereotypical gender divisions, sociohistorically conditioned by slavery, reconstruction, segregation, and ensuing poverty are implied in the women's turning to "religion" while their men accumulate "gambling debts." And sadly, the next generation's gender segregation remains cemented: "Her brother / doesn't // care. / He has / A Brain; he doesn't notice. . . . He never laughs. / He reads. He / shuts her out." Pearl's answer to (male) neglect and distress is excess. Layer by layer—she "oozes / everywhere"—her vulnerability is encapsulated within protective sedimentation. "When she was / young, she licked the walls free of chalk; she / ate the dust for the minerals. / Now she just / enjoys, and excess hardens on her like / a shell. She sheens." No longer just fat but sheening with a nacrous lustre, she turns into her own mother-of-pearl. The proverbial household pearl, she is not only generous toward her brainy brother—"She gives him her own / ham hock, plies him with / sweetened yams"—but ingeniously draws the best out of scarce resources as she "Unravels / ratted sweaters, reworks them / into socks . . . She tells him / it's the latest style." While her sibling climbs the ladder thanks to education and her silent support, she nourishes the dream of her own baby, without getting married of course. Next to eating, pregnancy is her other means of reaching merriment through excess. It is also her first step toward independence, although teenage childbearing, a severe problem of the 1990s, will remain endemic if inequality of gender, ethnicity, and class perpetuate oppressive patterns. Yet, "the stereotype of the black mother addicted to welfare is closely linked to resentment of her perceived autonomy—which is to say, her refusal to be dependent on a husband," Ellen Willis maintains.[8]

The programmatic stance of this introductory poem also presents the sequence of *RP* as an ongoing Bildungsroman in verse for African Americans both personally and collectively. And "Brain" is not enough, Dove states from the start. Soul food and food for the soul, "ham hock" and "sweetened yams," are as nurturing and creditable as food for thought proves to be.

For what does Pearl's brother learn in "Homework" (*RP* 20–21) but stale white encyclopedic wisdom on "the Negro's / entire being. Indeed / his love of rhythms / and melody, his / childish faith / in dreams . . ."! Only, the black boy prefers to "take Science, most / Exacting Art." He also graphically sets himself apart (in the left column) from white representations of blackness (in the right column) and refuses to be pigeonholed. He practices resistance instead. "In school when the teacher / makes him lead / the class in song, he'll cough straight through. / . . . Most of all / he'd like to study / the composition of the stars" as Benjamin Banneker (1731–1806) did, the "first black man to devise an almanac and predict a solar eclipse accurately" (*SP*, 93–94, 136). While "Homework" portrays her brother's frustrations with the white educational system, Pearl, in "Painting the Town" (*RP* 22–23), discovers her femininity as a (pro)creative asset. The second of two stanzas reads:

> She'd like to show
> her brother
> what it is to crawl
> up the curved walls

                    of the earth, or
                    to be that earth—but
                    he has other plans.
                    Which is alright. Which is
                    As It Should Be.
                    Let the boy reach manhood
                    anyway he can.

To incorporate roundness, "to be that earth" or "to crawl / up the curved walls / of the earth,"[9] has turned into a symbolic endeavor for Pearl to become and claim the world for herself, while her brother behaves "As It Should Be." Capitalization, a device Emily Dickinson and Dove borrow from German, nonetheless underscores Pearl's subtly mocking acceptance of male preferment: "Let the boy reach manhood / anyway he can."

Thus, the globular and oval shapes of pearl and cameo not only alternately signify fullness, pregnancy, obesity, even a sequence of "Holy Vessels" (*RP* 17), but a framing embrace in a larger sense: The poems of the couple, Lucille and Joe (in the beginning "July, 1925—Night—Birth—Lake Erie Skyline, 1930—" and in the end "Easter Sunday, 1940—Nightwatch. The Son") surround the poems of their children's growth ("Depression Years," "Homework," "Graduation," "Grammar School," "Painting the Town"). Furthermore, "Birth" (*RP* 16) and the final piece, "Nightwatch, The Son" (*RP* 24), display another form of bracketing. Womblike, the two parentheses enfold the newborn baby (left) as well as the adolescent child (right) in their mother's mental hug:

(So there you are at last—	(Aggressively adult,
a pip, a button in the grass.	they keep their
The world's begun	lives, to which
without you.	I am a witness.
And no reception but	At the other end
accumulated time.	I orbit, pinpricked
Your face hidden but your name	light, I watch
shuddering on air!)	I float and grieve.)

The motif of the strand of pearls, transformed into girls shining like "the points of a chandelier: // Corinna, Violet, Mary, Fay, // Suzanna, Kit and Pearl" also permeates "Lake Erie Skyline, 1930" (*RP* 16-18), particularly so in the following stanza, where sex and gender seem to determine destiny. In order to protect the girls, mother warns her son:

                    They were
                    Holy Vessels, mother said:
                    each had to wait
                    Her Turn. And he, somehow,
                    was part of the waiting, he was
                    the chain. He was, somehow,
                    his father.

"Holy Vessels" and the erotic connotation of "Turn," that is, virginity and its loss capitalized, are but flip sides of a coin doubly embossed with female connivance. Though both sexes must await their respective turn, girls somehow have to stay forever to conceive and serve in the Great Chain of Being, whereas the son, brother, lover, father *is* "the chain," the active link between female charms. Thus, the strand of pearl-image transmogrifies into gendered lineage and procreation.

In addition to the salient circular configurations, Dove also creates intriguing parallels. The first poem, "July, 1925" (*RP* 13–14), features the pregnant "Lucille among the Flamingos," as stark a contrast as the obese Pearl is to the depression years. Troublesome to both women are their male relations and their own bodies in excess juxtaposed to images of elongated pink birds or to an imaginary female ideal of weightless elegance catering to white male fantasies. How and when does woman ever step out of the vicious circle of gender, ethnicity, and class coercion?

FREEDOM: BIRD'S-EYE VIEW

The second section presents a new generation, a fresh speaking voice that emanates from the lyrical self's adolescence.[10] "Freedom: Bird's-Eye View" suggests critical distance right away and opens with "Singsong" (*RP* 27), a time of life when "the moon spoke in riddles," when shadows crouch into young years, when Grandma, in "Parlor" (*RP* 30) "insisted / peace was in what wasn't there, / strength in what was unsaid." Existential questions such as "How do you *use* life? / How do you *feel* it?" as well as experiences of blood ("I Cut My Finger Once on Purpose," *RP* 28–29), death (*RP* 30), and, above all, literature mark the young mind's mental growth. From "The First Book" (*RP* 31) to the "Maple Valley Branch Library, 1967" (*RP* 32–33), books are the colorful and colorblind passports[11] to the lyrical self's worlds beyond the local. "The First Book" proves the point: "Open it. (. . .) / Dig in: / you'll never reach bottom. // It's not like it's the end of the world— / just the world as you think // you know it." The voracious fifteen-year-old reader would "Browse the magazines, / slip into the Adult Section to see / what vast *tristesse* was born of rush-hour traffic, / décolletés, and the plague of too much money." This is the mature poet at her laconic best. Yet it is also the aspiring lyrical self's motto scrawled on a garage's boarded-up doors "I CAN EAT AN ELEPHANT / IF I TAKE SMALL BITES" that carries her beyond Pearl's domestic confinement and into the first "ars poetica" of the collection. "Dawn Revisited" (*RP* 36) not only foreshadows *RP's* ultimate ars poetica, "The Pond, Porch-View: Six P.M., Early Spring" (*RP* 88), but also consciously sets out to rewrite History through poetic revisions: "Imagine you wake up / with a second chance (. . .) If you don't look back, // the future never happens. / How good to rise in sunlight, / in the prodigal smell of biscuits— / eggs and sausage on the grill. / The whole sky is yours // to write on, blow open / to a blank page. Come on, / shake a leg! You'll never know / who's down there, frying those eggs, / if you don't get up and see."

Early in her training, the lyrical self feasts on spiritual and material break-fasts and grounds the universal in the particular. Poetry demands both diving into the depths of (book) wisdom and breakfasts as well as soaring above and beyond human knowledge in details, even if they refer to the March on Wash-ington in 1968. Rather than joining the masses in the parade, "the tops of 10,000 / heads[12] floating by on sticks," the lyrical I, too young or too unwilling to walk among the crowd of "magisterial wits," prefers to associate herself with nature, the sun that "flies over the madrigals," with the wind that "tucks / a Dixie cup up," with the hawks[13] that "wheel as the magistrates circle / below, clutching their hats." "Freedom: Bird's-Eye View," the title poem (*RP* 34), *is* the ultimate declaration of independence: "Life, liberty, and the pursuit of happi-ness," in Dove's words, "freedom, / and justice, / and ice cream for all."

BLACK ON A SATURDAY NIGHT

The third section of *RP* largely treats the black physical experience, vibrant black beauty as a steady escort and its exposure to the (white male) gaze. The opening poem is an emancipatory piece on Dove's mother,[14] or any woman of her gen-eration. "The Path to ABC Business School" paid by her daytime work as a seam-stress already evokes Parks, waiting in the wings to become Every(wo)man's seamstress-heroine. While stanza two of "My Mother Enters the Work Force" (*RP* 39) portrays the domestic "treadle machine / with its locomotive whir," the third moves on to "the office machines, their clack and chatter (. . .) ah, and then // no more postponed groceries, / and that blue pair of shoes!" Mother now earns her own money, her own ways, and blue dreams.[15] Blue as a color of hope is Dove's ingenious crossing of the vernacular blues tradition with the German romantic longing for the perennial blue flower ("die blaue Blume").

One major question remains: How does it feel to be bright, black, and beauti-ful within white culture ("The Venus of Willendorf," *RP* 48–50)? What is it to be gorgeously "Black on a Saturday Night," when the weekend connotes leisure, dancing, desire, and delight in one's body to counteract five weekdays of differ-ence, and of "we can't do it"? At first glance, the title poem "Black on a Saturday Night" (*RP* 40–41), obviously a lowdown nitty-gritty from a jitterbug queen,[16] walks a tight rope between a celebratory feat of negritude and an essentialist un-derstanding of color that would defy any valid attempt to view race as a mere construct and imaginary obsession dwelling in white heads. Among others, Henry Louis Gates, Jr., writes in his introduction to *"Race," Writing, and Difference*:

> Race, as a meaningful criterion within the biological sciences, has long been recognized to be a fiction. When we speak of "the white race" or "the black race," "the Jewish race" or "the Aryan race," we speak in biological misnomers and, more generally, in metaphors. (1986: 4)

But to Dove's persona black is "not a concept / nor a percentage / but a natural law" (*RP* 37). How should we interpret and contextualize this provoking statement of color as "a natural law"? Is it a revival of the Black Arts Movement? Or does Dove mockingly get over short-lived contemporary "theorizing"? Well, as grievous white Whitmanesque searchers for our own little truths, we are shut out from an exquisitely exclusive black world by an apt admonition:

> This is no place for lilac
> or somebody on a trip
> to themselves. Hips
> are an asset here, and color
> calculated to flash
> lemon bronze cerise
> in the course of a dip and turn.
> Beauty's been caught lying
> and the truth's rubbed raw:
> Here, you get your remorse
> as a constitutional right.
>
> It's always what we don't
> fear that happens, always
> not now and why are
> you people acting this way
> (meaning we put in petunias
> instead of hydrangeas and reject
> ecru as a fashion statement).
>
> But we can't do it—naw, because
> the wages of living are sin
> and the wages of sin are love
> and the wages of love are pain
> and the wages of pain are philosophy
> and that leads definitely to an attitude
> and an attitude will get you
> nowhere fast so you might as well
> keep dancing dancing till
> tomorrow gives up with a shout,
> 'cause there is only
> Saturday night, and we are in it—
> black as black can,
> black as black does,
> not a concept
> nor a percentage
> but a natural law.

Dancing ("Hips / are an asset here, / . . . in the course of a dip and turn") carries the poem from the first to the third stanza's "Saturday night, and we are in it—/ black as black can, / black as black does." Rhyming with "catch as catch can," this is the black version of any hold or approach that will do. Yet what is to be overcome? It is difference as fear of the other, grafted onto the black body, that delays advancement. Yet how ridiculous and simply a matter of taste "difference" is! The second stanza questions the eternal question: "why are / you people acting this way / (meaning we put in petunias / instead of hydrangeas and reject / ecru as a fashion statement)." Yet neither the refusal of pigeonhole, nor the most sophisticated rhetorical reasoning crafted as a climax or gradatio in the third stanza,

> and the wages of sin are love
> and the wages of love are pain
> and the wages of pain are philosophy

where the last word of one clause or sentence becomes the first of the following—like the rungs of a ladder—provokes significant change. "And an attitude will get you / nowhere fast so you might as well / keep dancing." Dancing then is not an ersatz activity but "a natural law," a genetic and generic gift of enjoyment, of *jouissance*, the delight of multiple identities, of excess rather than limitation. French feminist writers Hélène Cixous and Luce Irigaray have suggested that *jouissance* in this sense is characteristic of what they call "feminine" writing. Lacan contrasts it to "possession," for *jouissance* is fluid and unending; it involves using without using up, and as such exceeds a notion of possession based on some fixed value.[17] Giving freely and undermining notions of thrift or profit are indeed excessive steps toward liberation. Thus

> black as black can,
> black as black does,
> not a concept
> nor a percentage
> but a natural law

refers to black *jouissance* beyond sociocultural concepts, affirmative action, and the like. It simply and uniquely *is* a celebration of black nature in its beauty, humanity, and joy of life.

In a mock celebratory spirit Dove juxtaposes black folklore ("The Musician Talks about 'Process,'" *RP* 42–43) with a condescending traveler's praise of camels as "A rare commodity, these beasts— // who cannot know / what beauty wreaks, what mountains / pity moves" ("The Camel Comes to Us from the Barbarians," *RP* 46–47).[18] Autobiographical experiences color the two final poems of this section, "The Venus of Willendorf" (*RP* 48–50) and "Incarnation in Phoenix" (*RP* 51–52). They present two extreme physical experiences in terms of ethnicity and gender: A beautiful black woman visits an archaic Venus in Austria and feels exposed to the white, predominantly male gaze (*RP* 49).

> It was impossible, of course,
> to walk the one asphalted street
> without enduring a gauntlet of stares.
> *Have you seen her?* they asked,
> comparing her to their Venus
> until she could feel her own breasts

> settle and the ripening
> predicament of hip and thigh.

A tension between dead white art and live black beauty permeates the poem, but in the end the mystery of art transcends the color and gender division. Though the male gaze threatens to glut itself into the visitor's body, while "*Herr Professor*" confesses intimate details during his wife's absence, the target of scopophilia keeps wondering: "What made one sculpture so luscious / when there were real women, layered / in flesh no one worshipped? / The professor's wife, for instance." However, the question of art versus nature overrides the predicaments of exposure so that the lyrical self suddenly "understands what made / the Venus beautiful / was how the carver's hand had loved her, / that visible caress." Eros in art, and art in eros equally transform beauty into the worshipped rarity preserved in time. The discovery of the epiphanies of human creation and procreation run parallel. It is no coincidence in Dove's crafting of a sequence that the pairing of art and life occurs about halfway through the text, rounding off the opening and closure. Notice that *RP* sets out with a new-born baby (*RP* 16) and concludes with a poem in labor (*RP* 88).

Back in Phoenix, the lyrical self reincarnates in giving birth to her daughter Raven, a nice twist of the Poe-etic[19] tradition. No phoenix but a lustrous girl rises out of the ashes, the ultimate cameo—"her charcoal limbs emerging from crisp whites" (*RP* 51)—"dropped on our doorstep and ripening / before us, a miniature United Nations / 'Just like me,' Raven says, citing // the name of her mother's village / somewhere in Norway, her father / a Buffalo soldier. Now / of course, we can place her: / an African Valkyrie / who takes my breasts in her fists / grunting." The prevailing tendency to label and place someone within a black and white framework, even if the origins do not meet the stereotype of "an African Valkyrie," will thwart the very chance of ethnic integration.[20] However, the child as "a miniature United Nations" represents a fusion of multifarious spaces that outdate the temporal layers accumulated on the body of the archaic Venus of Willendorf. Throughout her oeuvre, Dove revises place and space against the pitfalls of pigeonholing.

REVENANT

With "Revenant," the penultimate chapter of *RP*, Dove's lyrical self travels to new realms of in-betweenness. She no longer straddles opposite cultures, ethnicities, or generations but, ghostlike, moves between life and death as a revenant, a person who returns as after a long absence.[21] Oscillating between the supernal and the uncanny, between creativity and destruction, the revenant searches for the beautiful and the sublime on the "*Journey to the Frontiers of Art.*" You sit "in front of the mirror, covered / . . . with plastic and copied on it / the outlines" of a new face, Ewa Kuryluk's epilogue to "On Veronica" (*RP* 53) indicates. Along these lines, the title poem "Revenant" emerges as an ars poetica beyond known worlds (*RP* 56):

Palomino, horse of shadows.
Pale of the gyrfalcon
streaking free,
a reckoning—

the dark climbing out a crack in the earth.

Black veils starched for Easter.
The black hood of the condemned,
reeking with slobber
The no color behind the eyelid
as the ax drops.

Gauze bandages over the wounds of State.

The canvas is primed, the morning
bitten off but too much to chew.
No angels here:
the last one slipped the room
while your head was turned,

made off for the winter streets.

This is Dove's powerful inscription of her name as an artist and historiographer in the tradition of Paul Celan, whose poem "Todesfuge" commemorates the shoah.[22] From "Palomino, horse of shadows," a dove-colored, gray, fallow horse[23]—in Latin "palumbinus," a pigeon, a ringdove—to the pale gyrfalcon—a gir-hawk is a greedy, fierce, strong, and large bird of prey who inhabits the arctic regions—"Revenant" turns into Dove's signature poem of this section, her wings and legs between inner and outer space. In addition, the two pale animals, hawk and horse, also represent Edmund Burke's distinction of the sublime and beautiful as in his *Philosophical Inquiry into the Origin of Our Ideas on the Sublime and Beautiful* (1756). And, as in "Cameos," her hybrid, dove-colored portrait as horse-bird rises from a dark background. "Streaking free," however, and from a bird's eye view, she cannot avoid reckoning "the dark climbing out a crack in the earth." Remembrances of the black holocaust are pervasive. Yet with their "Black veils starched for Easter," the victims are ready for resurrection. In Dove's striking gyre away from the masses onto the individual, the veil, synonymous with African-American double-consciousness, turns into the "The black hood of the lonely condemned," the one on whom "the ax drops." Individually or collectively these are "the wounds of State" that need to be bandaged by History and the saving grace of art. "The canvas is primed," the blank page ready to be rewritten and repainted. But the poet is alone, "No angels here" to help her paint the scene on a canvas of living skin.

The following poem, "On Veronica" (*RP* 57), however, reveals the picture in tercets:

Exposed to light,
the shroud lifts
its miraculous inscription—

a wound. Skin talking:
yes there, touch me there.
The stain of a glance,

a glance caught off-
guard, how it slices,
how each mirror imperils!

Time and again, Dove unites poetry with painting and depicts the poem and the picture in the making, or the picture in the making in the poem.[24] In "There Came a Soul" (*RP* 58–59), a model and muse, "Pretty Ida, out to earn a penny / for her tiny brood" restores the artist's creative powers so that "he kept to his task, applying paint / like a bandage to the open wound." The twin poems, "Against Repose" and "Against Self-Pity" (*RP* 62, 63), address the artist's ultimate loneliness and responsibility when "Nothing comes to mind" and any escape, even a glass of wine would stay bitter, "a mouthful of sin // in an inchful of hell." Self-pity also "gets you nowhere but deeper into / your own shit—pure misery a luxury / one never learns to enjoy. There's always some // meatier malaise, a misalliance ripe / to burst." And in "Götterdämmerung" (*RP* 64–65), a poem dedicated to the body in pain (Scarry 1987), personal and artistic discipline are of utmost help. In her study, *The Body in Pain*, Elaine Scarry (1987: 161ff) points to the connection between pain and imagining, a dialectics that permeates Dove's text:

> **The only state that is as anomalous as pain is the imagination. While pain is a state remarkable for being wholly without objects, the imagination is remarkable for being the only state that is wholly its objects**. . . . If, for example, a discussion of imagining takes either Pegasus or a unicorn as its instance of the imagined object, the imagination is then likely to be itself characterized by the qualities of the specified image. Although the unicorn or Pegasus expresses the imagination's freedom from natural occurrence, **its ability to rearrange wings and legs into new combinations,** and although it expresses as well the imagination's eventual capacity to create beyond "need," since neither the unicorn nor Pegasus is striking for its usefulness to people in the twentieth century, such an image, by its very frivolity, wrongly suggests that the activity itself is trivial or marginal: that is, discussions conjuring up this type of image tend also to underestimate the centrality and significance of imagining in everyday life. (162, 163, emphasis mine)

Both "Revenant" and "Götterdämmerung" move in the shadowy presence of death in life countered by the stimulating and salvaging power of imagination. Palomino, a Pegasus-like horse, and the gyrfalcon introduced in "Revenant" precisely embody the "ability to rearrange wings and legs into new combinations." "Götterdämmerung," the twilight of the Gods above and the earthbound gods of the artworld below—the German title adds a Brechtian alienation effect, that is, a sense of ironic detachment—shakes human beings into realizing that omnipotence might be short-lived and limiting.

> On good days
> I feel a little meaty; on bad,
> a few degrees from rancid.
> (Damn knee: I used it this morning
> to retrieve a spilled colander;
> now every cell's blowing whistles.)

> At least it's still a body.
> He'd never believe it son of mine,
> but I remember what it's like
> to walk the world
> with no help from strangers,
> not even a personal trainer
> to make you feel the burn.

The limitations of physical pain might also turn into imaginative expansion, as Elaine Scarry points out:

> Physical pain, then, is an intentional state without an intentional object; imagining is an intentional object without an experienceable intentional state. Thus, it may be that in some peculiar way it is appropriate to think of pain as the imagination's intentional state, and to identify the imagination as pain's intentional object. (164)

As if to prove Scarry's point, the lyrical self, the former gyrfalcon by now transmuted into an "ancient iron-clawed griffin," still produces sounds behind a colorful protective mask and declares medical wisdom simply inadequate.

> So I wear cosmetics maliciously
> now. And I like my bracelets,
> even though they sound ridiculous,
> clinking as I skulk through the mall,
> store to store like some ancient
> iron-clawed griffin—but I've never

> stopped wanting to cross
> the equator, or touch an elk's
> horns, or sing *Tosca* or screw
> James Dean in a field of wheat.
> To hell with wisdom. They're all wrong:
> I'll never be through with my life.

The ordeal of this resilient and powerfully imaginative poetic self overshadows the next poem, "Ghost Walk" (*RP* 66–68), dedicated to a "châtelaine-revenant"[25] who still haunts Lavigny Castle, which came to serve as a writers' retreat. Thus "Götterdämmerung" leads on to the emblematic penultimate poem of the section, "Lady Freedom among Us" (*RP* 69–70), the harbinger of Rosa Parks as a living Lady Freedom. Read by Dove during her poet laureateship, the poem commemorates the 200th anniversary of the U.S. Capitol and the restoration of the Statue of Freedom to the Capitol dome on 23 October,

1993 (*RP* 93). Dove's Lady Freedom is no empty female allegory ready to be filled with whatever culture calls for during a particular period, whether it be: vices, justice, peace, or nationhood: Britannia, Germania, Helvetia, Marianne, or Liberty and Freedom. This Lady invites and commands the gaze like nothing else in Washington, D.C.:

> with her oldfashioned sandals
> with her leaden skirts
> with her stained cheeks and whiskers and heaped up trinkets
> she has risen among us in blunt reproach
>
> she has fitted her hair under a hand-me-down cap
> and spruced it up with feathers and stars
> slung over one shoulder she bears
> the rainbowed layers of charity and murmurs
> *all of you   even the least of you*

Anaphorically clad "with" yet another trinket like a homeless person, she has "brought mercy back into the streets / and will not retire politely to the potter's field." In fact the public duty of Lady Freedom and Rosa Parks appropriates space and remains firmly placed.

> don't think you can ever forget her
> don't even try
> she's not going to budge
>
> no choice but to grant her space
> crown her with sky
> for she is one of the many
> and she is each of us

No punctuation hinders the flow of Lady Freedom's command when she finally comes to embody the motto embossed on U.S. currency: "e pluribus unum." What seems to be a mere realistic description of a statue animated by the poet's fancy—in this sense Lady Freedom is also a revenant between dead clay and imagined life—gains power by a subcutaneous closeness to an urban reality of tourism, government, poverty, and pollution. "[H]aving assumed the thick skin of this town / its gritted exhaust its sunscorch and blear," she is used to the capital's traffic. Thus Dove succeeds in anchoring an abstract idea in a lively public representation that refuses to accept people's multifarious excuses for ignoring her. As much as a cutting gaze should be avoided among human beings, this Lady invites contemplation: "don't lower your eyes / or stare straight ahead to where / you think you ought to be going."

ON THE BUS WITH ROSA PARKS

"All history is a negotiation between familiarity and strangeness," the title's epigraph by Simon Schama commends. History then does not primarily deal with time's chronology but with the dialectics of known and unknown territories: space and place granted, denied, appropriated, defended, exchanged, or expanded. Dove's extension of boundaries while endeavoring to recover the past, be it that of the European literary tradition or African-American history and culture, is at its best in the final chapter of her sequence *On the Bus with Rosa Parks*. Here she seeks to establish the role of Rosa Parks as the mother of the modern civil rights movement next and indeed prior to Martin Luther King, Jr. The living icon of peaceful perseverance, Parks's action on 1 December 1955, of sitting down to stand up for equal rights to ride the bus in Montgomery, Alabama, took on portentuous meaning. While the laws of black and white segregation in public transportation date back to the *Plessy v. Ferguson* decision of 1896, desegregation at large began in 1954 with *Brown v. the Board of Education of Topeka*, which ordered schools to integrate precisely by means of busing students from white to black neighborhoods and vice versa. Racial segregation, of course, went back to the origins of southern public education for African Americans during Reconstruction and had many earlier precedents in the North. The Supreme Court's *Plessy v. Ferguson* decision took the constitutionalizing of separate schools for granted, using the widespread tolerance of that practice to justify its opinion that separate railroad accommodation was constitutional. Its formula, "equal but separate" (usually recalled as "separate but equal"), was virtually ignored by politicians and educational administrators. Yet, the racist set of mind was not uniquely southern. Northern philanthropists were also willing to educate the races separately.[26] Within this historic perspective, Parks's insubordination also deserves respect as a timely act. Her legacy is alive in Spike Lee's film *Get on the Bus* (1997) and in Dove's most recent poetry collection *On the Bus with Rosa Parks*.

The title of the first poem, "Sit Back, Relax" (*RP* 75), in its double [i-a, i-a] singsong, suggests a treacherous moment of rest and peace after a long day's work. Parks, or any other black passenger who must traverse town to work in white neighborhoods and return to segregated living quarters in the evening, is hoping for a moment of peace. But the uncanny undermines the canny sense of homecoming right away:

> Lord, Lord. No rest
> for the wicked?
> Most likely no
> heating pads.
>
> (*Heat some gravy for the potatoes,*
> *slice a little green pepper*
> *into the pinto beans . . .*)
>
> Sometimes a body
> just plain grieves.
>
> *Stand by me in this, my hour—*

Religious invocations and the association of pain as a result of her daily chores ("Sometimes a body / just plain grieves") with the cooking at home intermingle with resistance: "No rest / for the wicked?" The reader is taken into "medias res" of a single mind and a collective situation that will be declared "intolerable" in official statements reflected in the following poem (*RP* 76). "The situation is intolerable," however, turns out to be a matter of sides. While African Americans are no longer willing to tolerate segregation, white supremacy cannot accept black resistance. Civilization remains a contested ground between familiarity and strangeness into which the poet, disguised as a "dovegray pleated trouser leg / a righteous sword advancing," places and inscribes herself next to Parks.

> *Intolerable:* that civilized word.
> Aren't we civilized, too? Shoes shined,
> each starched cuff unyielding,
> each dovegray pleated trouser leg
> a righteous sword advancing
> onto the field of battle
> in the name of the Lord . . .

The conclusion is: "Our situation is intolerable, but what's worse / is to sit here and do nothing." The subsequent poem, "Freedom Ride" (*RP* 71), changes the scene dramatically and with it the imagined space. The speaker, sitting behind the tinted glass of the bus from where the familiar "little houses with / their fearful patches of yard" appear like "rushing into the flames," expands her local world of constraints into a realm of bounty:

> As if, after High Street
> and left turn onto Exchange
> the view would veer onto
> someplace fresh: Curaçao,
> or a mosque adrift on a milk-fed pond.

"Freedom Ride" is a remarkable poem, for it succeeds in zooming in on and at the same time thwarting an intricate dialectics of the inside and outside, of the local and the global, the past and the present, of History with references to the murdered heroes of the coming civil rights movement—John and Robert Kennedy ("Dallas," "Bobby"), "Malcolm" (X), and Martin Luther King, Jr. ("Memphis")—and of History in the making.[27] Time and space race into freedom on this voyage away from illusions, daydreaming, and false promises. What has been and what is to come are one in this contested area of Jim Crow laws riding along with Dove and Parks, who knows where she is: "where you sit is where you'll be / when the fire hits." Imagining freedom is turning into political expansion right now, and bloodlines symbolized by bus stops to be picked or avoided are being redrawn. In including these single moments that led up to Parks's silent but powerful defiance in the Montgomery bus boycott, Dove merges a personal with a more general prospect of African-American emancipation.

At this point, Michel Foucault's general claim[28] to keep the field of dis-

courses radically open for any analysis and free from traditional concepts of
linearity or continuity comes to mind. History must be endlessly rewritten, in
particular by the voices hitherto unheard. It is from here that the dark voices of
the underground call in order to tell their histories of the small, unheard, and
unseen that throb underneath and beside the master narrative, those events
that led up to Parks's "Freedom Ride" in 1955. At this point Dove is but three
years old and most likely the child "Climbing In" (*RP* 78) to the bus. This poem
contains a change of perspective as well as a story within a story, a concrete situation wrapped into the fairy tale of "Little Red Ridinghood." But what History
is to Parks remains a mystery to Dove for the moment. In boarding the bus up
front, the child is holding the fare in her hand ready to tumble "head over tail /
down the clinking gullet." This recalls the wolf's

> Teeth.
> Metallic. Lie-gapped.
> Not a friendly shine
>
> like the dime
> cutting my palm as
> I clutch the silver pole
> to step up, up
>
> (sweat gilding the dear lady's
> cheek)—these are big teeth,
> teeth of the wolf
>
> under grandmother's cap.

Yet, the common underlying theme of danger likens the child's bus ride to
Parks's. In those days the driver, who had to be paid up front by all passengers—
while African Americans had to enter from the rear—would often leave the
stop without the paying paupers, and the coin's inscriptions, "Liberty, in God
We Trust" and "United States of America, e pluribus unum," magnified, could
flash in shame before Lady Freedom's stare.

"Claudette Colvin Goes to Work" (*RP* 79–80) and "The Enactment" (*RP*
81–82), which follows, are twin poems as they both highlight black women's
resilience and grace under pressure. Claudette Colvin, whose inner monologue
portrays her as an ambitious young woman—"I'm the crazy girl off the bus,
the one / who wrote in class she was going to be President"—awaits the
evening to "start out for work" so that "it's dark enough for my body to disappear." Though she helps "those who can't help themselves," Claudette, a "poor
black trash" teenager, is not considered adequate to embody and enact black resistance: "It's gotta be a woman, / someone of standing: / preferably shy, preferably married. / And she's got to know / when the moment's right. / . . . Then
all she's got to do is / sit there, quiet, till / the next moment finds her—and only
then / can she open her mouth to ask / *Why do you push us around?* / and his answer: *I don't know but* / *the law is the law and you* // *are under arrest.*" This woman
is Parks to whom Dove dedicates a subtle portrait of appropriate neatness in

four vignettes of tercets. Though Parks's personality might be particularly suited to meet white middle-class expectations, its natural dignity reaches beyond social and racial demarcations (*RP* 83).

"Rosa"

How she sat there,
the time right inside a place
so wrong it was ready.

That trim name with
its dream of a bench
to rest on. Her sensible coat.

Doing nothing was the doing:
the clean flame of her gaze
carved by a camera flash.

How she stood up
when they bent down to retrieve
her purse. That courtesy.

In its regularity, Parks's blazon touches on the tangible, the blameless, the eternal, and the miraculous. Furthermore, it acts as the prelude to the concluding group of four poems that entwine the *riding* and *writing* processes of Parks and Dove in a remarkable chiastic crossing. While the outer poems, "Rosa" and the ultimate ars poetica "The Pond, Porch-View: Six P.M., Early Spring" (*RP* 88), reveal both the political activist and the poet as historian in their existential loneliness to seize a moment of truth, the inner poems show off the two public figures touring the world: the poet—I consciously weld the lyrical self's experience to Dove at this point—is aboard the "QE 2. Transatlantic Crossing. Third Day" (*RP* 84–85), while the living legend Parks, "In the Lobby of the Warner Theatre, Washington, D.C." (*RP* 86–87), lends her grace to the screening of Steven Spielberg's film *Amistad*, that is, his vision of a slave mutiny aboard the *Amistad*, which took place in 1837.[29] Not only does Parks embody "*living* history" in any place, but in Washington, D.C., she actually becomes "Lady Freedom among Us" (*RP* 69–70), as if her deeds would finally enliven an allegorical or poetic shape to its fullest.[30] No longer riding the bus but a wheelchair "at the foot of the golden escalator, just right / of the movie director who had cajoled her to come" . . . "Not that he was using her / to push his films, but it was only right (wasn't it?) that / she be wherever history was being made." The irony is palpable, but Spielberg as the film historian of both the white and the black holocaust—from his films *The Color Purple* to *Schindler's List* to *Amistad*—is more than a white Jewish backdrop to Parks's bravery, another of Dove's cameos. He introduces the sister art of the silver screen into the picture by showing off a still curious and lively Parks, who "had learned to travel a crowd," and he reminds us at the same time of the ashes of the Jewish suffering. Commemorating the holocaust, Paul Celan's poem "Todesfuge," with its opening oxymoron of black and white, surfaces as well.[31]

Schwarze Milch der Frühe wir trinken sie abends
Wir trinken sie mittags und morgens wir trinken sie nachts
Wir trinken und trinken
Wir schaufeln ein Grab in den Lüften da liegt man nicht eng

. . .

Dein goldenes Haar Margarete
Dein aschenes Haar Sulamith

Familiarity and strangeness are engraved in these lines as the poem envisions two modes of being, death in life and life in death, which ultimately transcend all divisions. And Jewish and black victims do lie strangely close in their "graves," as slave ships were notorious for the stifling "familiarity" of their overcrowded quarters. However, Celan's double vision, I argue, is at the core of Dove's luxurious Middle Passage aboard the oceanliner *Queen Elizabeth 2*, a modern *Titanic* still afloat, where she sits "on the lap of existence," and both "neat dime or tarnished token" have been replaced by "chips and signatures."

Panel of gray silk. Liquefied ashes. Dingy percale tugged over
the vast dim earth—ill-fitting, softened by eons of tossing
and turning, unfurling its excesses, recalling its losses,
no seam for the mending, no selvage to catch and align
from where I sit and look out from this rose-colored armchair
along the gallery. I can hear the chime of the elevator,

the hush of trod carpet. Beyond the alcove, escorted widows
perfect a slow rumba. Couples linger by the cocktail piano,
enmeshed in their own delight as others stroll past,
pause to remark on the weather. Mist, calm seas.
This is a journey for those who simply wish to be
on the way—to lie back and be rocked for a while, dangled

between the silver spoon and golden gate. Even
I'm thrilled, who never learned to wait on a corner, . . .

A laconic final line, "Well. I'd go home if I knew where to get off"—there are no bus stops on the *QE2*—is preceded in five stanzas, a sea of superimposed images where contemporary luxurious leisure and past misery of the "midnight route" intersect. The "Panel of gray silk" turns immediately into "Liquefied ashes," as fast as Margarete's golden hair changes into Sulamith's ashen or dove-colored hair in Celan's poem. The poet, navigating between the Scylla of the "silver spoon" and the Charybdis of the "golden gate," passes through the positively discriminating ivory gate of art in evoking a Shakespearean tempest that likens the Atlantic Ocean to an ill-fitting "Dingy percale over / the vast dim earth." Even in her use of seamstress imagery ("no seam for the mending, no selvage to catch and align") and from her "rose-colored armchair," the poet pays tribute to Parks. Both ladies are now close to elevators that allow vertical journeys to the top rather than horizontal movements such as bus rides. In addition, the sea, "softened by eons of tossing / and turning, unfurling its excesses, recalling its losses," becomes the poet's own silver screen of intense remembrance as well as her element to move in ("I put this body into its sleeve of dark water"). While proving familiarity with the past, she opts for new territories ahead. In enjoying the freedom to do whatever she chooses, the lyrical self reverses the Middle Passage into a perfectly normal transatlantic passage to Europe—the only one that remains today—from where she will most likely fly back on the supersonic Concorde, stretching and compressing time and space at her leisure. This is her ultimate voyage out, her class act of liberation beyond a strange past that is no longer hers though she perfectly revisions and redeems it back into artistic reflection. In sharp contrast to the poetry of the Black Arts Movement ("And that, friends, is the difference— // I can't erase an ache I never had. // Not even my own grandmother would pity me"), she mitigates bitter experiences with humor and refuses to be caught in any restricting grid.

Parks's and Dove's journeys into unknown territory prove to be fruitful politically and poetically. But the political activist and the poet need to move in the world as well as to remain seated for the creative act that prepares the ground beyond "the hush of trod carpet."

And this is where the poet finds herself at the end of her journey, at the exact spatiotemporal coordinates of her porch, overlooking her own pond, as if it mirrored the ultimate blank page of a new poem (*RP* 88). Here and now, utopia and heterotopia[32] must suit content and form.

"The Pond, Porch-View: Six P.M., Early Spring"

I sit, and sit, and will my thoughts
the way they used to wend
when thoughts were young
(i.e., accused of wandering).
The sunset ticks another notch
into the pressure treated rails
of the veranda. My heart, too,
has come down to earth:
I've missed the chance
to put things in reverse,
recapture childhood's backseat
universe. Where I'm at now
is more like riding on a bus
through unfamiliar neighborhoods—
chair in recline, the view chopped square
and dimming quick. I know
I vowed I'd get off
somewhere grand; like that dear goose
come honking down
from Canada, I tried to end up
anyplace but here.
Who am I kidding? Here I am.

An iambic foot sets the pace for the poet's own look back, not in anger but regretful of missed chances "to put things in reverse, / recapture childhood's backseat / universe." Her longing shifts from spatial to temporal voyages down into the imaginative plenitude of her youth, whereas her life now seems "more like riding on a bus / through unfamiliar neighborhoods——." While the strange has become familiar by her growing into middle age and fame, the once familiar has become more remote. Instead of enjoying the nonselective wandering of a child's mind, the poet now has to will her "thoughts / the way they used to wend / when thoughts were young." But here she is: not "that dear goose" from Canada, but trusting her own legs and wings.

Dove closes her circle in various ways: In *RP* a baby's birth in the beginning parallels the birth of a poem in the end. Dove would not be the number fetishist she is if her strand of five chapter-pearls, beginning and ending with ten cameos, did not exactly match in number. Nowhere else do ten or five appear, as chapter 2 (eight poems), chapter 3 (seven poems), and chapter 4 (11 poems) all slightly differ from the regularity of the initial and the final section of ten poems. Yet numbers and form do not outshine the carefully wrought sequence that is one grand poem in itself. Predominantly enhancing the intricate web of female emancipatory acts, *On the Bus with Rosa Parks* is perhaps the first verse History of African-American women's achievements in the twentieth century. It is a tale that transcends race, class, and gender divisons through its razor-sharp gaze that highlights the poetic in politics, and the political in poetry. While *Thomas and Beulah* presents the lives of a couple one after the other, Dove now succeeds in weaving two lives together in constant exchange, reflection, and intertextuality. *On the Bus with Rosa Parks* is her homage to those who paved her way into political and artistic freedom as well as her poetic integration of a politically segregated world before her.

CONCLUSIONS

Crossing Color: Transcultural Space and Place in Rita Dove's Poetry, Fiction, and Drama represents the first monographic investigation of this major African-American author's writing (Pulitzer Prize, 1987; U.S. poet laureate, 1993–1995). It examines the linguistic devices through which Dove shapes her transcultural spaces and places, understood as a fusion of cultural backgrounds that provide "a home in art."

Crossing Color explores not only the vast range of Dove's thematic and formal means—she reaches out to the world's languages and learning and eludes marginalization and pigeonholing—but also her interest in crossing boundaries, be they geographical, racial, religious, or marked by class, gender, and genre. Moreover, her work crosses over to a broader public by means of reading, stage productions, and the media. Dove's oeuvre documents and enriches the American-European literary and humanist dialogue. Particularly intriguing and fruitful is Dove's fusion of African-American, German, and Greek backgrounds. These unusual trajectories of thought and creation open avenues of national and global artistic understanding and expand crosscultural discourses at a time when people(s), boundaries, and traditional views of national identity and literature are shifting.

Poetologically, Dove's incorporation of European thought is even more striking. Her poetic consciousness and sense of space is inspired by, among others, the French philosopher Gaston Bachelard's *Poetics of Space*. His basic elements of space, to Dove, are "imbued with time's urgency, the fleeting ache of time passing." Bachelard is important for her because he ties all fundamental spaces in with spiritual and metaphysical states of being. Bachelard's criteria, extended by Fritz Gysin's theory of borders and boundaries within recent African-American fiction, has provided a fruitful theoretical frame for Dove's transcultural spaces and places. Two aspects govern her worldmaking: Often the protagonists will find a way to expand the space that has been assigned to them by either assimilating or ignoring it, or by using it to their advantage. Often they succeed without the colonizer's noticing it. In terms of writing, of the technique itself—poetry is the tightest writing—Dove calls verse a "colonized space," a narrow rigid cage that represents confinement as well as a chance to challenge the walls and find an incredible freedom both in the mastery and expansion of a given frame.

Cultural space, as distinguished from place and location, is a space that has been seized upon and transmuted by imagination, knowledge, or experience. Both Dove's lyrical sequences as well as her individual poems reflect a conscious concern with borders and boundaries as *dividing line, area of contact or unilateral division, brink, edge,* and *threshold*. This increased awareness of constraints is balanced by a series of movements: *travelogues, sightseeing, flights into freedom, quests, metamorphoses,* and *imaginary voyages*. The psychotopology of *dreamscapes* and *mental expansion* prepared the ground for forceful instances of *transcultural enspacement*. Through the mediation of an African-American artist, European culture compellingly illuminates recent Caribbean history. Sometimes one right word will kill ("Parsley"), sometimes it will absolve ("Ö").

Dove's more recent works, *Through the Ivory Gate, Mother Love,* and *The Darker Face of the Earth,* particularly examine Greek myth within an African-American context. These trajectories of her transatlantic dialogue are revolutionary in yet another way: Within the African-American literary tradition, Dove's oeuvre represents a double reaction to the Black Arts Movement of the 1960s: she picks up its political impetus, that is, a sense of politics as the given starting point, but eschews and ironizes its clichéd political discourse and aesthetic dilettantism (for instance, in "Upon Meeting Don L. Lee, in a Dream"). Thus her aesthetic and thematic departure serves as a critique of the 1960s, offers a politicalization of the modernist tradition, and creates a more inclusive artistic realm of her own making. Moreover, with *On the Bus with Rosa Parks* Dove writes a local and global, a rural and urban history of African-American women's private, poetical, and political achievements in the twentieth century.

The sense of place Dove evokes in her poetry, fiction, and drama—even *IG*'s and *TB*'s Akron, Ohio, or, Montgomery, Alabama—is not fixed and reassuring, hence more truly attuned to regional and global changes. The emotional landscape in Dove is likewise both moored and unsettled: moments of deep intimacy and trust may be followed by disruption, threat, and death. Precisely through these cultural gaps, fissures, and fusions at the edge of the millennium, I argue, Dove embodies a sense of abiding dislocation in her art. Yet the shifting, conditional nature of space is always matched in her oeuvre by a precise sense of time and history: her fictional revision of facts in form. With a razor-sharp visual exactitude she surveys her rearranged territory and houses the displaced of all ages and places—protagonists and readers—in her lyrics.

In her desire to create harmony out of disjunction, Dove identifies herself with a generation of writers who find in their fragmented and hybrid cultural heritage not only frustration and invisibility but also richness and transcultural syncretism. Since her first published volume of poetry, *The Yellow House on the Corner* (1980), Dove has consistently demanded the liberty to move unfettered across boundaries and all facets of world culture. With the privilege of a cross-cultural perspective thrust upon her early on, she integrates these elements and fashions them into new coherence, healing the rifts and shifts in our own divisive culture, weaving the fragments into a fabric with a pattern, texture, and voice of her own.

IN CONVERSATION WITH RITA DOVE

Researching, collecting material is very much like interviewing: Ask
probing questions, talk to the subject for as long as you can before you get
thrown out. And since you've only got a limited space—say 750 words,
give or take a few—look for an angle. I call it the hinge, *that which*
swings open the door into the world of that poem—the color of a scarf, or
the number of upholstery studs (lynchpins) in a leather-backed office
chair.

Rita Dove

Selbst grosse Artefakte überleben ohne Resonanzen nicht. Ich möchte den
Resonanz- und Verständnisraum, den eigenen und den anderer Lesenden,
erweitern. Wie stehen sich Lesarten gegenüber? Interessiert, amüsiert,
gelegentlich nachsichtig, vielleicht wütend?

Therese Steffen

"A study of a living author cannot, properly speaking, have an ending," Werner
Sollors concludes his book on Amiri Baraka and LeRoi Jones (1978: 247). The
continuous reflexion on Dove's oeuvre has just begun. The possibility, however,
of entering into a dialogue with a living author is a unique chance. The following
conversation with Dove, on 1–2 June 1996[1] in her home near Charlottesville,
Virginia, invites her voice "live" into the formal framework of this investigation.

Therese STEFFEN: You are a historian. Many of your poems transport the reader
to a moment in the past. Sometimes it seems, your own past:

> *In the nigger night, thick with the smell of cabbages,*
> *Nothing can catch us.*
> *Laughter spills like gin from glasses,*
> *And "yeah" we whisper, "yeah"*
> *We croon, "yeah."*

But you are also an avowed syncretist, a mythographer whose work depicts characters and scenes from around the world. From your earliest days as a writer you have

sustained your imagination with the literature and culture of Germany: from "The Bird Frau" (1978) to "Agosta the Winged Man and Rasha the Black Dove" (1981) to "The Venus of Willendorf" (1992) to "Wiederkehr" (1995) to "Götterdämmerung" (1999). German words, personae, and syntax occupy a central place in your creative vision; you are presently at work on a sequence of poems on Albrecht Dürer. Your obsession began with your father's books: during World War II, he mastered Italian and German, "to know the language of the enemy." Your life-long affair with things German—including your husband—recalls Frederick Douglass's thirty-year relationship with Ottilie Assing, and W. E. B. Du Bois's enthusiasm for German history and the former East German government.

You have a similar affinity for ancient Greece. Your play, *The Darker Face of the Earth*, is a free-verse tragedy set in antebellum South Carolina—and an adaptation of Sophocles's Oedipus plays.

I wanted to start by asking about your varied interests and how they have affected your writing. What inspires you?

Rita DOVE: I try to remain ignorant of my influences, at least the literary ones. I think the way I was brought up was decisive. There were always books in the house, and the desire for knowledge was encouraged in our family. When we had questions about homework, my brother and I did our best to find answers on our own, since our father would invariably start out helping us only to get us interested in something else. He would demand that we look everything up in the encyclopedia, which would take hours: we'd learn a lot about the Roman Empire but still not know the answer to our question. That thrill of one thing leading to another, the excitement of seeing how things can come round full circle, has certainly influenced me as much as reading and listening to great storytellers has.

I grew up listening to the women in the kitchen telling their stories. The men had stories, but they belonged to another part of the world. Female storytelling was more intimate and chaotic, more fluid; the tales came out in bits and gobbets. The men used a much more deliberate, show-off style of narration, exaggerating the story in the tradition of "toasts." My father had a rather formal tradition of storytelling at Christmas; when we would wake up at five o'clock on Christmas morning, unable to fall asleep again, Dad would tell a very elaborate story about a little Italian girl named Marie who had helped the American troops during World War II. Every Christmas he would relate another episode about little Marie and the war. They were wonderful stories, very ritualistically presented: we had to beg for a prescribed amount of time before he would "relent" and start to spin his tale; and we knew when to be quiet and when to ask questions in order to spur on the telling.

Another influence is my serendipitous encounter with the German language. I met my husband, Fred, while practicing German at Iowa. German has influenced the way I write: I have tried to re-create in poems the feeling I had when I first began to speak the language—that wonderful sensation of being held hostage by a sentence until the verb comes along at the end. I can't imagine what it must be like for a German who grew up with this feeling, but I was fascinated by the way this grammatical device maintained the tension of any story. I wondered whether one could do that in English as well—make a poem's world cohere only at the very end, like the final piece in a jigsaw puzzle.

I am addicted to puzzles. Crossword puzzles are a dreadful habit; I have to ration mine out, one at the end of the day, for relaxation. I'm not as crazy about jigsaw puzzles, but I do sometimes find it soothing to come home after an incredibly hectic day or a long plane ride and sit there for half an hour, piecing one together.

I think my puzzle fetish has something to do with the way poems are constructed. Poems work in a temporal sense—that is, they proceed from the beginning to the end. But at the same time, there are words that reverberate throughout the poem on a different level—a more vertical axis. Words start to reverberate by virtue of their proximity to one another. That's a spatial thing as well as a temporal one. Sometimes when I get stuck working on a poem, I lay words out like they are pieces in a jigsaw puzzle and see what happens. It sounds irreverent, but it's not. I am laying out a cage, an emotional and linguistical gridwork.

TS: What are your ambitions as a writer?

RD: I try to remain passionate about whatever I am writing, no matter how small or supposedly insignificant it is, no matter how large. That's the only way to be honest, to get to the ur-experience. Ur-experience connects completely nonverbal experiences with the world—you and your consciousness and your body interact as one with something outside of the self. It happens in that instant before we start thinking as educated human beings—that feeling when you're on the verge of a revelation. It happens most often when you are a child.

I was watching a little girl today as she ate her first grape. You could see the expectation on her face before she tasted it, the concentration as she tried to match it to what she had already experienced in life. There are all these Platonic experiences, but we don't remember them unless we see them repeated in children.

One of the tasks of poetry is to create these ur-experiences by artificial means—by language.

TS: I wanted to ask you about the Black Arts Movement. It seems to me that the idea of "black art" has inspired generations of writers and artists at least since the Harlem Renaissance. Do you create black art?

RD: It's so confusing, so complicated, this notion of "black art." The concept is not pure: the insistence on black art is just a device, a way of establishing territory or generating publicity. It was necessary at one time to underscore that "otherness" in order to get any kind of respect whatsoever, but the insistence on difference also requires one to erect certain walls or obey certain rules—all of which is anathema to the artist. When I was growing up, I did not think in terms of black art or white art or any kind of art; I just wanted to be a writer.

On the other hand, when I became culturally aware, in the late sixties, I was incredibly excited about some aspects of the Black Arts Movement. I was amazed by the Last Poets—their mix of political poetry and black music anticipated the hip-hop scene by a decade. It was exciting to recognize heretofore secret aspects of my experience—the syncopation of jazz, the verbal one-upmanship of signifying or the dozens—not only to acknowledge their legitimacy, but to see them transformed into art. They showed me more possibilities for the English language.

But I tried to keep out of the political fray. I was young enough to be able to do that. I shied away from publishing early poems like "Agosta the Winged Man and Rasha the Black Dove" because I didn't think I was strong enough to withstand the political fallout. I didn't want to have to answer questions from Black Arts people like, "Why are you writing about a white—German!—artist?" I waited; I stepped out as a writer later, when things had become more tolerant.

And yet there are always difficulties. In the mid-seventies, a couple of my poems appeared in an anthology of American poetry. One day I got a phone call from one of the editors; it turned out that Alice Walker had refused to read at the book launch in San Francisco because a "racist poem" had been published in the anthology. The poem in question was mine: "Nigger-Song. An Odyssey." Alice objected to the use of the word "nigger," even by a black writer. I wrote her a letter explaining my philosophy about the word; my concern was to redeem the word, to reimagine it as a black concept. She responded with a polite, dignified letter in which she acknowledged my right to use whatever words I choose but argued that we should not use such words in the company of white people. My immediate reaction was: "No one's going to put me in that kind of cage—not whites, not blacks, not even myself. I am trying to make the best poem I possibly can, a poem that will defy whatever nefarious purposes people may want to use it for." So in spite of my precautions, the very thing I feared—being called to task by the Black Arts Movement—happened early in my career.

TS: I wonder if the tension between you and Walker doesn't reflect a conflict over methodological approach rather than race. Werner Sollors has described an opposition in Black Arts, going back to the twenties and thirties, between an anthropological approach to the world—exemplified by Zora Neale Hurston—and a sociological approach, typified by Richard Wright.

RD: You are absolutely right. People have always assumed that racial tension was behind Hurston's discomfort with the Harlem Renaissance scene—all because she wouldn't behave in a certain genteel manner and because she described what she lived. But she was an anthropologist: for her, it was a matter of recording things accurately, not imposing your beliefs onto the reality. An anthropologist is there to report.

TS: You're something of an anthropologist yourself. And the complexities you present are not always or primarily racial.

RD: All of the discussions about schools and movements in this country are saturated with race. But I think that many of the tensions among black artists—even among the partisans of the Black Arts Movement—are more class-based than racial. Yet no one dares to say so. Class has to be the next battleground. Consider the vehemence with which people react to Terry McMillan's work—as if she had somehow betrayed something. Everyone criticizes her on aesthetic grounds, but if you compare her novels—*Mama, Disappearing Acts, Waiting to Exhale, How Stella Got Her Groove Back*—with the bestsellers of John Grisham or Danielle Steele, hers are much better written. We screen everything through aesthetics, but I think that we're really ashamed of showing our tail feathers, as it were. The issue is not how brilliant or apt a passage is, but whether the race will be judged by the classiness of the fictional characters. It's how the characters talk and dress, whether they display an artistic or an intellectual approach.

I think right now is an exciting time to be a black artist, because we are finally getting to the point where a black artist is defined by differences more than rules. Afrocentric, Eurocentric—there are so many different artists out there, so we can finally move a bit more freely in the field. We have surmounted what Langston Hughes called "the racial mountain."

TS: So many of today's black artists are engaged with foreign cultures and languages. Your own work incorporates "foreign" cultures—German, French, Italian, Jewish, Chinese, Greek; Hortense Spillers and Maya Angelou have embraced French; Ishmael Reed is interseted in Yoruba and Japanese. What do you think about multiculturalism in the United States today, and how does that relate to writing—your own and others'?

RD: As as child, I experienced the world as a kind of feast, a banquet. All the books on the shelves, all these different cultures that swirled around me, in the streets, on television—they all spoke to me. One of the greatest tragedies of the Black Arts Movement was its insistence upon Afrocentric arts to the exclusion of others. There was the constant questioning: is this (painting, poem, dance) really African? Why should you bother to read Dostoyevski? As if using all the world's resources were traitorous, somehow.

There is a difference between what happens when Ishmael Reed uses Haitian or West African cultures in his novels and what happens when someone like Hemingway goes off to Spain and writes about it. Hemingway's Spain is a backdrop— something to highlight the drama of the American male, like whipped cream on top of the cake. But with an Ishmael Reed or a Derek Walcott or an Ai, different cultures are incorporated into the artistic fabric. So Reed doesn't just mention hoodoo for flash; he mixes the arcane perceptions of voodoo into the text. Ai writes from all her experiences, all of her heritages: the Southwestern, the Indian, the Japanese, and the African American. It's another way of improvising, rooted in the African American experience of being bought over the Atlantic on slave ships and arriving in a terrifying foreign country, not knowing the language, not knowing what happened to your parents or children. How do you survive in such a situation? Well, you make do—cherish what you remember, and absorb what you can of the new cultures, making them part of your own culture. Think of great jazz musicians, like Coltrane, who could take a syrupy song like "My Favorite Things"—sung by Julie Andrews in *The Sound of Music* (1961)—and make it jazz. He actually transforms the song; it becomes part of his music. And that's been done in African American literature.

I believe that one of the most liberating revelations for this country would be to recognize that all of us are in a diaspora—not just blacks or immigrants, but every one of us. This nation is founded on the concept of diaspora. Here in this country, people want to say: "We are Americans. This is where we stand. I fit in here." But the ground isn't really stable. And once you've recognized that it's unstable, you can stop being afraid.

TS: I'm interested in your relationship to the Greeks. You've made repeated use of figures from Greek mythology: Hades, Demeter, and Persephone are protagonists in *Mother Love,* and *The Darker Face of the Earth* is patterned on Sophocles's Oedipus plays. There is a long-standing tendency among black artists to make use of Greek mythology: Melvin Tolson, Richard Bruce Nugent, Derek Walcott, Langston Hughes, Robert Hayden, June Jordan, and Michael Harper, among others. What is it about Greek mythology that makes it such an important frame (or foil) for you and for the black experience?

RD: Since I wrote the play *The Darker Face of the Earth,* I have been asked, "How did you come to write this?" I can't explain how such a thing could happen. I was fascinated by the way the concept of fate in Greek myth was analogous to the African American experience. If there's any group of people that knows what it's like to try to find a certain amount of freedom within a cage, it's the African Americans.

Then there are the Greek gods, who tend to make war for sport and are capricious to boot, using human beings as pawns in their bickerings with each other— which means that things on Earth are apt to change without warning. If a god decides something's going to happen this way, a human being really can't do much about it. Doesn't it sound a lot like the whimsy of a white plantation mistress and the punishments of the white master? What was interesting to me were the ways human beings—like Odysseus, like Augustus in my play—trick the gods. How does an individual struggle against overwhelming fate? Greek mythology is a natural kind of thing for African Americans.

In *Oedipus Rex*, a bold and arrogant leader is brought down. He's lost everything: he's lost his people, he's lost his home. At the end, he says, "Make me into an example." I've always felt that when he says, "Tell the world this story," it is, in a sense, a kind of triumph, because he has made himself into a work of art. At the conclusion of *The Darker Face*, Augustus proves that he can be a leader; it appears that he has chosen his people over personal love. The community makes him a hero, turns him into a legend. And yet he knows exactly what he did and didn't do, and in this moment of glory he has, in fact, just realized how little he has been able to do in his life. My play turns the notion of immortality on its head. It doesn't follow the Greek plot, but it is another view of the Greek moral.

TS: You first published the text of *The Darker Face of the Earth* in 1994. In that version, Augustus, the leader of the slave revolt, fails. But in the first full stage production in 1996, Augustus heroically succeeds.

RD: Well, he succeeds in a sense. When the play was workshopped in Oregon in 1994, people complained about the death of Augustus, and their argument was that in the original, Oedipus lives. To me, that was no argument to change the ending. It wasn't until I began working through the play again that I realized that the tragedy of the original Oedipus is that he is a living dead man. So it doesn't really matter whether Augustus lives or dies; either he dies and that's it, or he lives, but in a nihilistic sense. Ultimately we know only what history tells us: this slave rebellion will fail, has failed. Since we know how slavery ended, we can also imagine the end of Augustus; though he is still alive at the end of the play, we know what the immediate future holds. Only when he is finally executed will he come to life again as legend. When I recognized this final irony, I was able to change the ending so that Augustus lives, and the impact was much more heartbreaking. There is a bitter optimism to the piece. Regardless of what happens to Augustus after the play closes, he is a hero, and his example will influence the history that follows. But should one think about—a brilliant defeat? Augustus has become a role model, but he is also dead. I think of Medgar Evers and Emmett Till, Malcolm X, and Martin Luther King, Jr.—throughout history, heroes get destroyed.

I've had numerous discussions with directors and dramaturges about whether Augustus was manly enough. Black males were particularly interested in this question. Things seem just to happen to Augustus, they would say, instead of his instigating the action. But the important thing that happens to Augustus is that he becomes human. He messes up everything else, but he's human—humane—by play's end. Male heroes don't achieve that very often, and I wanted Augustus to find that humanity in himself. Still, a lot of people may be uncomfortable with this; I can imagine some who will ask, "What kind of hero is this?"

TS: Derek Walcott directed the stage reading of a shortened version of *The Darker Face* at the 92nd Street Y theater in New York. How did you go about altering the play, and why?

RD: The shortened version was a matter of practicality. The Y had done stage readings before, and they said that their audiences could not sit longer than ninety minutes. So when the Y reading came along, Derek thought it would be heartbreaking for me to trim the play. But I knew it had to be done. The whole process was less painful than I had anticipated, because it reminded me of writing poetry under conditions of absolute economy.

It was wonderful to work with Derek Walcott. Because he is a poet and a playwright, he understood instinctively what I was trying to do with both the music of the text and the whole staging of the piece. I never felt I had to explain things to him; twenty minutes spent talking to Derek was worth more than three weeks of workshopping with the theater, with people who understood the stage but had very little experience with a verse play, much less with poetry.

Derek guided me to the recognition that theater is not merely the handmaiden of real life. I was getting away from a vision of theater as a melting pot of language and thought and body, all presented on a stage; I was beginning to work with a much more traditional notion of theater, where words are secondary to their embodiment. I didn't want theater as illusion—"Oh, honey, it looks so *real!*" Rather, I wanted the audience to always be aware that the time is not real time, and that the reality they're seeing is metaphorical. I think what happens in *The Darker Face* is powerful because the language is so heightened. We cannot forget for a minute that we are in an abstract situation. It's a more continental European notion of theater, more in the tradition of Brecht or even Arrabal or Ionesco.

TS: What do you think about the works of Afrocentrists like Martin Bernal, who trace the origins of Greek civilization back to Egypt? Does the idea of Egypt interest you? Why write about or exploit the Greeks rather than the Egyptians?

RD: For a vision to work, poetically, one must make use of myths one has grown up with. There is a storehouse of common knowledge and lore which all of the poems in *Mother Love*, as well as the unfolding conflicts in *The Darker Face of the Earth*, play off of. This knowledge is the groundwork, and the improvisation comes on top of that. It makes no sense, emotionally, to go further and trace Greek myths back to the Egyptians, because in our American culture—which includes African American culture—the emotional connections are not to the Egyptians, but to the Greeks. For better or for worse, this is what we have been brought up with. At one point while I was working on *Mother Love*, I did consider following Martin Bernal's example: I dabbled briefly with poems that explored the origins of the Egyptian myth of regeneration, Isis and Horus and Osiris. But I discovered that such a journey was primarily an intellectual one, with little emotional or psychological resonance for postmodern America.

Of course, it may be that African American children today, who are growing up with African fables like Anansi the spider, will develop emotional attachments to them. But for the contemporary reader, a mere allusion to Egyptian myth or African fable bears no mysterious urgency, no compelling presence. These stories were not part of our cosmology during the crucial period when we were growing up, acquiring language and discovering the world for the first time.

On the other hand, one of my current projects entails a group of poems based on the ancient Egyptian board game of Senet, which literally means "passing." Senet was very popular during pharaonic Egypt; it was based on the Egyptian depiction of the journey after death through the resurrection into whatever form the newly blessed soul desired. I've put the project on a back burner because I've had my fill of the underworld for a while—Egyptian, Greek, or otherwise. But I am intrigued by this ritualized journey into death. Senet was an entertaining method of inculcating beliefs into the social fabric—commoners and rulers played the game for fun; even children played it. Much the way Monopoly instructs today's children in the ways of capitalism, so Egyptian children familiarized themselves with the path to death and rebirth: this is what will happen when you die, this is how you go away from the material world in order to find your true selves. We lack precise instructions, and many of the playing tiles have been either obliterated or partially effaced, so we don't know exactly how to play the game, but the thread of the journey is decipherable. Senet is a wonderful narrative, a beautiful story, full of the wisdom and mystery of great myth. Hopefully, my sequence of poems will embrace the journey toward dying; how we prepare for death and how we either confront it or pass into it. I fear it's going to take a long while to find the heartbeat of those poems, but I'm excited at the prospect.

TS: Your novel *Through the Ivory Gate* is an account of one black girl's erotic and artistic coming of age, a hymn to life and growth through education. Virginia King becomes an adult and an artist, a puppeteer. In its subject matter and its optimism, the book stands apart from the majority of African American novels of youth.

RD: I had grown impatient with what I had come to see as the African American bildungsroman. I thought, "Every black child's life is not dark and tortured." Not that tragedies don't happen. But there are many African Americans who had relatively normal childhoods, and there is a need, I think, to portray such people. *Through the Ivory Gate* is the poetic bildungsroman of a young artist, and this artist is a black woman. And even though there are dark things that happened in Virginia's past, the tragedies are not the crux of her fate; they don't drag her down. I was much more influenced by Thomas Mann's *Buddenbrooks* and by Joyce's *Portrait of the Artist as a Young Man*, even Hermann Hesse's *Steppenwolf*, than by Richard Wright's *Native Son*. My experience was very different from Wright's, as you know: I did not grow up in the ghetto or the South. And though there were instances of discrimination, the general tenor of my childhood was more nourishing than confrontational. So I wanted to pay tribute to this kind of upbringing as well. If I, a middle-class black girl from the American Midwest, could respond to the situation of an oppressive family in pre–World War I Lübeck [*Buddenbrooks*], then I thought it was possible to write about a black woman puppeteer and still believe that her life would find resonance across gender, race, and class lines.

TS: Incest seems to be a recurring motif in African American writing, from Ralph Ellison to Alice Walker to Toni Morrison to Sapphire. It also appears in your work: in *Through the Ivory Gate* in the person of Virginia's Aunt Carrie, and again in *The Darker Face of the Earth*, with Augustus/Oedipus and his mother.

RD: One of the things I was trying to do in *Through the Ivory Gate* was to present Aunt Carrie's narrative as a perfectly normal story that just happens to be about incest. What shakes Virginia upon hearing it is that she *isn't* shocked. Incest appears as an almost natural outcome for people who know each other very well.

Even in *The Darker Face of the Earth*, it's not the overwhelming concern. I don't want the audience to think, "Oh no, it's incest," but that it's a shame that Augustus and Amalia can't stay together. In that sense it's similar to what happens in *Through the Ivory Gate*, the emotion that's called up is not "How horrible—she slept with her brother," but "How sad that this ruined her life." It's a different take on incest, that's true.

TS: You introduce a choice of artistic activities: music, drama, pantomime, writing, training to twirl batons, puppeteering. Is this a kind of competition between the arts?

RD: No. Rather, I was interested in how arts can influence and complement one another. Not every budding artist knows what he or she wants to do from the time of birth. Not everyone grows up thinking, "I will become a concert pianist." This is another myth, I believe many artists start out interested in several different aspects of the arts; they kind of browse.

Why we have gotten into this incredible mess with the genres I just don't know. I suspect academia's partly to blame. Creative Writing programs exacerbate the problem: a student must choose between becoming a fiction writer or a poet before actually doing the groundwork in either genre. It's a serious problem. And it leads to intensely self-indulgent poetry and formulaic fiction.

My notion of how the discussion of art should proceed is closer to the revelation Virginia has in *Ivory Gate*, where she discovers how to approach performing a Bach suite while doing mime. These are two completely disparate things, yet when the mime instructor tells her that her mimicry of cello performance is *accurate*, but doesn't *look right*, Virginia realizes that the secret to interpreting music is similar. You have to know the rules, but then you must bend them.

TS: America is a performance-oriented society. Americans seem to be constantly testifying to what they are or would like to become. There is a need to play with identities. Is Virginia the puppeteer a representative American?

RD: Virginia actually hides behind her puppets; she is not a born show-off. Her puppets become a way of talking about dangerous things without risking exposure. I never think of her as quintessentially American, although she is trying to "find herself." But you are absolutely right: this country is performance-oriented, and it's getting worse. We've always loved our celebrities, but the notion that an ordinary person can snatch a moment of glory by showing off is a recent phenomenon, starting with Andy Warhol's performance pieces. Today, there is the talk show. Everybody wants to confess and testify to total strangers. In Virginia's era, the seventies, it was slightly different. There wasn't quite that level of desperate exhibitionism.

The saving grace of art is that it offers a home for all who are dispossessed. [And we are all dispossessed in some way.] I think that's one reason why viewing art that deals with tragedies can be uplifting; you can never feel completely lost if, in this sad space of time, you feel connected with all the others who appreciate that particular artistic expression.

TS: Form is still considered suspect in African American writing, as too far from the real world, whatever that means. Gwendolyn Brooks said recently, "This is no time for tight-faced poetry." Yet self-censorship, as you have pointed out repeatedly, is good for neither the artist nor the race. Knowing and playing up to received ideas is always a way of repressing and cheating on form. How do you respond to this?

RD: What has happened with free verse in this country is tragic. People have come to believe that concentrating on themes releases them from the necessities of form. In returning to form, I've had to address the question of why pattern exists. Why do meter and rhythm beguile us? Conversely, what are we denying in language by going against formal verse? If we are trying to address emotions, surely we must admit that so much verbiage stands for the ineffable, what you can't really "get at." There is a lot of rather arrogant free verse that ignores this inarticulate core of language; these poets believe that what they're able to express in words is the truth, and there wells up a smug feeling of "I've gotten it." I always feel that I've never gotten it. You catch a glimpse, but you don't quite see it; the "event" of a poem always has resonances that you can't control.

Still, the boundary between formalist poetry and free verse is really just a crutch; it allowed you to feel safe in your chosen territory. If you are a formulist, you can say, "My poetry is much more rigorous because I am addressing the formal aspect of the language"; one is relieved from thinking deeply. The free verse poet, on the other hand, can think his or "deep" thoughts without considering the formal shape of the phrase, the line, the sentence, the poem. I caught myself doing it; the idea of writing sonnets for *Mother Love* filled me at first with horror. But when I turned the question around—when I asked, "Why don't I want to do sonnets, what does this say about my relationship with language?"—the fear dissolved. In a sense, the space of the poem is a narrow cage whose bars I am always trying to bend. It goes back to my love of crossword puzzles. I relish the challenge of the walls and the fact that an incredible freedom can be found within.

TS: Some have attacked your work and its formalism as "aesthetic." How do you respond to the charge that your work is apolitical?

RD: What people really mean is that my writing is not propagandistic. When I write, I may not be aware of the implications of my writing, but this is not the concern of the artist. I would falsify the writing itself to figure out the implications beforehand; not only would it narrow artistic expression, but the very essence of art would be compromised. We have a thousand political analysts to deal with the crude aspects of politics; they put their spin on trends and results, what was, is, will or should be. They are perpetually trying to analyze the reactions of the "people" to leaders and events, and trying to put these reactions into some kind of ordered context. But the true political moment is a disjointed and intensely personal experience.

TS: Where does truth emerge for you, amid all the competing narratives your work offers?

RD: I don't think the truth is absolute or static. And though I'm not bothered by the notion that a poem can project an absolute truth, I don't think you can put absolute meaning into a poem. Like the New Critics, I believe a poem has to stand on its own, that the reader will extract from it what she needs—the truths that are important to her, the memories that are awakened in her, all those inaccurate memories that serve us perfectly well. That's what I hope will happen when I give up a poem, though I'm also hoping that a reader's interpretation of the poem will be close to what I put into the poem.

I'm not an insistent or indignant sort of writer. It's not interesting to be a dictator. If there is any kind of truth, then it occurs in that instant of intense emotion when actions emerge that carry their own conviction, which may be completely at odds with the general view. If, however, we acknowledge that intense emotion is one of the most precious experiences we can have, and that we wish to experience such intensity, this admission will help us understand what is true. You can be appalled or amazed at what a character or narrator does, but this embedded truth is what makes the actions or the emotions of another in a particular moment understandable. At that moment, truth is absolute, it is a point in space. But it moves.

TS: You are often written about—praised—by white critics as a black writer whose work addresses universal concerns. What do you think about "universalism" and the literary imagination?

RD: I don't think a universalism that lacks a sense of the specific can be very powerful; at the same time, any culturally drenched perception isn't going to be powerful if it doesn't have some kind of universal reverberation. I guess what I am saying is that "the universal" is a bogus concept. We've come to believe that being "universal" is to transcend difference—again, the incredible trauma of difference in modern society has made us yearn for conformity. Why can't we find the universal in those differences?

NOTES

Preface

1. The Black Arts Movement's credo has just been revived by the playwright August Wilson's claim for a stage "for blacks only"; see Henry Louis Gates, Jr. (1997), "The Chitlin Circuit."

2. Dudley Randall's image of a "white unicorn" aims to critcize the position of universalism in African American literature. Cf. Stephen Henderson(1973), *Understanding the New Black Poetry: Black Speech and Black Music as Poetic References: 234*.

3. "The Black Unicorn" refers to the title of Audre Lorde's 1978 collection of poetry. The text is a quote from her 1979 speech "The Great American Disease," in the *Black Scholar* 10.8: 17.

4. In "Developing Diaspora Literacy: Allusion in Maryse Condé's *Heremakhonon*," paper delivered at the African Literature Association Conference, in Baltimore, 1984. Printed in *Out of the Kumbla: Caribbean Women and Literature*, ed. Carole Boyce Davies and Elaine Savory Fido (Trenton, N.J.: Africa World Press, 1990), 303–19.

Introduction

1. Helen Vendler's critique of "Ars Poetica" as a poem that "doesn't deal with the making of poems, only with the stance from which they are made" . . . and "doesn't get to the heart of Dove's talent" because it is not "about arrangement and what it yields," though in tune with Vendler's definition of the function of poetry as "to clothe common perceptions in striking language, not to enunciate striking perceptions," should not interfere with our analysis in a non-judgmental context. See Vendler's "A Dissonant Triad: Henri Cole, Rita Dove, and August Kleinzahler," rpt. in her 1995 *Soul Says*, 148, and her 1988 collection of essays *The Music of What Happens*, 37. To Bonnie Costello "Ars Poetica" is "one writer's desire to merge with the elemental, another's desire to master it." See "Scars and Wings: Rita Dove's *Grace Notes*," 436.

2. Cf. Jacques Derrida's (1987) comment on the crossing sign in *The Truth in Painting*, trans. G. Bennington and I. McLeod (Chicago: University of Chicago Press), 166: "The form of the chiasmus, the X [Chi], interests me greatly, not as the symbol

of the unknown but because there is here a sort of fork (the series *crossroads, quadri-furcum,* grid, grill, key, etc.) which is moreover unequal, one of its points extending its scope [*portée*] further than the other: a figure of the double gesture and the crossing."

3. In his 1978 portrayal of twelve American poets (Ai, Dove [by far the youngest], Norman Dubie, Susan Feldman, Carolyn Forché, Daniel Halpern, Laura Jensen, Erica Jong, Larry Levis, Elizabeth Libbey, Gregory Orr, and Greg Pape), Rafael Lozano confirms this notion of diversity in young poets: "Esos poetas jóvenes no tienen nada en común. Màs bien se distinguen por la diversidad de sus actitudes mentales, de sus temas y de sus formas poéticas [These young poets have nothing in common. In fact they represent a conspicuous diversity of mental attitudes, themes and poetic forms]" ("Doce Poetas Jóvenes de Los Estados Unidos," 101).

Dove has portrayed both the African-American and white mainstream literary scene; cf. "Geschichte ist unser Herzschlag. Tendenzen der afroamerikanischen Lyrik der Sechziger und Siebziger Jahre [History Is Our Heartbeat. Tendencies in African-American Poetry of the 60s and 70s]," with Fred Viebahn, and "A Black Rainbow: Modern Afro-American Poetry," with Marilyn Nelson Waniek, *Poetry after Modernism,* ed. Robert McDowell (Brownsville, Oreg.: Story Line Press, 1991). "'Was man wissen sollte, um ein Dichter zu sein'—Aspekte zeitgenössischer Lyrik in den USA ['What one should know to be a poet'—aspects of contemporary poetry in the USA]," *Grenzüberschreitungen oder Literatur und Wirklichkeit,* deals with recent trends in American poetry but opposes categorizations like "Beat," "New York School," "Black Mountain," "Confessional," or "Deep Image." As a few common traits in American poetry, Dove mentions "knappe, direkte Ausdrucksweisen, Vorlieben für Visualisierungen, Abneigung gegen Abstraktionen" [tight, direct modes of expression, preferences for visualizations, aversion for abstractions], traits that characterize her own writing as well.

4. Those authors who spoke or still speak to her include, among others, William Shakespeare, Emily Dickinson, James Baldwin, Sara Teasdale, Hans Magnus Enzensberger, Paul Celan, Langston Hughes, Michael Harper, Robert Hayden, Claude McKay, Anne Spencer, Melvin Tolson, Gwendolyn Brooks, and Muriel Rukeyser. Cf. Helen Vendler (1990), "An Interview with Rita Dove"; *Newsletter,* D. C. Heath and Company, College Division, 125 Spring Street. Lexington, Mass., n.d., 9; and Steven Bellin (1995), "A Conversation with Rita Dove," 17. Dove most obviously shares her description and remapping of contemporary and past worlds with Elizabeth Bishop (*Geography III*), Adrienne Rich (*An Atlas of the Difficult World*), and Jorie Graham (*Region of Unlikeness*). A capacity to live up to "Wittgenstein's statement, 'The world is everything that is the case,'" Dove also attributes to "Adrienne Rich and Philip Levine, Yusef Komunyakaa and Sandra Cisneros, Maxine Kumin and Stanley Kunitz, C. K. Williams and Audre Lorde, Shirley Kaufman and Stephen Dunn, Gerald Stern and Toi Derricotte, Margaret Atwood and Seamus Heaney, just for starters" (*The Poet's World,* 40).

5. For an extended discussion of this period see. Abby Arthur Johnson and Ronald Johnson (1994), "Charting a New Course: African American Literary Politics since 1976," *The Black Columbiad: Defining Moments in African Amerian Literature and Culture,* ed. Werner Sollors and Maria Diedrich (Cambridge: Harvard University Press), 369–81; David Lionel Smith, "Chicago Poets, OBAC [Organization of Black American Culture], and the Black Arts Movement," *The Black Columbiad,* 253–64, and Theodore O. Mason, Jr. (1994), "African-American Theory and Criticism." An excellent survey from an African-American and feminist perspective is Deborah E.

McDowell's 1995 essay "Transferences," in *The Changing Same: Black Women's Literature, Criticism, and Theory,* 156–75.

6. In "Chicago Poets, OBAC, and the Black Arts Movement," David Lionel Smith balances the unfavorable view of the movement toward women: "Contrary to some characterizations of the Black Arts Movement, women always had a strong and vocal presence in OBAC, beginning with Carolyn Rodgers, Ronda Davis, and Jewel Lattimore [Johari Amini] in the early years. By the late 1970s OBAC was predominantly female. Certain issues, however, were constants in OBAC—in particular, a concern with the relationship of writers to their audience, the accessibility of the work, and the saturation of the work with black culture. This last point especially focused on the issue of how to use vernacular language in poems and the limitations of the vernacular." Cf. e.g. Carolyn Rodgers's "muthafucka" (ibid. 259). See also Madhu Dubey's 1994 study *Black Women Novelists and the Nationalist Aesthetic,* 1–32.

7. In 1987 Gates and Baker joined forces to answer Joyce A. Joyce's attack in the name of a true black American criticism. See her discussion "The Black Canon: Reconstructing Black American Literary Criticism," Gates's commentary "'What's Love Got to Do with It?': Critical Theory, Integrity, and the Black Idiom," Baker's commentary "In Dubious Battle," and finally Joyce's reply "'Who the Cap Fit': Unconsciousness and Unconscionable-ness in the Criticism of Houston A. Baker, Jr. and Henry Louis Gates, Jr.," in *New Literary History* 18, no. 2 (1987): 335–83.

8. Cf. her 1994 interview with William Walsh, "Isn't Reality Magic?": "Marvin Bell was good in the workshop. Louise Glück was extremely good one-on-one; she was uncanny. Stanley Plumly's Forms of Poetry course was absolutely liberating: we read prose, all sorts of prose—not just fiction, but imaginative nonfiction memoire, travelogues. It was a class of poets discussing the strategies of prose. Bill Matthews was brilliant at finding the technical turn to open up a stalled poem. I can't remember who remarked, 'Bill Matthews would be the one to choose to interview God.'" Dove further evaluated her formative years in her 1985 interview with Gretchen Johnsen and Richard Peabody, "A Cage of Sound": "Iowa was both a good and a very bad experience. It was a good experience in that I met lots of people. . . . Iowa was bad in the sense that I think what everybody says is true about that place: there is an Iowa Writer's Workshop poem, . . . and you can find yourself slipping into that stuff very easily. It's simply that old idea of positive reinforcement. . . . Though I did learn some things technique-wise in Iowa, particularly in my first year there, which was very good, I also found myself starting to write these kind of safe poems. . . . and as a consequence, after Iowa, for over a year I really didn't write any poems. Instead, I wrote fiction. Let's say I didn't finish any poems, because whenever I tried to write one, it didn't sound like me. It sounded like a poem from some composite person." On the influence of "Iowa" cf. also Robert McDowell (1986), "The Assembling Vision of Rita Dove," 61: "Passing through a graduate writing program (Iowa) in the mid-seventies, Dove and her peers were schooled in the importance of sensation and its representation through manipulation of The Image. The standard lesson plan, devised to reflect the ascendancy of Wallace Stevens and a corrupt revision of T. S. Eliot's objective correlative, instructed young writers to renounce realistic depiction and offer it up to the province of prose; it promoted subjectivity and imagination-as-image; it has strangled a generation of poems." Despite these drawbacks, McDowell concludes, Dove became not a "dissembler" but an "assembler."

9. Cf. Fred Viebahn (1969), *Die Schwarzen Tauben, oder Gitarren schiessen*

nicht (Hamburg: Merlin Verlag), and e.g. Dove (1995), "How They Met," *Washington Post.*

10. Based on: Dove (1995), *Fact Sheet;* (1995), "Autobiography"; (1995), *The Poet's World,* 73–107; and *Contemporary Authors Autobiography Series,* vol. 19: 97–115. For life-cum-work portraits cf. also: Steven Bellin (1995), "A Conversation with Rita Dove" Tom Brazaitis (1995), "Poet in Motion"; Walt Harrington (1995), "The Shape of Her Dreaming"; Kirkland C. Jones (1992), "Rita Dove," American Poets since World War II,. 3d ser., *Dictionary of Literary Biography.* vol. 120 (Detroit: Gale Research), 47–54; Therese Steffen (1996), "Rita Dove"; Helen Vendler (1990), "An Interview with Rita Dove"; Vendler (1995), "The Black Dove. Rita Dove: Poet Laureate," *Soul Says,* 156–66; and William Walsh (1994), "Isn't Reality Magic?"

11. E.g. in Vendler, ed. (1985), *The Harvard Book of Contemporary American Poetry;* Donald McQuade, et al., eds. (1987), *The Harper American Literature;* Nina Baym, et al., eds. (1989), *The Norton Anthology of American Literature;* Vendler, ed. (1992), *The Faber Book of Contemporary American Poetry;* Gerald Costanzo and Jim Daniel, eds. (1993), *The Carnegie Mellon Anthology of Poetry;* Margaret Ferguson, Mary Jo Salter, Jon Stallworthy, eds. (1996), *The Norton Anthology of Poetry.*

12. Cf. e.g. Paul Lauter, and James A. Miller, eds. (1995), *"Syllabi in African-American Literature"* prepared for the Transatlantic Passage Conference, Tenerife, 15–19 February, 3. Representative for a range of core courses in poetry of the twentieth century is, e.g., *Courses of Instruction 1995–96.* Harvard University, Faculty of Arts and Sciences: 60, 311.

13. Cf. bibliography.

14. Interestingly enough, Dove does not appear in the regionally organized anthology by Edward Field, Gerald Locklin, and Charles Stetler, eds. (1992), *A New Geography of Poets* (Fayetteville: University of Arkansas Press).

15. Like Jon Stallworthy, Vendler (1995) "sees the reader as the true speaker of the lyric" rather than envisioning the interplay of a reader overhearing a lyric persona. Cf. *The Given and the Made,* xi.

16. "Dove balances opposites, bridges conventional divisions . . . . , and transcends boundaries of space and time. . . . She speaks with the voice of a world citizen who places her personal, racial, and national experience within the context of the human experience as a whole." Cf. Ekaterini Georgoudaki (1991), "Rita Dove: Crossing Boundaries," 430.

17. "Postcolonial," as emphasized by Ashcroft, Griffiths, and Tiffin (1989) in *The Empire Writes Back,* 8. The term "emergent" was proposed by Wlad Godzich in the mid-1980s, notably during a conference at the University of Witwatersrand in 1986, to denote literature in English surfacing outside the United States, United Kingdom, or Canada, and to replace problematical labels such as "commonwealth" or "postcolonial." Cf. his "Introduction to Emergent Literatures," unpublished lecture course at University of Zürich, winter term 1995–1996, 30 October 1995.

18. "Heteroglossia" and "glossalia," M. G. Henderson's tropes for intertextuality and revision, follow Bakhtin and Gadamer's terminology as well as religious practices of the "Afro-American Sanctified Church." Yet, Dove transgresses such African-American theories as e.g. Gates does in *Figures in Black* and *The Signifying Monkey,* M. G. Henderson in *Speaking in Tongues,* G. Smitherman in *Talkin' and Testifyin,'* or H. A. Baker in *Workings of the Spirit.*

19. "The performative introduces a temporality of the 'in-between' through the 'gap' or 'emptiness' of the signifier that punctuates linguistic difference. The boundary that marks the nation's selfhood interrupts the self-generating time of

national production with a space of representation that threatens binary division with its difference." Cf. Homi K. Bhabha (1993), *Nation and Narration*, 299. As to the role of the "griot" see Eric J. Sundquist (1993), *To Wake the Nations*, 489–90.

Chapter 1

1. I adhere to Kant in a historical context—Gaston Bachelard is challenging Kant and the ideology of things—and only in view of the subjectivity (opposed to an objectivity derived from experience and observation) and flexibility his concepts of time and space lend to spatiotemporal poetic revisions. Kant actually did not perceive space and time, spatiality and temporality, as interconnected. To quote Kant in an African-American context is another matter. Together with David Hume and Thomas Jefferson, Hegel and Kant—in the Age of Enlightenment, which is also the Age of Scientific Racism—came to conclude that blacks were incapable of intelligence. In *Observations on the Feeling of the Beautiful and Sublime* (1764), commenting on Hume's essay, Kant claims that "so fundamental is the difference between [the black and white] races of man, . . . it appears to be as great in regard to mental capacities as in color." See *Observations on the Feeling of the Beautiful and Sublime*, trans. John T. Goldthwait (Berkeley: University of California Press, 1960), 111.

2. Notice that despite its title, *The Location of Culture*, Homi Bhabha's 1994 collection of essays defines "the borderline work of culture" as a "contingent 'in-between' *space*" (7; emphasis mine).

3. According to Webster's *New World Dictionary*, 1) of or pertaining to culture; specif., of the training and refinement of the mind, interests, tastes, skills, arts, etc; 2) obtained by breeding or cultivation.

4. See Antonio Benítez-Rojo (1995), *The Repeating Island: The Caribbean and the Postmodern Perspective.*

5. See Michel Fabre (1991), *From Harlem to Paris: Black Americans in France, 1840–1980.*

6. On first seeing the island women, Dove thought: "Yes, that's the way *all* of us should walk. We should all be so proud to exist in our skins, as to say: 'Isn't it amazing that human beings are walking on the face of this earth!' Their natural sense of themselves and their worth as human beings reminded me of how often many of us actually seem apologetic for existing. (. . .) They never *seem* [emphasis mine] to be going somewhere because someone sent them there. They invent their destinations themselves." Cf. Bill Moyers (1995), "Rita Dove," *The Language of Life: A Festival of Poets*, 115.

7. See Linda Hutcheon (1994), "Die Politisierung der Präfixe," *Multikulturelle Gesellschaft. Modell Amerika* ["The Politicization of Prefixes," *Multicultural Society. Model America*], ed. B. Ostendorf (München: Wilhelm Fink Verlag), 155–66. It is important to note that "multicultural" cannot be equated with "multiethnic." Ethnicity is but one component of multiculturalism.

8. Berndt Ostendorf cites the unmasking of power structures (Nietzsche / Foucault), a tendency toward decentralization, a predilection for the patchwork of minorities (Lyotard), a critique of the aporias of the enlightenment (Heidegger), a revaluation of difference in feminism and pedagogy (Derrida). See his 1994 introduction to *Multikulturelle Gesellschaft*, 11.

9. In his 1975 essay "Colonialist Criticism," Chinua Achebe would like "to see the word *universal* banned altogether from discussions of African literature until such a time as people cease to use it as a synonym for the narrow, self-serving

parochialism of Europe." See Ashcroft, Griffiths, and Tiffin (1989), *The Empire Writes Back*, 127. Cf. also Ernesto Laclau (1992), "Universalism, Particularism, and the Question of Identity."

10. Cf. also Henry Louis Gates, Jr. (1993), "Beyond the Culture Wars: Identities in Dialogue." In examining the paradoxes of pluralism and considering some of the limitations of multiculturalism considered, Gates raises questions about the historically recent triumph of "ethnicity" as a paradigm or master code for human difference where multicultural is substituted for multiracial (7–8). He considers the newer lexeme, i.e., the shift from race to ethnicity, a salutary one, a necessary move away from the essentialist biologizing of a previous era.

Most appropriate would be Arjun Appadurai's term "ethnoscape," which includes "tourists, immigrants, refugees, exiles, guestworkers and other moving groups and persons." See his 1990 essay "Disjuncture and Difference in the Global Cultural Economy," 7.

11. "I see no single thread / That binds me one to all; / Why even common dead / Men took the single fall. // No universal laws / Of human misery / Create a common cause / Or common history / That ease black people's pains / Nor break black people's chains."

12. Wlad Godzich proposed the term "emergent" during a conference at the University of Whitwatersrand in 1986 to denote literature in English outside the United States, United Kingdom, or Canada, and to replace problematic labels such as "commonwealth" or "postcolonial." Cf. his "Introduction to Emergent Literatures," unpublished lecture course at Zürich University, 30 October 1995.

13. "I had just entered third or fourth grade; the novel had forty-three chapters, and each chapter was twenty lines or less because I used each week's spelling list as the basis for each chapter, and there were twenty words per list. In the course of the year I wrote one installment per week, and I never knew what was going to happen next—the words led me, not the other way around" (*SP* xx–xxi). Cf. also her account in *Contemporary Authors Autobiography Series*, vol. 19, 98–99.

14. The books *YH*, *M*, and *GN* will be discussed in Chapter 2, whereas *TB*, *FS*, *IG*, *ML*, and *DF* will be examined as specific units in the following chapters.

15. Geneva Smitherman (1986), *Talkin' and Testifyin': The Language of Black America*, 147–48. On the new concept of "black" in the 1960s see also p. 35: "The summer of 1966 marked the beginning of the nationwide shift from 'Negro' to 'black' as a term of racial identification for Black Americans." This was a major departure from the original term "Negro" (Portuguese for "black"), adopted by the explorers to designate their newfound property.

16. Dove outlines Tolson's sequence in her 1985 essay "Telling It Like It I-S *IS*: Narrative Techniques in Melvin Tolson's *Harlem Gallery*," 110: "*Harlem Gallery, Book I: The Curator* is the first part of a proposed five-part poem delineating the odyssey of the black man in America. Book II, *Egypt Land*, was to be a delineation of slavery; Book III, *The Red Sea*, an analogy of the Civil War; Book IV, *The Wilderness*, was to deal with Reconstruction; and Book V, *The Promised Land*, a gallery of highbrows and middlebrows and lowbrows against the ethnological panorama of contemporary America (from Tolson's *Notebooks*)." A quotation from Melvin Tolson's *Harlem Gallery*, "Black Boy, O Black Boy, / is the port worth the cruise?" introduces Thomas's part in *TB* (*SP* 139).

17. The publisher, Carnegie Mellon, effected the change without asking the author's consent.

18. Langston Hughes's early poem "The Negro Speaks of Rivers" cites the Eu-

phrates, the Congo, the Nile, and the Mississippi as the great waterways along which Africans and people of African-American descent have lived their lives. See the 1995 *Collected Poems of Langston Hughes*, ed. Arnold Rampersad, and David Roessel (New York: Knopf), 23. In *ML* Dove will add the river Styx to her poetic waterland.

19. Cf. Gaston Bachelard (1957), *La poétique de l'espace*. (*The Poetics of Space*).

20. The house counts among the elements of spatial description in the Western world and its epistemological function is of utmost importance as it allows us to consider and reconsider various levels of time, lifestyles, family and community patterns, and history. Literary examples are legion: e.g. E. A. Poe's "The Fall of the House of Usher" (1840), Nathaniel Hawthorne's *The House of the Seven Gables* (1851), Charles Dickens's *Bleak House* (1853), William Faulkner's *The Mansion* (1959).

21. In *The Poet's World* (1995) she names the following authors "just for starters": "Adrienne Rich, Philip Levine, Yusef Komunyakaa, Sandra Cisneros, Maxine Kumin, Stanley Kunitz, C. K. Williams, Audre Lorde, Shirley Kaufman, Stephen Dunn, Gerald Stern, Toi Derricotte, Margaret Atwood, Seamus Heaney, Muriel Rukeyser, and Rainer Maria Rilke" (40).

22. Place, of course, is also central to Audre Lorde's work. Yet hers is a didactic stance against a "white Western, phallocentric pencil." All place-names scattered over the world are there to renegotiate positions from where she can speak and write. They mark the wide area of her political and personal concerns, whereas Dove's world-mapping deliberately abstains from any direct social comment. See Lorde's 1968 collection *The First Cities*, and Gloria T. Hull (1989), "Living on the Line: Audre Lorde and *Our Dead Behind Us*," *Changing Our Own Words*, ed. Cheryl A. Wall, 150–72.

23. I follow both Fritz Gysin's principles of distinction presented in "Passage to Which India? The Enigma of the Return" (unpublished lecture, Berne: SAUTE Conference, November 1994) as well as Coco Fusco's examination of borders as lines of division and sites for potential hybridity; see Fusco (1989), "The Border Art Workshop-Interview with Guillermo Gomez Pena and Emily Hicks," *Third Text* 7: 53–76. In "Predicaments of Skin: Boundaries in Recent African American Fiction," *The Black Columbiad* (Cambridge, Mass.: Harvard University Press, London, 1994, 286–97), Gysin discusses some recent works of African-American fiction that do pay attention to the phenomenon of boundaries by highlighting it in fresh and unusual ways. In contrast to a number of fashionable cultural theories, Gysin calls for "a more complex mode of boundary formation, one that takes into consideration that the cultural blends within an ethnic group are utilized to formulate the dividing issues within the same group as well as those between this group and the mainstream or the majority at large" (287).

24. For an extended discussion of Bachelard's thought, see Lutz Baumann (1987), *Gaston Bachelards materialistischer Transzendentalismus* [Gaston Bachelard's Materialistic Transcendentalism] (Frankfurt Lang), 196f, or Mary McAllester Jones (1991), *Gaston Bachelard, Subversive Humanist: Texts and Readings*.

25. See Henri Lefebvre (1994), *The Production of Space*, 121, 166n., 172n., 184n., 298n.; Beatriz Colomina, ed. (1992), *Sexuality & Space*, 53, on Laura Mulvey's use of Bachelard in film theory; Steve Yates, ed. (1995), *Poetics of Space: A Critical Photographic Anthology*, 1–6, 23–33.

26. As developed by Ferdinand de Saussure in his *Cours de lingustique générale*. (Wiesbaden: Harrassowitz, 1916).

27. Cf. Katerina Clark and Michael Holquist (1984), *Mikhail Bakhtin*, 7, 79–80.

See also Bakhtin's definition of the literary artistic chronotope, which fuses spatial and temporal indicators "into one carefully thought-out, concrete whole. Time, as it were, thickens, takes on flesh, becomes artistically visible; likewise, space becomes charged and responsive to the movements of time, plot and history. This intersection of axes and fusion of indicators characterizes the artistic chronotope" (*The Dialogic Imagination: Four Essays by M. M. Bakhtin*, 84).

28. Rita Dove read the poem at the threshold of a commencement at Harvard University, where she was the Phi Beta Kappa Poet of 1993. See also "Teach Us to Number Our Days" (*SP* 13), which reads: "In the old neighborhood, each funeral parlor / is more elaborate than the last."

29. "Rich has placed us, quite literally in . . .—a space of intervention—*in between* past and present, haunted memory, its 'individuating' intensity and some version of historical 'accounting for . . .'" Homi Bhabha evaluates Adrienne Rich's work in his 1996 essay "Unpacking my Library . . . again," *The Post-Colonial Question*, 204.

30. Raccoons or coons, like rabbits or monkeys, are part of the African-American folklore.

31. Cf. Paul Celan's concept of "Sprachgitter"; Dove studied his poetry in Tübingen.

32. Cf. Jacques Lacan (1977), *The Four Fundamental Concepts of Psychoanalysis* (Harmondsworth: Penguin), 279–80: "Henceforth it is the symbolic, not the imaginary, that is seen to be the determining order of the subject."

33. Section III of *M*, which deals with the poet's growing detachment from her father, offers an interesting parallel. There he also tends his roses outdoors. "Under the Rose," Dove's 1995 short story, describes a family under the spell of the rose, the beautiful daughter *deflowered*. See *Ancestral House*, 151–55. Cf. also Sharon Olds's 1995 collection of poems dedicated to her father's illness and death, *The Father* (New York: Knopf).

34. *Brenda Starr®* was a classic soap-opera strip, a pioneering comic strip featuring a strong female lead character created by the female artist Dale Messick. Brenda's big-city newsroom assignments usually led to adventure and romance. The strip began in 1940.

Chapter 2

1. In her introduction to *The Body in Pain*, Elaine Scarry bespeaks similar complications when she tries to separate the difficulty of expressing physical pain, the political and perceptual complications that arise as a result, and the nature of both material and verbal expressibility, i.e. the nature of human creation.

2. All classificatory and evaluative structures are inherent in Dove's oeuvre.

3. See Elleni Tedla (1995), "*Sankofa*. African Thought and Education" (New York: Lang), 3: "SANKOFA means that as we move forward into the future, we need to reach back into our past and take with us all that works and is positive." Cf. also Albert W. Kayper-Mensah (1978), *Sankofa: Adinkra Poems* (Tema: Ghana), 4: "Sankofa: That bird is wise, / Look. Its beak, back tuned, picks / For the present, what is best from ancient eyes, / then steps forward, on ahead / To meet the future, undeterred."

4. Presented in "Passage to Which India? The Enigma of the Return" (unpublished lecture, Berne: SAUTE Conference, November 1994; forthcoming in *Centralizing the Marginal: Boundaries in Contemporary African American Fiction*, ed. Josef Jarab

and Jeffrey Melnick [New York: Oxford University Press]). See also Fritz Gysin (1994) "Predicaments of Skin: Boundaries in Recent African American Fiction," *The Black Columbiad*, ed. Werner Sollors and Maria Diedrich, 286–97.

5. Frederick Barth (1969), *Ethnic Groups and Boundaries: The Social Organization of Culture Difference*, 15.

6. As Dove told Rohan B. Preston (*Chicago Tribune*, 5 July 1993), she still recalls her inability to understand why the members of her family, who were the only people at the beach that day, were supposed to remain on the side reserved for blacks.

7. The image of the crab barrel was quite popular in certain segments of the black community as a descriptive tale of black internalized self-hatred; the teller of the tale may or may not have bought into this mode of action (personal communication with Anthony Glenn Miller).

8. For a similar process of liquefaction, here with biblical undercurrents, see "In the Bulrush" (*GN* 95), "Strike the stone / to see if it's thinking / of water," or Beulah's thawing out of memories in "Dusting" (*SP* 179–80).

9. Wilson Harris (1973), "A Talk on the Subjective Imagination," *New Letters* 40 (Autumn): 37–48; Kirsten Holst Petersen and Anna Rutherford (1995), "Fossil and Psyche," *The Post-Colonial Studies Reader*, ed. Bill Ashcroft, et al., 185–89.

10. See also Gaston Bachelard (1942), *L'eau et les rêves*. (Paris: Corti).

11. In the famous case of *Plessy v. Ferguson* (1896), the Supreme Court held that enforced separate facilities for Negroes did not imply that they were inferior. "Separate but equal" did not violate the Fourteenth Amendment.

12. "It's the perfect blue of a forbidden, because segregated, swimming pool. It's also the blue of redemption. It gives equal time to the blue sky, the Fourth of July picnics that her daughters have invited her to, as well as the blue sky over the heads of the Civil Rights demonstrators marching through Washington, D. C. in 1963." (Dove, National Press Conference, 17 March 1994, 172).

13. See Robert D. Crassweller (1966), *Trujillo: The Life and Times of a Caribbean Dictator* (New York: Macmillan), 154–56; Hubert Fichte (1988), *Petersilie. Die afroamerikanischen Religionen, Santo Domingo, Venezuela, Miami, Grenada, 1980* (Frankfurt/M: Fischer), epigraph, 46–47; Ulrich Fleischmann (1994), "Petersilie am Massaker-Fluss. Die Geschichte einer Grenze," *Dominikanische Republik, 1991* (Köln: DuMont), 144–45; S. Weise, ed. (1994), *Die Dominikanische Republik, 1991* (Köln: Mundo), 81.

14. Not in 1957 as various sources, e.g. *SP* 136; Rubin and Ingersoll (1986), 229; or *The Norton Anthology of Poetry*, 4th ed. (1996), 1858, erroneously indicate.

15. An example of parsley as a paradigmatic sign of life in modern poetry can be found in William Carlos Williams's poem "Good Night" (1916).

The epigraph in Hubert Fichte's enlightening study, *Petersilie*, reads:

Am 2. Oktober 1937 liess Trujillo, der Staatschef der Dominikanischen Republik, 20.000 Neger ermorden. Sie wurden von den Exekutionskommandos gezwungen, das spanische Wort für "Petersilie"—"Perejil" auszusprechen; Trujillo gab vor, die dominikanischen Schwarzen zu schützen—nur die haitianischen Zuckerarbeiter sollten ausgerottet werden. Man behauptet, dass die Haitianer kein R sprechen können. Jedem, der "Pelejil" sagte, wurde der Kopf abgeschlagen. Kein dominikanischer Neger sagt "Perejil." Schon die spanischen Eroberer nannten Katharina "Catalina."

Und die Gileaditer namen ein die furt des Jordans fur Ephraim. Wenn nu sprachen die flüchtigen Ephraim / Las mich hin über gehen / So sprachen die Menner von Gilead zu jm / Bistu ein Ephraiter? Wenn er denn antwortet/ Nein / So hiessen si jn sprechen / Schiboleth / So sprach er / Siboleth / und kunds nicht recht reden / So griffen si Jn und schlugen Jn an der furt des Jordans / Das zu der zeit von Ephraim fielen zwey und vierzig tausent." *Das Buch der Richter* XII, 5.6.

Fichte further elaborates the incident on pp. 46-47:

Am 2. Oktober 1937 liess Trujillo in 36 Stunden 20 000 Neger mit Macheten ermorden. Es waren Siedler und Saisonarbeiter, die sich diesseits und jenseits der nie eindeutig festgelegten Grenze zwischen der Dominikanischen Republik und Haiti niedergelassen hatten. Die Flüsse färbten sich rot. Strassen und Täler waren mit Leichenteilen voll. Um jedoch vorgeblich die Neger dominikanischer Nationalität zu schützen, hatte Trujillo den Auftrag erteilt, die Schwarzen, die in Haufen zusammengetrieben, Männer, Frauen, Kinder, Vadoupriester, Spiegelmänner, ihre Enthauptung erwarteten, das Wort "Petersilie"—"Perejil" aussprechen zu lassen. Alle sagten "Pelejil" wie sie es als Kinder oder als Einwanderer gelernt hatten. 40 Dollar zahlte Trujillo später dem haitianischen Staat als Entgelt pro Kopf.

16. Confirmed by Fred Viebahn in personal communication.

17. See "Das Heterogene, Das Werk," *Lettre International* 27.4 (1994): 60–61.

18. According to *Webster's*, a short poem of fixed form, French in origin, consisting usually of five three-line stanzas and a final four-line stanza and having only two rhymes throughout. See also Dove's comments on the formal aspects of "Parsley" in J. Kitchen, and S. S. Robin, "A Conversation with Rita Dove 230f.

19. The tropes of cane—as in Jean Toomer's *Cane*—and of the swamp loom large in African-American literature, though with varied, even opposed signification. Whereas in W. E. B. Du Bois's *Quest for the Silver Fleece* the swamp figures as uncontrolled chaos that must be plowed under and controlled, for Zora Neale Hurston (*Their Eyes Were Watching God*) the swamp is the trope of the freedom of erotic love, the antithesis of the bourgeois life and order to which her protagonist flees but to which Du Bois's characters aspire. See also Dove's (1996) version of *DF* (II.4: "The Swamp"), and for an extensive discussion of the trope, see H. L. Gates, Jr. (1989), *The Signifying Monkey*, 193.

20. "Sie sprechen 'L' für 'R.' Sie können nicht richtig schreiben. Sie schreiben 'L' für 'R.' Das behaupten die weissen Dominikaner. Es ist falsch . . . Alle Dominikaner, die weissen und schwarzen sagen 'Amol' statt 'Amor,' 'pol favol' für 'por favor' . . . wie schon die Spanier statt 'Katharina' 'Catalina' schrieben." See Hubert Fichte (1988), *Petersilie*, 46–47.

21. Paul Celan's shibboleth "No pasaràn," also in Spanish, reads as follows "Herz: / gib dich auch hier zu erkennen, / hier, in der Mitte des Marktes. / Ruf's, das Schibboleth, hinaus / in die Fremde der Heimat: / Februar. No pasaràn. "*In Eins,* quoted in Jacques Derrida (1986), *Schibboleth*, 58.

22. Particularly in her verse play, *DF*, Dove combines elements from Judaism and Christianity in antebellum South Carolina, highlighting parallels between the biblical book of Exodus and the flight from slavery to freedom as exemplified in the Negro spiritual "Go Down Moses, and Tell Ole Pharaoh to Let My People Go." Dove's

poem "In the Bulrush" alludes metonymically to Moses in exile: "Strike the stone / to see if it's thinking / of water." Zora Neale Hurston and Ishmael Reed have also written myths of Moses. Both draw on black sacred and secular mythic discourse as metaphorical and metaphysical systems; see H. L. Gates, Jr. (1989), *The Signifying Monkey*, 111. Paul Celan's poetry also enters "Zabriah" in *Fifth Sunday*.

23. "The backlit plumes of smoke and murky variations of exhaust and light were exciting, a negative snapshot of power and hope; the mere sight of a belching smokestack at night made me think of evening gowns and diamond lavaliers." Dove (1990), "The Epistle of Paul the Apostle to the Ephesians," *Incarnation*, ed. Alfred Corn (New York: Viking), 167. In the poem Dove describes the silos from the perspective of various beholders. To children they are but "a fresh packet of chalk, / dreading math work."

24. "Turning and turning in the widening gyre / The falcon cannot hear the falconer; / Things fall apart; the centre cannot hold; / Mere anarchy is loosed upon the world, / The blood-dimmed tide is loosed, and everywhere / The ceremony of innocence is drowned; / The best lack all conviction, while the worst / Are full of passionate intensity. // Surely some revelation is at hand; / Surely the Second Coming is at hand." *The Collected Poems of W. B. Yeats*, ed. R. J. Finneran (New York: Macmillan), 187.

25. See also Aleida Assmann and Jan Assmann (1993), "Schrift und Gedächtnis," *Schrift und Gedächtnis*, ed. Aleida Assmann, Jan Assmann, and Chr. Hardmeier (München: Wilhelm Fink), 265–81.

26. Concepts also elaborated by Jonathan Hufstader in "Coming into Consciousness: Lyric Poetry as Social Discourse in the Work of Charles Simic, Seamus Heany, Tom Paulin, Tony Harrison, and Rita Dove," diss., Harvard University, 1993, 337.

27. In 1829 David Walker published his *Appeal: in Four Articles, Together with a Preamble, to the Coloured Citizens of the World, but in Particular, and Very Expressly to Those of the United States of America.*

28. See also "Catherine of Siena's" journey in *SP* 80: "You walked the length of Italy / to find someone to talk to. . . . No one stumbled across your path / No one unpried your fists as you slept."

29. At Villa Serbelloni, the "Study and Conference Center" of the Rockefeller Foundation on Lake Como, Italy.

30. Elisabeth Bronfen (1999), *Dorothy Richardson's Art of Memory: Space, Identity, Text*. Manchester: Manchester University Press. The term micro-structure refers less to Bronfen's terminology than to the sensitive differentiation through which she raises the awareness of multifarious textual spatializations and their semantic values.

31. This is Gwendolyn Brooks's definition of "black literature," cf. Brooks (1975), *A Capsule Course in Black Poetry Writing*, 3. Cf. as well Larry Neal in *The Black American Writer*, ed. C. W. E. Bigsby, vol. 2 (Deland, Fla.: Everett/Edwards, 1969), 203. Cf. Don L. Lee's runs as follows:

Blackpoetry is written for / to / about & around the lives / spiritactions / humanism & total existence of blackpeople. Black poetry in form / sound / word / usage / intonation / rhythm / repetition / definition / direction& beauty is opposed to that which is now (&yesterday) considered poetry, i.e., white poetry . . . Whereas, blackpoets deal in the concrete rather than the abstract (concrete: art for people's sake; black language or Afro-american language in contrast to standard english, &tc.). Blackpoetry moves to define and legitimize blackpeople's reality (*that* which is real to us.)

See "Black Poetics / For the Many to Come," in *Nommo: A Literary Legacy of Black Chicago (1967–1987)*, ed. Carole A. Parks (Chicago: OBAhouse, 1987), 13.

32. In "Gender and Afro-Americanist Literary Theory and Criticism," Valerie Smith cites Don L. Lee's appraisal of the protagonist of one of Mari Evans's poems: "The woman herein . . . is not fragmented, hysterical, doesn't have sexual problems with her mate, doesn't feel caught up in a 'liberated womanhood' complex/bag—which is to say she is not out to define herself (that is, from the position of weakness, as the "others" do) and thus will not be looked upon as an aberration of the twentieth-century white woman." See *Speaking of Gender*, ed. Elaine Showalter (New York: Routledge, 1989), 60.

33. A range of female poets, however, e.g. Gwendolyn Brooks, Mari Evans, Nikki Giovanni, Sonia Sanchez, and Carolyn Rodgers, stand tall with Don L. Lee as powerful poetic proclaimers of the new black awareness. In her all-inclusive view, however, Dove seems much closer to poets like Robert Hayden, Michael S. Harper, or Derek Walcott and novelists like Ralph Ellison, Paule Marshall, or Wilson Harris, who all disapprove of a didactic and ideological fixation. It should be noted that Don L. Lee (pseudonym H. R. Madhubuti), in *Black Men: Obsolete, Single, Dangerous?* (Chicago: Third World Press, 1990), not only gratefully acknowledges Margaret Walker and Gwendolyn Brooks as "the two writers who signaled to me the possibilities of poetry" (132), but he praises black women writers as a "major and positive historical force in the Black struggle" (83). As the director of positive education, editor of Third World Press, poet, critic, and essayist of reknown, Haki R. Madhubuti works especially toward the improvement of the black male to become responsible, stabilizing members of family and society.

34. *On Poetic Imagination*, 19, in James Hillman (1979), *The Dream and the Underworld*, 128.

35. In *DF* (1996), 49, Dove includes a possum folk rhyme. See the slightly different version in the 1994 ed. of *DF*, which includes "Old Mr. Coon," 41.

36. In Jonathan Hufstader's interpretation, "Thomas retreats from the risky business of artistic invention, sheds the bardic mantle while keeping the mantle of age, and recalls how the possum tasted. The grandfather cannot function as *griot*, storyteller, or sage—it is too late in black cultural history for that" (diss., Harvard University, 1994), 316. As one certainly agrees with Hufstader that times have changed, his point is hardly in tune with Thomas's guiding and thoughtfully protective passing on information and stories to his grandchildren throughout the poem. He is not dropping out of storytelling but seeks an elegant and telling way out of a story.

37. See Anna Maria Stuby (1992), *Liebe, Tod und Wasserfrau. Mythen des Weiblichen in der Literatur* (Opladen: Westdeutscher Verlag).

38. First published posthumously in *Imago* 25 (1940), 105; rpt. in *The Standard Edition of the Complete Psychological Works of Sigmund Freud*, trans. and ed. James Strachey et al., vol. 18, 273–74. The manuscript is dated 14 May 1922. See also Elisabeth Bronfen (1992), *Over Her Dead Body*, 255.

39. Hélène Cixous (1976), "The Laugh of the Medusa," *Signs* Summer: 875–93; a revised version of "le rire de la méduse," which appeared in *L'arc* (1975), 39–54; or, (1981), "Castration or Decapitation?" *Signs* Autumn: 41–55.

40. From "The Other Side of the House," reprinted as heading for section III in *GN.*

41. Gaston Bachelard refers to a poem by R. Cazelles that features a house "as a sort of airy structure that moves about on the breath of time. It really is open to the wind of another time" (*The Poetics of Space,* 1994: 54).

42. In speaking of "The Silence of Polyglots," Julia Kristeva quotes Hölderlin's experience with Greek; see *Strangers to Ourselves,* 16.

43. Cf. Louise Erdrich's revisions of the lives of saints in part one of *Baptism of Desire* (New York: Harper & Row, 1989; rpt. 1991).

44. Sander L. Gilman's *Difference and Pathology: Stereotypes of Sexuality, Race and Madness* offers an excellent discussion of the role of the black as an icon of sexuality, a source of fascination so that "the black female literally becomes her genitalia" (115, 121). Cf. especially chapter 4, "Black Sexuality and Modern Consciousness."

Chapter 3

1. Cf. Haki M. Madhubuti (1990), *Black Men: Obsolete, Single, Dangerous? African American Families in Transition: Essays* (Chicago: Third World Press); Andrew Billingsley (1993), *Climbing Jacob's Ladder: The Enduring Legacy of African-American Families* (New York: Simon & Schuster); or Deborah E. McDowell (1989), "Reading Family Matters," *Changing Our Own Words,* ed. Cheryl A. Wall, 75–97. In "Allegories of Black Female Desire; or, Rereading Nineteenth-Century Sentimental Narratives of Black Female Authority" (Changing Our Own Words, p. 103), Claudia Tate highlights the value attributed to marriage in the antebellum South: "To vote and to marry, then, were two civil responsibilities that nineteenth-century black people elected to perform; they were twin indexes for measuring how black people collectively valued their civil liberties."

2. Thomas as a reversal of Mark Twain's Tom moving South in *Huckleberry Finn* is a likely twist, while "Old Lem," the protagonist of a poem by Sterling A. Brown in the collection *Southern Road* (1932), reflects black powerlessness in the face of white supremacy during the Great Depression.

3. The seemingly disparate spheres of Thomas's wheel and Beulah's canary find a striking equation in Gaston Bachelard's *La poétique de l'espace,* X: "La phénoménologie du rond," 208–14. Bachelard quotes Jules Michelet (*L'Oiseau*) as saying "L'oiseau, presque tout sphérique, est certainement le sommet, sublime et divin, de concentration vivante. On ne peut voir, ni imaginer même un plus haut degré d'unité. Excès de concentration qui fait la grande force personnelle de l'oiseau, mais qui implique son extrême individualité, son isolement, sa faiblesse sociale" [The bird, almost spherical, is certainly the culmination, sublime and divine, of living concentration. One can neither see nor even imagine a higher degree of unity. Excess of concentration which constitutes the great personal strength of the bird, but also implies its extreme individuality, its isolation, its social weakness].

4. "The wheel is a worldwide mode of taking the measure of time, representing it as a cycle in which the days and nights turn. We turn with time and, as Bachelard said, space is our friend, but time has death in it." See James Hillman (1979), *The Dream and the Underworld,* 161.

5. See Booker T. Washington (1996), *Up from Slavery,* 28–29: "I swept the recitation-room three times. Then I got a dusting-cloth and dusted it four times. All the woodwork around the walls, every bench, table, and desk, I went over four times with my dusting-cloth. . . . The sweeping of that room was my college examina-

tion, and never did any youth pass an examination for entrance into Harvard or Yale that gave him more genuine satisfaction."

6. Aunt Jemima is part of America's racial background noise. She flourished in minstrel shows before she became a corporate brand name on pancake-mix boxes: the archetypal "mammy" who represents the mythic Old South of benign slavery, grace, and abundance. Aunt Jemima has an opposite, Jezebel, as sexy as the mammy is neutral, figured not by the traits of the kitchen but the delights of the bedroom. She is not a mother but a prostitute. Diane Roberts offers an excellent account of the racial stereotype in her 1995 study *The Myth of Aunt Jemima: Representations of Race and Regions*, 1–2. Cf. also Don L. Lee's poem "Move Un-Noticed to Be Noticed: A Nationhood Poem," which "transforms Beulah from a maligned stereotype to a hurricane of the Black nation reborn" (in Stephen Henderson [1973], *Understanding the New Black Poetry*, 340–43).

7. From Harriet Beecher Stowe's *Uncle Tom's Cabin* to Richard Wright's *Native Son*, with its "Bigger Thomas," a "nigger" who failed in a white man's world.

8. Toni Morrison, herself from Lorain, Ohio, testifies to the geographic and demographic mediating role of her native state: "Ohio is right on the Kentucky border, so there's not much difference between it and the 'South.' It's an interesting state from the point of view of black people because it is right there by the Ohio River, in the south, and at its northern tip is Canada. And there were these fantastic abolitionists there, and also the Ku Klux Klan lived there. And there is only really one large city. There are hundreds of small towns and that's where most black people live" ("'Intimate Things in Place.' A Conversation with Toni Morrison," 215). Cf. also the exchange between Virginia and Mrs. Voltz in *IG* 72–73: "It's from the Greek. *Akros*." . . . "Tell me where it's high," Virginia demanded. "I don't see no high." "Course you don't. Cities don't like for their hills to show. More tea?"

9. See Denise Riley, "Does a Sex Have a History?" *"Am I That Name?": Feminism and the Category of "Women" in History* (Minneapolis: University of Minnesota Press, 1988), 1.

10. *Beloved*, in Toni Morrison's words, "was not a story to pass on," suggesting quite the reverse.

11. Beulah, whose color of redemption is blue (cf. e.g. "Pomade," *SP* 192–93), reappears anonymously as a young woman in the prologue "Summit Beach, 1921" of Dove's following volume *GN*. Cf. also Jonathan Hufstader's unpublished dissertation, "Coming into Consciousness: Lyric Poetry as Social Discourse in the Work of Charles Simic, Seamus Heany, Tom Paulin, Tony Harrison, and Rita Dove" (Harvard University, 1993).

Chapter 4

1. "Fifth Sunday," "The Zulus," "The Spray Paint King," "Second-Hand Man," "Damon and Vandalia," "The Vibraphone," "Zabriah," and "Aunt Carrie."

2. Kelly Cherry (1992) calls *IG* "almost shocking in its sweet optimism, its willingness to forgive. Here is narrative prose whose first impulse is to describe its world precisely, without preconception. Such writing is felt by the reader as a kind of caress. It is as if the book reaches out to the reader, saying 'Join me in this venture; we're side by side here.' . . . In fact, it is a pleasure to read a contemporary novel that does not depend on irony to establish a sense of collusion or complicity between author and reader. And it may be this lack of irony that accounts for the certain sweet purity (not puritanism) that suffuses the story, runs through like a melodic

line—and it is a relief, too, from postmodernism's insistence on being in the know, one up, too cool for words." See "A State of Independence," *Los Angeles Times Book Review*, 8.

3. See Wayne Ude (1993), "An Interview with Rita Dove," 3.

4. "How It Feels to Be Colored Me," *I Love Myself When I Am Laughing* (New York: Feminist Press, 1979).

5. As Anthony K. Appiah argued in his 1995 talk at Harvard University on "African-American Popular Theories," *An American Dilemma Revisited*, An Investigation of Gunnar Myrdal's 1944 Landmark Study "The Negro Problem and Modern Democracy" (30 Sept.)

6. Radio interview with Dove, "Through the Ivory Gate," *All About Books*, KFPK Los Angeles, 12 Dec. 1992.

7. The roots of the name "Sambo" were both African and Hispanic—from the Hausa fashioning of a spirit or the second son, and "Zambo," meaning a type of monkey—but the English "Sam" had an important role in transposing it into popular lingo. From the mid-nineteenth century to the early decades of the twentieth century, Sambo became the nickname for the black male. The essential features of Sambo consisted of two principal parts. He was childish and comical, employed outlandish gestures, and wore tattered clothes. Irresponsibility was a cardinal characteristic and buffoonery an inherent trait. On the flip side, he was the natural slave and servant who displayed the qualities of patience, humility, nonbelligerence, and faithfulness. Here responsibility was expected and smartness rewarded, though both virtues were carefully monitored by whites.

The two separate forms eventually became transplanted into theatrical forms. The child became the "plantation darky" called Jim Crow; the servant became the urban mulatto known as "Zip Coon" or "Jim Dandy." See *Encyclopedia of African-American Culture and History*, vol. 5, ed. Jack Salzman, David Lionel Smith, and Cornel West (New York: Simon & Schuster, 1996), 2566–69.

8. Radio interview with Dove, "Through the Ivory Gate," *All About Books*, KFPK Los Angeles, 12 Dec. 1992.

9. "The back door is the door of childhood. Countless movies and TV sitcoms have exploited the real-life possibilities of this symbolism. A slamming screen door signals the child's defiance of parents and the adult world—what child hasn't run out the back door in tears, vowing to go away and never come back and then they'll be sorry? And the vista from the backyard is also many children's first—albeit sheltered and contained—vision of a larger world to explore. They can catch a glimpse of the possibilities of the Open" (*PW* 21).

10. See, e.g., Laura Sue Fuderer (1990), *The Female Bildungsroman in English*; Gunilla Theander Kester (1995), *Writing the Subject*; Geta Leseur (1995), *Ten Is the Age of Darkness*; Randolph P. Shaffner (1984), *The Apprenticeship Novel*. Cf. also Annis Pratt (1995), "Bildungsroman and Künstlerroman," *The Oxford Companion to Women's Writing in the United States*, ed. Cathy N. Davidson and Linda Wagner-Martin, 104–6.

11. Dove, Shange, Brooks, and Jordan belong to a smaller subset still: June Jordan's *His Own Where* (1971) is an adolescent love story, while Brooks's *Maud Martha* (1952) and Shange's two novels *Sassafrass, Cypress and Indigo* (1982) and *Betsey Brown* (1985) are all coming-of-age stories of memory, pain, and discovery with young black girls at their centers.

12. E.g., in the work of Terry McMillan, Sapphire, or Jamaica Kincaid.

13. E.g., Alice Walker and Toni Morrison.

Chapter 5

1. *Callaloo* 14.2 (1991): 396–418, features *The Siberian Village*, a play in one act by Dove. The title refers to a "Professor's" report of the Siberian village of Kibirsk, which housed convicts. The "professor" was gunned down when he tried to escape. The roleplay on empathy and survival unites a woman and two former convicts in an attempt to recreate the grim circumstances of betrayal, death, and survival against all odds.

2. A copy is extant at the Library of Congress, Washington D.C.

3. Cf. *E&A The Register-Guard*, 2–8 August 1996, 17.

4. In the 92nd Street Y reading, Dove explained, "I decided to write in an ancient version of my own real role, that of poet troubadour" ("Chronicle," *New York Times*, 20 Nov. 1995). "I am not exactly the narrator but an all-seeing chorus who comments on the action" (ibid.).

5. The members of the chorus in Athenian tragedy always act out marginal members of society in the world of heroes, such as old men, young girls, prisoners of war, and the like. In Gregory Nagy, "Notes on Athenian Tragedy," *The Concept of the Hero in Hellenic Civilization*, unpublished lecture, Harvard University, n.d.

6. The image of Moses as political leader within the African-American community is powerfully suggested by many spirituals, including the well-known "Go Down, Moses." Various activists, especially Martin Luther King, Jr., phrased their agenda for civil rights in terms of the biblical Exodus.

7. Snakes link Hector with Sophocles's seer Teiresias who, while killing copulating snakes, changed sex whenever he would strike a male or a female. His androgynous nature allows him to recognize the essence of truth. Dove, however, delegates the power of foreknowledge to the conjure-woman Scylla.

8. "Walker's Appeal No. 1," *Liberator*, 8 Jan. 1831, 6. See also Elizabeth McHenry (1995), "Dreaded Eloquence." For the "Appeal"'s influence in the South cf. Jane Pease and William Pease, "Walker's Appeal Comes to Charleston: A Note and Documents," *Journal of Negro History* 59 (1974): 287–92.

9. Two important sources for the study of Denmark Vesey's conspiracy are James Hamilton, Jr. (1822), *An Account of the Late Intended Insurrection Among A Portion of the Blacks of This City* (16 Aug.) and Lionel H. Kennedy and Thomas Parker (1822), *An Official Report of the Trials of Sundry Negroes, Charged with an Attempt to Raise an Insurrection in the State of South-Carolina* (22 Oct.; cf. footnote above). I consulted a copy of the latter at Houghton Library, Harvard University. For notes on executions, see also the *Republican Star* (Easton, Md.), 16 July 1822; the *Richmond Enquirer* (Richmond, Va.), 19 July and 6 August 1822. For a more extended reading, see Herbert Aptheker (1967), *American Negro Slave Revolts*, 1943 (New York: International Publishers); John Lofton (1983), *Denmark Vesey's Revolt*, 1964 (Kent, Ohio: Kent State University Press); Robert S. Starobin, ed. (1970), *Denmark Vesey: The Slave Conspiracy of 1822* (Englewood Cliffs, N.J.: Prentice-Hall).

10. Son of Odysseus and Penelope who helped his father to slay his mother's suitors.

11. St. Thomas, with its capital Charlotte Amalie, was Danish at that time.

12. The playwright of the same name will figuratively "seize" the rebel in her play.

13. During the premiere of *DF*, the Ashland Oregon Shakespeare Festival also played Shakespeare's *The Winter's Tale*. The former, a tragedy with melodramatic infusions, and the latter, a romance, share structural parallels as well: both feature

abandoned children, Augustus and Perdita, who will reappear twenty and sixteen years later, respectively. In Shakespeare, Time the Chorus bridges the gap; in Dove a dream-sequence combining all major voices, desires, and deadly contradictions (II.1) mediates between the first and second halves. In contrast to *The Winter's Tale*, *DF* denies its hero redemption and salvation.

14. *Oedipus Tyrannus* (between 429, the year of the plague, and 425): *Oedipus at Colonus* (401 postum). See Charles Segal (1993), *Oedipus Tyrannus* (New York: Twayne), xiii and xv, and Kurt Steinmann (1995), "'Meine Taten hab' ich mehr erlitten als verübt.' Notizen zum 'Oedipus auf Kolonos' von Sophokles," *Neue Zürcher Zeitung* 18 / 19 Nov.: 69.

15. Cf. also the fate of St. Gregory. Discovering the truth of his incestuous marriage, he is overwhelmed by guilt and has a fisherman lock him up in a cellar where he lives in solitary penance. Later he is miraculously found and named Pope.

16. Notice the German distinction between marked by pain, *gezeichnet*, and marked out, *ausgezeichnet*.

17. The tightened and reorganized plot of the 1996 edition—the seventh scene featuring Amalia and Augustus's romance in the 1994 plot has been relegated to the end of the first act—differs not so much in phrasing but in content. Biblical reflections of Augustus (*DF* 1994: 46–47) and of Henry Blake (1994: 81), the parts of Ned and of the old prayerwoman are shed. The chorus's function to provide explanation and elaboration has been transferred to the narrator, who links the scenes with short vignettes: "A sniff of freedom's all it takes / to feel history's sting; / There's danger by-and-by / when the slaves won't sing" (*DF* 1996: 76). Augustus no longer divulges his past to Scylla but to Amalia. Most important, he has become a leader throughout the play, though he is drawn into action rather than seeking to command. Instead of a double defeat in the verse play of 1994—there he gets shot as a bloody traitor—he faces a short-lived triumph in the 1996 version. His mother stabs herself and Augustus's mission seems fulfilled. First directed by Derek Walcott as a stage reading (New York, 21 Nov. 1995), the shortened version brilliantly succeeded in providing a straightened plot with a favorable ending for the rebels' cause.

18. See Juan Francisco Manzano, *Obras* (Habana: Instituto Cubano del Libro, n.d.), vii, and his *Poems by a Slave in the Island of Cuba*, ed. and trans. R. R. Madden (London, 1840), 101.

19. When asked whether she was Wheatley's spiritual heir, Dove stressed sociological rather than literary parallels (interview with Mike Hammer and Christina Daub [1996]: 30–31).

20. See Countee Cullen in *Black Poets of the United States*, ed. Jean Wagner, 301; Langston Hughes, "Seven Moments of Love," subtitled "An Un-sonnet Sequence in Blues," in *The Collected Poems of Langston Hughes*, ed. Arnold Rampersad and David Roessel (New York: Knopf, 1995), 217–20.

21. In her foreword, Dove states that "the Olympians disapprove of the abduction," but in the *Homeric Hymn*, Helios, who greatly respects Demeter and feels sorry for her, also informs her of Zeus's explicit sanction of the deed. See Pindar's *Homeric Hymn to Demeter*, trans. Gregory Nagy, lecture script Harvard University, Fall 1992, 75–80. Cf. also Hesiod's *Homeric Hymn to Demeter*, trans. H. G. Evelyn-White (Cambridge, Mass.: Harvard University Press, 1982), 289-325. An excellent survey of plot variants is still Richard Foerster's 1874 study *Der Raub und die Rückkehr der Persephone* [The Abduction and the Return of Persephone] (Stuttgart: Heitz).

22. Cf. Pindar's *Homeric Hymn to Demeter*, l. 1–495, especially ll. 445f. Here Persephone divides the year differently: Zeus "assented that her daughter, every

time the season came round, would spend a third portion of the year in the realms of dark mist underneath, and the other two thirds in the company of her mother and the other immortals."

23. Margaret E. Atwood (1961), *Double Persephone* (Toronto: Hawkshead); and Jorie Graham (1987), "Self-Portrait as Demeter and Persephone," *The End of Beauty* (New York: Ecco), 59–63. Cf. also Gerburg Treusch-Dieter (1984), "Der Mythos von Demeter und Kore [The Myth of Demeter and Kore]," *Mythos Frau. Projektionen und Inszenierungen im Patriarchat* [Mythos Woman. Projections and Dramaturgies in Patriarchal Society] (Berlin: Publica), 176–212.

24. On Dove's punning on her own name see "The Event" and "Courtship," *Thomas and Beulah* (141, 146), and Stephen Cushman's 1996 essay "And the Dove Returned," 131.

25. Before a young headhunter can be permitted to marry and father children, he must go forth and have his sacred kill. "Unless there is death, there cannot be birth." See Joseph Campbell and Bill Moyers (1988), *The Power of Myth* (New York: Doubleday), 111.

26. See Elaine Scarry (1985), *The Body in Pain*: "Because the person in [physical] pain is ordinarily so bereft of the resources of speech, it is not surprising that the language for pain should sometimes be brought into being by those who are not themselves in pain but who speak *on behalf of* those who are" (6).

27. Robert Graves maintains that "it may have been at Sicilian Enna; or at Attic Colonus; or at Hermione; or somewhere in Crete, or near Pisa, or near Lerna; or beside Arcadian Pheneus, or at Boeotian Nysa, or anywhere else in the widely separated regions which Demeter visited in her wandering search for Core" (*The Greek Myths*, vol. 1, 90).

28. Arcadia, the Greek vale of undisturbed bliss, also features various entrances for Hades. It is Death who says "et in arcadia ego." Death and bliss are always intertwined.

29. Stephen Cushman observes "that the key to Dove's sonnets lies not in accentual-syllabic meter or regular rhyming but in their various arrangements based on the number fourteen . . . for Dove counts lines and stanzas and strophic groupings" ("And the Dove Returned," 132).

30. Upon Zeus's suggestion, Demeter must have taken poppyseeds to forget her pain. Cf. R. Foerster (1874), *Der Raub und die Rückkehr der Persephone* (Stuttgart: Heitz), 62. See also Ovid, *Fasti IV*, 531, where Demeter is said to have broken her lent because she has eaten poppy.

31. In order to complete an orphic circle, the poet must experience the worlds of both joy and sorrow. See Rainer Maria Rilke (1993), *The Sonnets to Orpheus*, 19.

32. A quote from Jorie Graham's 1987 "Self-Portrait as Demeter and Persephone" (*The End of Beauty*, 61).

33. Introduced and developed to perfection by Robert Browning.

34. The Italian "fica," "fig," is a slang term for female genitals.

35. See Gerburg Treusch-Dieter (1983), "Das Märchen von Amor und Psyche," *Manuskripte. Zeitschrift für Literatur* 1983 (Graz: Forum Stadtpark), and Dove's "Fifth Sunday," 8–9.

36. Notice that "Mexico" in Robert Lowell's sonnet cycles—he too writes about father, mother, and daughters—is no place of art but one of erotic initiation and rejuvenation. See *Selected Poems* (New York: Noonday, 1995), 201–6.

37. In *Der Raub und die Rückkehr der Persephone*, R. Foerster traces the myth from its attic Greek origin to Sicily (65).

Chapter 6

1. See Beverly Maeder, "Performance, Lyric, and the Audience's Demands in Wallace Stevens' 'The Man with the Blue Guitar,'" *SPELL* 11 (1999), 129.

2. On the relativity of History read e.g. Trinh T. Minh-Ha, *Women, Native, Other*:

> Historians have, for several decades now, been repeating that History with a capital H does not exist and that it has never constituted the *a priori* reasoning of their discourse but, rather, its result. Like the anthropological study whose information may always be reordered, refuted, or completed by further research, the historical analysis is nothing other than the reconstruction and redistribution of a pretended order of things, the interpretation or even transformation of documents given and frozen into monuments. The re-writing of history is therefore an endless task, one to which feminist scholars have devoted much of their energy. The more they dig into the maze of yellowed documents and look into the nonregistered facts of their communities, the more they rejoice upon discovering the buried treasures of women's unknown heritage. (84)

3. Cf. W. Augustus Low and Virgil A. Clift, eds., *Encyclopedia of Black America*, 228–72, 486–89, 565, 862–66, and Darlene Clark Hine, Elsa Barkley Brown, and Rosalyn Terborg-Penn, eds., *Black Women in America: An Historical Encyclopedia*, 2 vols. (Bloomington: Indiana University Press, 1993), vol. 2, 807–9, 907–9.

4. It appeared first in *Georgia Review* (Winter 1998).

5. On iconicity or ekphrasis, cf. W. J. T. Mitchell, *Iconology: Image, Text, Ideology* (Chicago: University of Chicago Press, 1986).

6. Pearl as Papa's girl also appears in "Taking in Wash," the first poem of Beulah's section in *TB*. See *SP* 175. Cf. as well the poem "Pearls" in *SP* 50.

7. A proven method to keep one's distance both for uneducated female black angels and for such renowned writers as Henry James. When his overprotective mother wrote to him in London, "Your life must need this [my own] succulent, fattening element more than you know yourself" (Edel, vol. 1, 47), he gained weight and replied defensively: "I am as broad as I am long, as fat as a butter-tub and as red as a British *materfamilias*" (Edel, vol. 2, 343). In Leon Edel, *Henry James*, 5 vols. (Philadelphia: Lippincott, 1953–1972).

8. In "The Up and Up. On the Limits of Optimism," *Transition* 74 (1998): 44–61, 56.

9. Compare *TB* (*SP* 192–93) where Beulah "feels / herself slowly rolling down the sides of the earth."

10. Cf. Dove's exquisitely crafted poems on the topic: "Adolescence I," "Adolescence II," "Adolescence III" in *SP* 42–44.

11. In 1967 Dove was a fifteen-year-old girl attracted to all things written and printed in this library. Harold's purple crayon left an indelible mark on her, as it would draw any space the little girl dreamed of. Cf. "In the Old Neighborhood," *SP* xxii–xxvi.

12. Officially, 250,000 people participated in the March on Washington.

13. In her poem "Ars Poetica" (*GN* 48) Dove imagines the lyrical self hawklike, "a traveling x-marks the spot."

14. Dove's mother once earned a grant but did not attend business school.

15. Blue is also Beulah's color of hope in *TB*.

16. "Singsong" and "Black on a Saturday Night" are part of *Seven for Luck*, a song cycle for soprano and orchestra, lyrics by Dove, music by John Williams, that premiered with the Boston Symphony Orchestra at Tanglewood on 25 July 1998. See Notes, *RP* 93–94.

17. Cf. Hélène Cixous, "The Laugh of the Medusa," trans. Keith Cohen and Paula Cohen, in *New French Feminism*, ed. Elaine Marks and Isabelle de Courtivron (Amherst: University of Massachusetts Press, 1980); Luce Irigaray, *This Sex Which Is Not One*, trans. Catherine Porter (Ithaca, N.Y.: Cornell University Press, 1985); Julia Kristeva, *Desire in Language*; Jacques Lacan, *Ecrits: A Selection*, trans. Alan Sheridan (New York: Norton, 1977).

18. Cf. Notes in *RP* 91: An allegorical poem inspired by the Aesop fable "The First Appearance of the Camel"; it relates how man's terror of this strange and powerful creature gradually turns to contempt once the means to control and domesticate the animal were discovered. Slavery, of course, is the key to this passage.

19. Cf. Edgar Allan Poe's poem "The Raven."

20. See Orlando Patterson, *The Ordeal of Integration* (Washington, D.C.: Civitas, 1997).

21. Persephone in *ML* divides her time between upper- and underworld; Goethe's "Erlkönig" and Stoker's "Dracula" cannot find peace as revenants or "Wiedergänger."

22. Dove often compares her artistic self to a hawk and inscribes her last name in her work; cf. e.g. *SP*, 98–100, 141; *RP* 77.

23. Cf. the antic horse Pegasus that sprung from Medusa's head. It is a winged horse that travels the world. Pegasus's significance remains caught between an underwater realm linked to Poseidon and heavenly spheres.

24. See e.g. "Agosta the Winged Man, and Rasha the Black Dove" (*SP* 98–100).

25. The ghostwalker is Mrs. Rowohlt, a German publisher's dead widow. The couple bequeathed the Château de Lavigny on the Lake of Geneva to the Rowohlt foundation. Dove was the recipient of a Rowohlt grant in August 1996. See Notes, *RP* 94.

26. See e.g., Louis R. Harlan, *Separate and Unequal* (1958), Studies in American Negro Life (New York: Atheneum, 1969), and the more recent Oxford University Press publication of the same title.

27. Cf. "Geometry," *SP* 17.

28. To no longer regard historical documents as material manifestations of an underlying idea, truth, or tradition (Foucault 1981: 12), but rather to describe the series and layers apparent in them and set them in relation to one another (ibid.: 16) means to dispense with the notion of a global history and to turn to the diversity of a general history (ibid.: 18–19) consisting of layers and relations, emplacements and displacements, to moments of resistance (ibid.: 20).

29. Information by Dove. The screening was held in December 1997.

30. The book's launch also took place at the National Museum for Women in the Arts in Washington, D.C., on 24 March 1999.

31. Dove studied and translated Paul Celan. Cf. *Poetry* 173.1 (Oct.–Nov. 1998).

32. Foucault outlined his notion of "heterotopias" as the characteristic spaces of the modern world, superseding the hierarchic "ensemble of places" of the Middle Ages and the enveloping "space of emplacement" opened up by Galileo into an early-modern, infinitely folding "space of extension" and measurement. Moving away from both the "internal space" of Bachelard's brilliant poetics and the inten-

tional regional descriptions of the phenomenologists, Foucault focused our attention on another spatiality of social life, an "external space," the actually lived (and socially produced) space of sites and the relations between them. See Edward Soja, (1989), *Postmodern Geographies*, 17, and Michel Foucault (1998), *Aesthetics, Method, and Epistemology*, 178–79.

In Conversation with Rita Dove

1. First published as *"The Darker Face of the Earth. A Conversation with Rita Dove,"* in *Transition* 74 (Nov. 1998): 104–23.

WORKS CITED

Primary Sources

Poetry

Dove, Rita (1989). *The Yellow House on the Corner.* 1980. Pittsburgh: Carnegie Mellon Press.
———(1992). *Museum.* 1983. Pittsburgh: Carnegie Mellon Press.
———(1986). *Thomas and Beulah.* Pittsburgh: Carnegie Mellon Press.
———(1989). *Grace Notes.* New York: Norton.
———(1993). *Selected Poems.* New York: Vintage Books.
———(1995). *Mother Love. Poems.* New York: Norton.
———(1999). *On the Bus with Rosa Parks.* New York: Norton.

Limited Editions

Dove, Rita (1977). *Ten Poems.* Lisbon, Iowa: Penumbra Press.
———(1980). *The Only Dark Spot in the Sky.* Tempe, Ariz.: Porch Publications.
———(1982). *Mandolin.* Athens: Ohio Review Poetry Series.
———(1988). *The Other Side of the House.* Tempe, Ariz.: Pyracantha Press.
———(1993). "Lady Freedom among Us." *Congressional Records* 23 Oct. (1994). Rpt. commissioned by the University of Virginia Libraries. West Burke, Vt.: Janus Press (1995). Rpt. in *Rita Dove. Poet Laureate Consultant in Poetry 1993–95. The Poet's World.* Washington, D.C.: Library of Congress. 11.
———(1994). "Elevator Man, 1949." *Des Moines Sunday Register.* 24–30 April: 4.
———(1994). "The First Book." *Richmond Times Dispatch* 21 Apr.
———(1996). "Umoja: Each One of Us Counts." Opening poem of the 1996 Atlanta Summer Olympics Arts Festival. Music by Alvin Singleton; poem read by Andrew Young.
———(1998). *Evening Primrose.* Minneapolis, Minn.: Tunheim Santrizos Company.
———(1998). "Seven for Luck." A cycle of seven poems sung by Cynthia Haymon. Music by John Williams. Tanglewood: Boston Symphony Orchestra Program. World Premiere, 25 July.

Fiction

Rita Dove (1990). *Fifth Sunday*. 1985. Callaloo Fiction Series, University of Kentucky. Charlottesville: University Press of Virginia.
——— (1992). *Through the Ivory Gate*. New York: Pantheon.
——— (1995). "Under the Rose." *Ancestral House: The Black Short Story in the Americas and Europe*. Ed. Charles H. Rowell. Boulder, Colo.: Westview Press. 151–55.

Plays

Dove, Rita (1980). *Oedipus Rex. A Black Tragedy*. Washington, D.C.: Library of Congress.
——— (1991). "The Siberian Village." *Callaloo* 14.2: 396–418.
——— (1994). *The Darker Face of the Earth*. A verse play in fourteen scenes. Three Oaks Farm, Brownsville, Ore.: Story Line Press.
——— (1995). *The Darker Face of the Earth*. A play in a prologue and two acts. Shortened stage version for 92nd Street "Y" stage reading. Directed by Derek Walcott.
——— (1996). *The Darker Face of the Earth*. Completely revised 2d ed. Brownsville, Ore.: Story Line Press.

Reviews, Essays

Rita Dove (1985). "Telling It Like It I-S *IS*. Narrative Techniques In Melvin Tolson's *Harlem Gallery*." *New England Review and Bread Loaf Quarterly* 8.1: 109–117. [Title refers to Amiri Baraka's "tell it like it is"]
——— (1987). "'*Either I'm Nobody, or I'm A Nation'*." *Parnassus* 14.1: 49–76.
——— (1988). "The Laureate of Black America." *New York Times Book Review* 9 Oct.: 1, 48–49. [On Langston Hughes]
——— (1988). "Notes to the Earth: The Poems of Lucille Clifton." *Gettysburg Review* 1.3: 501–57.
——— (1989). "In Nigeria, Ohio is Exotic." *New York Times Book Review* 12 Nov.: 11. [On Wole Soyinka]
——— (1990). "The Epistle of Paul the Apostle to the Ephesians." *Incarnation: Contemporary Writers on the New Testament*. Ed. Alfred Corn. New York: Viking. 162–74.
——— (1990). Foreword. *Jonah's Gourd Vine*. By Zora Neale Hurston. Ed. Henry Louis Gates, Jr. New York: Harper & Row.
——— (1991). "A Black Rainbow: Modern Afro-American Poetry." With Marilyn Nelson Waniek. *Poetry after Modernism*. Ed. Robert McDowell. Brownsville, Ore.: Story Line Press.
——— (1991). "The House That Jill Built." *The Writer on Her Work*. Ed. Janet Sternburg. Vol. 2. New York: Norton.
——— (1993). "JFK: Kennedy. 30 Years after the Assassination." *Akron Beacon Journal* 21 Nov.: A1, A16.
——— (1993). "To Make A Prairie." *The* [Phi Beta Kappa] *Key Reporter* 59.
——— (1994). "Bearing Witness. A Tribute [to Gwendolyn Brooks] from Poet Laureate of the United States Rita Dove." *Humanities* (magazine of the National Endowment for the Humanities) May/June: 8–9.

———— (1994). "Rita Dove." Autobiographical Essay. Contemporary Authors Series. Vol. 19. Gale Research. 97–115.

———— (1994). "Speaker: Rita Dove, Poet Laureate of the United States." *National Press Club Luncheon* 17 Mar.: 169–74.

———— (1994). "What Does Poetry Do for Us?" *UVA Alumni News* Jan./Feb.: 22–27.

———— (1995). "ALA Keynote Address." American Library Association. Chicago, 24 June.

———— (1995). "How They Met. Poet Laureate Rita Dove, Married to Fred Viebahn since 1979." *Washington Post* 14 Feb.

———— (1995). *The Poet's World.* Washington, D.C.: Library of Congress.

———— (1996). "Who's Afraid of Poetry?" *Writer's Yearbook.* 40–43.

————(2000). "Poet's Choice." *Washington Post* Jan. 2000.

Translations into German

Dove, Rita, and Fred Viebahn (1977). "Geschichte ist unser Herzschlag. Tendenzen der afro-amerikanischen Poesie der 60er und 70er Jahre." *Akzente* 6: 514–35.

Dove, Rita (1979). "Anläßlich einer Begegnung mit Don L. Lee—im Traum"; "Kentucky, 1833" ["Upon Meeting Don L. Lee, in a Dream"; "Kentucky, 1833" in *The Yellow House on the Corner*]. Trans. Fred Viebahn. *Akzente* 5: 577f.

———— (1979). "David Walker," "Die Vogelfrau" ["David Walker," "The Bird Frau" in *The Yellow House on the Corner*]. Trans. Rolf Eckart John. *Literaturmagazin* 10.

———— (1980). "Die Vogelfrau" ["The Bird Frau"]. Trans. Fred Viebahn. *Die Horen* 120: 177.

———— (1981). "Jugendzeit die erste," "Jugendzeit die zweite," "Jugendzeit die dritte" ["Adolescence—I," "Adolescence—II," "Adolescence—III" in *The Yellow House on the Corner*]. Trans. Uli Becker, Stefan Tomas Gruner, Werner Völker. Schreibheft 16: 22f.

———— (1981). "Pamela" [Pamela in *The Yellow House on the Corner*]. Trans. Fred Viebahn. *Kürbiskern* 3.

———— (1981). "Schreiben, aber nicht lesen? Wovon amerikanische Dichter leben." Trans. Fred Viebahn. *Frankfurter Rundschau* 29 Apr.: 11.

———— (1982). "Agosta, der Flügelmensch und Rasha, die schwarze Taube" ["Agosta the Winged Man and Rasha the Black Dove" in *Museum*]. Trans. Fred Viebahn. *Litfass* 23.

———— (1982). "Sklavenkritik an der praktischen Vernunft" ["The Slave's Critique of Practical Reason" in *The Yellow House on the Corner*]. Trans. Uli Becker, Stefan Tomas Gruner, Werner Völker. Ed. Walter Neumann. *Grenzüberschreitungen.* Bremerhaven: Wissenschaftsverlag NW.

———— (1982). "Was man wissen muß, um ein Dichter zu sein. Aspekte zeitgenössischer Dichtung in den U.S.A." Trans. Fred Viebahn. Ed. Walter Neumann. *Grenzüberschreitungen.* Bremerhaven: Wissenschaftsverlag NW. 59–76.

———— (1983). "Ralph Ellison." Trans. Fred Viebahn. *Kritisches Lexikon zur fremdsprachigen Gegenwartsliteratur.* München: text & kritik.

———— (1984). "Dann bleiben wir verschont." Sechs Gedichte: "Petersilie," "Fiammetta bricht ihren Frieden," "Geometrie," "Nachtwache," "Abgang der Gamben," "Der Fisch im Stein" ["Geometry," "Night Watch" in *The Yellow House on the Corner*; "The Fish in the Stone," "Fiammetta Breaks Her Peace," "Exeunt the Viols," "Parsley" in *Museum*]. Trans. Klaus Birkenhauer. *Die Horen* 136: 95–99.

—— (1987). "Frauen, Sprache und Macht." Trans. Fred Viebahn. *Die Tageszeitung* 12. Nov.

—— (1988). "Die morgenländische Tänzerin" ["The Oriental Ballerina"]. Trans. Karin Graf. Reinbek: Rowohlt. [Contains parts of *Museum* and the complete *Thomas and Beulah*.]

—— (1989). "Die gläserne Stirn der Gegenwart." Trans. Fred Viebahn. Eisingen: Heiderhoff.

—— (1994). "Das Vibraphon" ["The Vibraphone" in *Fifth Sunday*]. Trans., and ed. Terry McMillan. *Breaking Ice*. Rogner & Bernhard. 349f.

Selected Audiovisual Material

(1985). *Rita Dove. Poetry Reading*. Cambridge, Mass., Woodberry Poetry Room. 1 sound tape reel.

(1986). *A Celebration of Black Women Poets*. With Lucille Clifton, Rita Dove, Gloria Olden and Sherley Anne Williams. Introduced by Gloria Naylor. New York: Academy of American Poets.

(1987). *Welcome Home, Rita Dove*. Live from E. J. Thomas Hall at the University of Akron, 2 Oct. University of Akron Media Productions. Broadcast by Northern Ohio PBS affiliates.

(1988). *Poetry Reading by Rita Dove and Rosanna* Warren. New York: Academy of American Poets. 2 sound tape reels.

(1988). *Rita Dove. Poetvision presents Rita Dove*. Videorecording. Philadelphia, Penn.: Rohm and Haas.

(1988). *USIA Program for South Africa*: May.

(1989). *Six Pages on Rita Dove*. Produced by University of Akron Media Productions. Ohio Public TV stations.

(1989). *Thomas and Beulah*. Produced by Video Press, Cave Creek, Ariz. Narrated by the author, with documentary photographs. [Broadcast on PBS in 1990 and 1991.]

(1990). *Author-to-Author. Contemporary Poets*. Rita Dove, Elizabeth Spires, and Henry Taylor. Series Host, George Garrett.

(1990). Interview with Charlie Rose. *CBS Night watch*. 20 Feb.

(1991). *Rita Dove in Conversation with Helen Vendler*. Series on American Poets and Their Art. Chicago: Modern Poetry Association.

(1992). *Through the Ivory Gate*. All About Books. KFPK, Los Angeles. 12 Dec.

(1993). *Charlie Rose in Conversation with Rita Dove*. PBS. 22 Oct.

(1993). *A Conversation with Poet Laureate Rita Dove*. With Susan Stamberg. Library of Congress Video Production. 15 Oct.

(1993). "Interview with Rita Dove, Poet Laureate Designate." With Charlayne Hunter-Gault: *The McNeil/Lehrer Newshour*.

(1993-95). Rita Dove. Telecasts of the Poet Laureate. Washington, D.C.: Library of Congress. 15 June 1993; 7 Oct. 1993; 3 Feb. 1994 [Poetry Readings: Michael S. Harper and Quincy Troupe]; 5 May 1994; 3 Oct. 1994 [Crow Indian Poetry Reading]; 6 Oct. 1994; 4 May 1995.

(1993). *Selected Poems*. New York: Random House Audio Publishing.

(1993). "The Souls of Black Folk." Harvard University. 17 Oct.

(1993). *Talk of the Nation*. National Public Radio. 2 tapes. 6 Oct.

(1994). *Bill Moyers' Journal: Poet Laureate Rita Dove*. PBS. 22 Apr.

(1994). *Network Earth*: "Changing our Minds." n.d., n.p.

(1994). *Poet Laureate Rita Dove: Who's Afraid of Poetry?* National Press Club. 17 Mar. Broadcast on C-Span (TV) and NPR (radio).

(1994). *Shine Up Your Words: A Morning with Rita Dove.* A poetry teleconference simulcast live from the Rotunda Dome Room at the University of Virginia and from Norton Elementary School to thousands of American classrooms. 20 Apr. Rita Dove, host and executive producer. Virginia State Library and Archives and the Virginia Center for the Book.

(1994). *Woman to Woman on Lifetime.* 10 animated Poems. 29 Apr.

(1995). *CNN Newsroom.* With Kathleen O'Connor. 17 Feb.

(1995). *Fine and Mellow: The Artistry of Billie Holiday.* Hosted: by Rita Dove. Produced by: Elizabeth Blair. Washington, D.C. (National Public Radio). 22 June.

(1995). Sesame Street. Show #3359. 13 Feb.

(1995). *"Virginia Currents."* WCVE, Charlottesville, Va. Television News Office. 23 June.

(1996). *Gateways.* Judith Shatin, Rita Dove. Charlottesville, Va.: Televisions News Office. n.d.

(1996). *UMOJA—Each One of Us Counts.* Text by Rita Dove; composed by Alvin Singleton. The World Youth Orchestra; text spoken by Andrew Young. Atlanta, Ga.: Olympic Arts Festival, Atlanta Symphony Hall. 21 July. Recorded and broadcast, with interviews of Singleton and Dove, on National Public Radio's "Performance Today." 23 July.

Selected Studies and Reviews

Anshaw, Carol (1992). "Pulling Strings." Newsday 1 Nov.

Bagby, George F. (1995). "Rita Dove Uses Analogy to Frame Mother-Daughter Poems." *Newsclips from the University of Virginia Office of University Relations* 8 June. n.p.

Baker, Houston A. (1990). "Rita Dove. *Grace Notes.*" Black American Literature Forum 24.3: 574–77.

Barker, Elspeth (1995). "Dear Mom, Love Persephone." *Independent on Sunday* 6 Aug.: 34.

Berger, Charles (1997). "The Granddaughter's Archive: Rita Dove's *Thomas and Beulah.*" *Western Humanities Review* 50–51.4–1: 359–63.

Booth, Alison (1996). "Abduction and Other Severe Pleasures: Rita Dove's *Mother Love.*" *Callaloo* 19.1: 125–30.

Chappel, Fred (1995). "Dove in Hades." *News & Observer* [Raleigh, N.C.] 7 Feb.: 4G.

Cherry, Kelly (1992). "A State of Independence. *Through the Ivory Gate.*" *Los Angeles Times Book Review* 22 Nov.: 8.

Cook, Emily Walker (1995). "'But She Won't Set Foot / In His Turtle-Dove Nash': Gender Roles and Gender Symbolism in Rita Dove's *Thomas and Beulah.*" *College Language Association Journal* 38.3: 322–30.

Costello, Bonnie (1991). "Scars and Wings: Rita Dove's Grace Notes." *Callaloo* 14.2: 434–38.

Cushman, Stephen (1996). "And the Dove Returned." *Callaloo* 19.1: 131–34.

Edmundson, Mark, ed. (1996). "Rita Dove's *Mother Love*: A Discussion." *Callaloo* 19.1: 125–34. [Readings by Alison Booth, Stephen Cushman, and Lotta Lofgren]

Erickson, Peter (1996). "Rita Dove's Two Shakespeare Poems." *Shakespeare and the Classroom* 4.2: 53–55.

——— (1999). *Transforming Shakespeare: Contemporary Women's Re-Visions in Literature and Performance.* Ed. Marianne Novy. New York: St. Martin's.

Foreman, Gabrielle (1993). "Miss Puppet Lady." *Women's Review of Books* 10.6: 12.

Georgoudaki, Ekaterini (1991). *Race, Gender, and Class Perspectives in the Works of Maya Angelou, Gwendolyn Brooks, Rita Dove, Nikki Giovanni, and Audre Lorde.* Thessaloniki: Aristotle University of Thessaloniki.

——— (1991). "Rita Dove: Crossing Boundaries." *Callaloo* 14.2: 419–33.

Greening, John (1995). "Vendler's List." *Poetry Review* Summer: 41–42.

Gregerson, Linda (1984). "*The Yellow House on the Corner and Museum.*" *Poetry* 145.1: 46–49.

Grosholz, Emily (1987). "Marriages and Partings." *Hudson Review* 40.1: 156–64.

Hampton, Janet Jones (1995). "Portraits of a Diasporan People: The Poetry of Shirley Campbell and Rita Dove." *Afro-Hispanic Review* 14.1: 33–39.

Harrington, Walt (1995). "The Shape of Her Dreaming: Rita Dove Writes a Poem." *Washington Post Magazine* 7 May. 12–19, 28–29.

Harris, Peter (1988). "Four Salvers Salvaging: New Work by Voigt, Olds, Dove, and McHugh." *Virginia Quarterly Review* 64.2: 262–76.

Hernton, Calvin (1985). "The Tradition." *Parnassus: Poetry in Review* 13.1: 543–49.

Hoge, Heide (1982). "Nur Liebesgedichte kommen nicht vor" [Only love-poems are missing]. *Kölner Stadt-Anzeiger* 22 June: 19.

Howard, Ben (1996). "Review of *Mother Love* and *The Darker Face of the Earth.*" *Poetry* Mar.: 349–53.

Hull, Akasha (Gloria) (1994). "When Language Is Everything." *Women's Review of Books* 11.8: 6–7. [On *Through the Ivory Gate*]

Jablon, Madelyn (1994). "The African American Künstlerroman." *Diversity. A Journal of Multicultural Issues* 2: 21–28. [On *Through the Ivory Gate*]

Jones, Kirkland C. (1992). "Folk Idiom in the Literary Expression of Two African American Authors: Rita Dove and Yusef Komunyakaa." *Language and Literature in the African American Imagination.* Ed. Blackshire-Belay and Carol Aisha. Westport, Conn.: Greenwood Press. 149–65.

Keene, John (1994). "Rita Dove's *The Darker Face of the Earth*: An Introductory Note." *Callaloo* 17.2: 371–73.

Lofgren, Lotta (1996). "Partial Horror: Fragmentation and Healing in Rita Dove's *Mother Love.*" *Callaloo* 19.1: 135–42.

Love, Steve (1995). "Love and Dove Are Mother's Connection." *Beacon Journal* 21 May: G4.

Lozano, Rafael (1978). "Doce Poetas Jóvenes de Los Estados Unidos." *Revista Nacional de Cultura* 39.237: 100–119.

Maguire, Sarah (1995). "Sailing round Sicily." *Times Literary Supplement* 17 Nov.: 29. [On *Mother Love*]

McDowell, Robert (1986). "The Assembling Vision of Rita Dove." *Callaloo* 9.1: 61–70.

McGraw, Erin (1986). "Review of *Fifth Sunday.*" *North America Review* 271.1: 72–73.

Muske, Carol (1995). "Breaking out of the Genre Ghetto." *Parnassus: Poetry in Review* 23: 409–23.

Ostrom, Hans (1992). "Poet Turns Novelist with Puppeteer's Tale." *News Tribune.* [Tacoma, Wash.] 29 Nov.

Proitsaki, Maria (1997). "Seasonal and Seasonable Motherhood in Dove's *Mother Love.*" *Women, Creators of Culture.* Ed. Ekaterini Georgoudaki, and Domna Pastourmatzi. Thessaloniki: Hellenic Association of American Studies. 143–52.

Rampersad, Arnold (1986). "The Poems of Rita Dove." *Callaloo* 9.1: 52–60.

Ryman, Geoff (1992). "Nothing Succeeds Like Virginia." *New York Times Book Review* 11 Oct.: 11–12.

Sample, Maxine (1994). "Dove's *Thomas and Beulah*." *Explicator* 52.4: 251–53.

Shaughnessy, Brenda (1999). "Rita Dove: Taking the Heat." *Publishers Weekly*, 12 Apr: 15, 48–49.

Shoptaw, John (1987). "Review of *Thomas and Beulah*." *Black American Literature Forum* 21.3: 335–41.

——— (1990). "Segregated Lives: Rita Dove's *Thomas and Beulah*." *Reading Black, Reading Feminist*. Ed. Henry Louis Gates, Jr. Harmondsworth, U.K.: Penguin. 374–81.

Silberg, Richard (1995). "*Mother Love*, by Rita Dove." *Poetry Flash* July/Aug.: 32.

Smith, Dave (1982). "Some Recent American Poetry: Come All Ye Fair and Tender Ladies." *American Poetry Review* 11.1: 36–46.

Smith, Patricia (1992). "Rita Dove's Lyrical *Through the Ivory Gate*." *Boston Globe* 13 Nov.

Steffen, Therese (1996). "Movements of a Marriage, or Looking Awry at U.S. History: Rita Dove's *Thomas and Beulah*." Ed. Werner Senn. *SPELL* 9, *Families*: 179–96.

——— (1996). "Rita Dove." *Kritisches Lexikon zur fremdsprachigen Gegenwartsliteratur–KLfG*.

——— (1997). "Beyond Ethnic Margin and Cultural Center: Rita Dove's 'Empire of Mother Love.'" Ed. John G. Blair, and Reinhold Wagnleitner. *SPELL* 10, *Empires*: 225–41.

——— (1998). "Theme and Form: Rita Dove's Sonnet Cycle *Mother Love*." *Freedom and Form: Essay in Contemporary American Poetry*. Ed. Esther Giger and Agnieszka Salska. Lodz, Poland: Wydawnictwo Uniwersytetu Lodzkiego. 104–19.

——— (1999). "Rooted Displacement in Form: Rita Dove's Sonnet Cycle *Mother Love*." *The Furious Flowering of African American Poetry*. Ed. Joanne V. Gabbin. Charlottesville: University of Virginia Press. 60–76

Stein, Kevin (1995). "Lives in Motion: Multiple Perspectives in Rita Dove's Poetry." *Mississippi Review* 23.3: 51–79.

Steinman, Lisa M. (1987). "Dialogues between History and Dream." *Michigan Quarterly Review* 26: 428–38.

Stitt, Peter (1986). "Review of *Thomas and Beulah*." *Georgia Review* 40.4: 1031–33.

Tarasevich, Andrew W. (1995). "Maternal Instinct. Rita Dove Explores 'mother love.'" *Minnesota Daily* 19 May.

Throne, Robin (1995). "A Grecian Tragedy in South Carolina." *Iowa Woman Book Reviews* Spring/Summer: 56–57.

Van-Dyne, Susan R. (1999), "Siting the Poet: Rita Dove's Refiguring of Traditions." *Women Poets of the Americas: Toward a Pan-American Gathering*. Ed. Jacqueline Vaught-Brogan and Candelaria Cordelia-Chavez. Notre Dame: Notre Dame University Press.

Vendler, Helen H. (1986). "In the Zoo of the New." *New York Review of Books* 23: 47–52.

——— (1988). "Louise Glück, Stephen Dunn, Brad Leithauser, Rita Dove." *The Music of What Happens: Poems, Poets, Critics*. Cambridge: Harvard University Press. 437–54. [Rpt. of "In the Zoo of the New"]

——— (1991). "A Dissonant Triad: Henri Cole, Rita Dove, and August Kleinzahler." *Parnassus: Poetry in Review* 16.2: 391–404. [Rpt. in *Soul Says*]

———— (1993). "Rita Dove. America's Poet Laureate." *Ideas from the National Human-ities Center* 2.1: 27–33.

———— (1994). "Blackness and Beyond Blackness." *Times Literary Supplement* 18 Feb.: 11–13.

———— (1995). "Rita Dove: Identity Markers." *The Given and the Made: Strategies of Poetic Redefinition.* Cambridge: Harvard University Press. 61–88. [First published in 1994 Callaloo 17.2: 381–98]

———— (1995). *Soul Says.: Recent Poetry.* Cambridge: Harvard University Press.

———— (1995). "Twentieth-Century Demeter." *New Yorker* 15 May: 90–92.

Wallace, Patricia (1993). "Divided Loyalties: Literal and Literary in the Poetry of Lorna Dee Cervantes, Cathy Song and Rita Dove." *MELUS: The Journal of the Society for the Study of the Multi-Ethnic Literature of the United States* 18.3: 3–19.

Waller, Gary (1983). "I and Ideology: Demystifying the Self of Contemporary Po-etry." *Denver Quarterly* 18.3: 123–38.

Ward, Scott (1995). "No Vers Is Libre." *Washington and Lee University Review.*.

Selected Interviews with Rita Dove

Bellin, Steven (1995). "A Conversation with Rita Dove." *Mississippi Review* 23.3: 10–35.

Carroll, Rebecca, ed. (1994). "Rita Dove." *I Know What the Red Clay Looks Like: The Voice and Vision of Black Women Writers.* New York: Crown Trade. 82–90.

Cavalieri, Grace (1995). "Rita Dove: An Interview by Grace Cavalieri." *American Po-etry Review* 24.2: 10–15.

Hammer, Mike, and Christina Daub (1996). "Interview with Rita Dove." *Plum Re-view* 9: 27–41.

(1994–1995). "An Interview with Rita Dove. Poet Laureate 1993–1995." *Reverse Im-ages*: 10–14.

Johnsen, Gretchen, and Richard Peabody (1985). "A Cage of Sound: Interview with Rita Dove." *Gargoyle* 27: 2–13.

Kirkpatrick, Patricia (1995). "The Throne of Blues: An Interview with Rita Dove." *Hungry Mind Review* 35: 36–37, 56–57.

Kitchen, Judith, and Stan Sanvel Rubin (1986). "A Conversation with Rita Dove." Ed. and updated by Earl G. Ingersoll. *Black American Literature Forum* 20.3: 227–40.

Klein, Gil (1994). "Questions and Answers." *National Press Club Luncheon* 17 Mar.: 175–81.

Lloyd, Emily (1994). "Navigating the Personal. An Interview with Poet Laureate Rita Dove." *Off Our Backs: A Women's Newsjournal* 24.4: 1, 22.

Moyers, Bill (1995). "Rita Dove." *The Language of Life. A Festival of Poets.* Ed. J. Haba. New York: Doubleday. 109–28. (Published version of *Bill Moyers' Journal: Poet Laureate Rita Dove.* PBS. 22 Apr. 1994)

Pereira, Malin (1999). "An Interview with Rita Dove." *Contemporary Literature.* 40.2: 183–213.

Plumley, Stanley (1995). "A Reminiscence." *Mississippi Review* 23.3: 7–9.

Schneider, Steven (1989). "Coming Home: An Interview with Rita Dove." *IOWA Re-view* 19.3: 112–23.

Steffen, Therese (Nov. 1998). "*The Darker Face of the Earth*: A Conversation with Rita Dove." *Transition* 74: 104–23.

Taleb-Khyar, Mohamed B. (1991). "An Interview with Maryse Condé and Rita Dove." *Callaloo* 14.2: 366–74.

Thomas, Wynn M. (2000). "Rita Dove Talks to M. Wynn Thomas, Aug. 12, 1995." *Swansea Review* 19: 158–63.

Ude, Wayne (1993). "An Interview with Rita Dove." *AWP Chronicle. A Publication of the Associated Writing Programs* 26.2 (Oct./Nov.): 1–8.

Vendler, Helen (1990). "An Interview with Rita Dove." *Reading Black, Reading Feminist.* Ed. Henry Louis Gates, Jr. Harmondsworth, U.K.: Meridian. 481–91.

Walsh, William (1994). "Isn't Reality Magic? An Interview with Rita Dove." *Kenyon Review* 16.3: 142–54.

Dissertations

Davis, Susan Shibe (1994). "Creative Composing: The Verbal Art of Rita Dove, the Visual Art of Stephen Davis and the Filmic Art of Stanley Brakhage." Diss. Arizona State University.

Hufstader, Jonathan (1993). "Coming into Consciousness: Lyric Poetry as Social Discourse in the Work of Charles Simic, Seamus Heany, Tom Paulin, Tony Harrison, and Rita Dove." Diss. Harvard University.

Selected Newspaper and Magazine Coverage

Boen, Donna (1993–1994). "The Power of the Fast-paced Poet." *Miamian* Winter: n.p.

Brazaitis, Tom (1995). "Poet in Motion." *Plain Dealer* 26 Feb.: 14–17.

Craig, Patricia (1993). "Rita Dove Wants to Sell the Public on Poetry." *Library of Congress Gazette* 5 Nov.: 7.

———— (1994). "The Myths of Poetry: Rita Dove Addresses National Press Club Audience." *Library of Congress Information Bulletin* 17 Mar.: 172.

DeLavan, Joanne (1995). "In Search of the Olympic Spirit. A Union of Art." *Sky*: Apr.: 26–27.

Dixon-Williams, Gail (1995). "Broadening the Possibilities: Rita Dove Says She Has Fulfilled Her Mandate." *Library of Congress Information Bulletin* 29 May: 235–37.

D'Ooge, Craig (1994). "Native American Poetry: Crow Nation Children Read Their Work at the Library." *Library of Congress Information Bulletin* 18 Apr.: 147–48.

Gray, Paul, and Jack E. White (1993). "Rooms of Their Own: Toni Morrison, Rita Dove." *Time* 18 Oct.: 86–89.

Kastor, Elizabeth (1994). "Rita Dove: The People's Poet." *Washington Post* 22 Apr.: C1, C2.

Merritt, Judy (1994). "Rita Dove and the Crow Poets." *Winds of Change* Summer: 72–77.

Miller, Mark (1993). "Nation's Poet Seeks Ties to White House." *Washington Times* 19 May: A5.

Otto, Mary (1993). "A Poet for the People: Rita Dove Takes Her Lyrical Message to the Streets." *Detroit Free Press* 3 Dec.: 4D.

Sholiton, Faye (1994). "Poetry in Motion Rita Dove." *Avenues* Jan.: 29.

Smith, Jeanne (1994). "Poetry and All That Jazz: Innovative Program Combines Both Art Forms." *Library of Congress Information Bulletin* 4 Apr.: 128–29.

———— (1995). "The Black Diaspora: Symposium Participants Discuss Effects on Their Work." *Library of Congress Information Bulletin* 29 May: 238–39.

Smith, Patricia (1993). "Poetry in Motion." *Boston Globe* 25 May: 61, 66.

Streitfeld, David (1995). "Continental Drift. At Library of Congress, Deconstructing the African Diaspora." *Washington Post* 21 Apr.: D1, D4.

Tell, Bernice (1995). "End of Term. Rita Dove Gives Final Reading as Poet Laureate." *Library of Congress Information Bulletin* 29 May: 232–33.

Wilkerson, Elizabeth (1994). "Dove Makes Poetry 'Fun': She Leads Va. Pupils in Exercises during Teleconference." *Richmond Times Dispatch* 21 Apr.: n.p.

Anthologies of Primary Sources

Allison, Alexander W., et al., eds. (1983). *The Norton Anthology of Poetry.* New York: Norton.

Barksdale, Richard, and Keneth Kinnamon eds. (1972). *Black Writers of America: A Comprehensive Anthology.* New York: Macmillan.

Baym, Nina, et al., eds. (1989). *The Norton Anthology of American Literature.* 2 vols. New York: Norton.

Cade, Toni, ed. (1970). *The Black Woman.* New York: New American Library.

Costanzo, Gerald, and Jim Daniel, eds. (1993). *The Carnegie Mellon Anthology of Poetry.* Pittsburgh: Carnegie Mellon University Press.

Edelberg, Cynthia Dubin, ed. (1995). *Scars: American Poetry in the Face of Violence.* Tuscaloosa: University of Alabama Press.

Ferguson, Margaret, Mary Jo Salter, and Jon Stallworthy, eds. (1996). *The Norton Anthology of Poetry.* 4th ed. New York: Norton.

Field, Edward, Gerald Locklin, and Charles Stetler, eds. (1992). *A New Geography of Poets.* Fayetteville: University of Arkansas Press.

Gwynn, R. S., ed. (1992). *American Poets since World War II.* Detroit: Bruccoli Clark Layman.

Honey, Maureen, ed. (1989). *Shadowed Dreams: Women's Poetry of the Harlem Renaissance.* New Brunswick, N.J.: Rutgers University Press.

Johnson, James Weldon, ed. (1959). *The Book of American Negro Poetry.* 1931. New York: Harcourt.

Knopf, Marcy, ed. (1993). *The Sleeper Wakes: Harlem Renaissance Stories by Women.* Serpent's Tail.

Lauter, Paul, et al., eds. (1990). *The Heath Anthology of American Literature.* 2 vols. Lexington, Mass.: Heath.

McMillan, Terry, ed. (1990). *Breaking Ice: An Anthology of Contemporary African-American Fiction.* Abr. 1992. New York: Viking.

McQuade, Donald, et al., eds. (1987). *The Harper American Literature.* 2 vols. New York: Harper & Row.

Miller, Ethelbert E., ed. (1994). *In Search of Color Everywhere: A Collection of African-American Poetry.* New York: Stewart.

Randall, Dudley, ed. (1988). *The Black Poets.* 1971. New York: Bantam.

Sherman, Joan R., ed. (1988). *Collected Black Women's Poetry.* 4 vols. Schomburg Library of Nineteenth-Century Black Women Writers. New York: Oxford University Press.

——— (1989). *Invisible Poets: Afro-Americans of the Nineteenth Century.* 1974. Urbana: University of Illinois Press.

Stetson, Erlene, ed. (1981). *Black Sister: Poetry by Black American Women, 1746–1980.* Bloomington: Indiana University Press.

Vendler, Helen, ed. (1985). *The Harvard Book of Contemporary American Poetry.* Cambridge, Mass.: Belknap Press of Harvard University.

————, ed. (1992). *The Faber Book of Contemporary American Poetry*. London: Faber & Faber.

Watson Sherman, Charlotte, ed. (1994). *Sisterfire: Black Womanist Fiction and Poetry*. New York: Harper Perennial.

Secondary Sources

General Studies

Abbott, Edwin A. (1992). *Flatland: A Romance of Many Dimensions*. 1884. New York: Dover.

Abrahams, Roger D. (1970). *Deep Down in the Jungle: Negro Narrative Folklore from the Streets of Philadelphia*. Chicago: Aldine.

———— (1976). *Talking Black*. Rowley, Mass.: Newbury House.

Altieri, Charles (1973). "From Symbolist Thought to Immanence: The Ground of Postmodern American Poetics." *Boundary* 2 1.3: 605–41.

Anderson, Benedict (1991). *Imagined Communities*. 1983. London: Verso.

Angelou, Maya (1970). *I Know Why the Caged Bird Sings*. New York: Bantam.

Appadurai, Arjun (1990). "Disjuncture and Difference in the Global Cultural Economy." *Public Culture: Society for Transnational Cultural Studies* 2.1: 1–24.

Appiah, Kwame Anthony (1991). "Is the Post- in Postmodernism the Post- in Postcolonial?" *Critical Inquiry* 17.2: 336–57.

———— (1992). *In My Father's House: Africa in the Philosophy of Culture*. New York: Oxford University Press.

Appiah, Kwame Anthony, and Henry Louis Gates, Jr., eds. (1992). "Identities." *Critical Inquiry* 18.4: 625–843.

Appiah, Kwame Anthony, and Amy Gutmann (1996). *Color Conscious: The Political Morality of Race*. Princeton, N.J.: Princeton University Press.

Appignanesi, Lisa, ed. (1987). *The Real Me: Post-Modernism and the Question of Identity*. ICA Documents 6. London: Institute of Contemporary Arts.

Arendt, Hannah (1989). *The Human Condition*. 1958. Chicago: University of Chicago Press.

Ashcroft, Bill, Gareth Griffiths, and Helen Tiffin (1989). *The Empire Writes Back: Theory and Practice in Post-Colonial Literatures*. London: Routledge.

————, eds. (1995). *The Post-Colonial Studies Reader*. London: New York: Routledge.

Awkward, Michael (1989). "Appropriative Gestures: Theory and Afro-American Literary Criticism." *Gender and Theory: Dialogues on Feminist Criticism*. Ed. Linda Kauffman. London: Blackwell. 238–46.

Bachelard, Gaston (1957). *La poétique de l'espace*. Paris: Presses Universitaires de France.

———— (1970). *Le droit de rêver*. Paris: Presses Universitaires de France.

———— (1971). *The Poetics of Reverie*. Trans. Daniel Russell. Boston: Beacon Press.

———— (1994). *The Poetics of Space*. Trans. Maria Jolas. Boston: Beacon Press.

Baker, Houston A., Jr. (1980). *The Journey Back: Issues in Black Literature and Criticism*. Chicago: University of Chicago Press.

———— (1981). "Generational Shifts and the Recent Criticism of Afro-American Literature." *Black American Literature Forum* 15.1: 3–21. [Rpt. in *Blues, Ideology, and Afro-American Literature*]

———— (1987). *Blues, Ideology, and Afro-American Literature: A Vernacular Theory*. 1984. Chicago: University of Chicago Press.

———— (1987). *Modernism and the Harlem Renaissance.* Chicago: University of Chicago Press.

———— (1991). *Workings of the Spirit: The Poetics of Afro-American Women's Writing.* Chicago: University of Chicago Press.

Bakhtin, Mikhail (1992). *The Dialogic Imagination.* 1981. Ed. Michael Holquist. Trans. C. Emerson and M. Holquist. Austin: University of Texas Press.

Baldwin, James (1984.). "Stranger in the Village." 1955. *Notes of a Native Son.* Boston: Beacon Press.

Barth, Frederick (1969). *Ethnic Groups and Boundaries: The Social Organization of Culture Difference.* Boston: Little, Brown.

Barthes, Roland (1985). "Introduction à l'analyse structurale des récits." *L'aventure sémiologique.* Paris: Editions du Seuil. 167–206.

———— (1994). "Myth Today." *Mythologies.* 1957. New York: Hill & Wang.

Benitéz-Rojo, Antonio (1995). *The Repeating Island: The Caribbean and the Postmodern Perspective.* 1992. Trans. James E. Maraniss. Durham: Duke University Press.

Benko, Georges, and Ulf Strohmayer, eds. (1997). *Space and Social Theory: Interpreting Modernity and Postmodernity.* Oxford: Blackwell.

Bercovitch, Sacvan (1986). *Reconstructing American Literary History.* Cambridge, Mass.: Harvard University Press.

Bhabha, Homi K. (1984). "Representation and the Colonial Text: Some Forms of Mimeticism." *The Theory of Reading.* Ed. Frank Gloversmith. Brighton: Harvester. 93–122.

———— (1990). "Articulating the Archaic: Notes on Colonial Nonsense." *Literary Theory Today.* Ed. Peter Collier, and Helga Geyer-Ryan. Ithaca, N.Y.: Cornell University Press. 203–18.

————, ed. (1993). *Nation and Narration.* London: Routledge.

———— (1994). *The Location of Culture.* London: Routledge.

———— (1996). "Unpacking My Library . . . Again." *The Post-Colonial Question. Common Skies, Divided Horizons.* London: Routledge. 199–211.

Billeter, Erika, ed. (1993). *Das Blaue Haus. Die Welt der Frida Kahlo.* Frankfurt: Ausstellungskatalog Kunsthalle Schirn.

Blackshire-Belay, Carol Aisha (1992). *Language and Literature in the African American Imagination.* Westport, Conn.: Greenwood.

Blanchot, Maurice (1982). *The Space of Literature.* 1955. Trans. Ann Smock. Lincoln: University of Nebraska Press.

Bloom, Harold (1973). *The Anxiety of Influence: A Theory of Poetry.* New York: Oxford University Press.

———— (1976). *Poetry and Repression. Revisionism from Blake to Stevens.* New Haven: Yale University Press.

———— (1994). *The Western Canon: The Books and Schools of the Ages.* New York: Harcourt. [Includes Rita Dove]

Bonnefoy, Yves (1989). "The Act and the Place of Poetry." *The Act and the Place of Poetry.* Trans. Jean Stewart and John T. Naughton. Chicago: University of Chicago Press. 101–17.

————, ed. (1993). *American, African, and Old European Mythologies.* 1991. Trans. Wendy Doniger. Chicago: University of Chicago Press.

Braxton, Joanne M., and Andrée Nicola McLaughlin, eds. (1990). *Wild Women in the Whirlwind: AfroAmerican Culture and the Contemporary Literary Renaissance.* London: Serpent's Tail.

Brelich, Angelo (1969). *Paides e Parthenoi.* Rome: Edizioni dell' Ateneo.

Broich, Ulrich, et al. (1985). *Intertextualität. Formen, Funktionen, anglistische Fallstu-dien.* Tübingen: Max Niemeyer.

Bronfen, Elisabeth (1992). "From Omphalos to Phallus: Cultural Representations of Femininity and Death." *Women: A Cultural Review* 3.2: 145–58.

———— (1992). *Over Her Dead Body: Death, Femininity and the Aesthetic.* Manchester: Manchester University Press.

———— (1999). *Dorothy Richardson's Art of Memory: Space, Identity, Text.* Manchester: Manchester University Press.

Brooks, Gwendolyn, et al. (1975). *A Capsule Course in Black Poetry Writing.* Detroit: Broadside.

Brooks Higginbotham, Evelyn (1992). "African-American Women's History and the Metalanguage of Race." *Signs* 17.2 (Winter): 251–74.

Bucknell, Brad (1990). "Henry Louis Gates, Jr. and the Theory of 'Signifyin(g).'" *Ariel* 21.1: 65–84.

Burkert, Walter (1979). *Structure and History in Greek Mythology and Ritual.* Berkeley: University of California Press.

———— (1987). *Ancient Mystery Cults.* Cambridge: Harvard University Press.

Butler, Judith (1990). *Gender Trouble: Feminism and the Subversion of Identity.* New York: Routledge.

———— (1993). *Bodies That Matter: On the Discursive Limits of "Sex."* New York: Routledge.

Carby, Hazel V. (1987). *Reconstructing Womanhood: The Emergence of the Afro-American Woman Novelist.* New York: Oxford University Press.

Carter, Erica, James Donald, and Judith Squires (1993). *Space and Place: Theories of Identity and Location.* London: Lawrence & Wishart.

Caruth, Cathy, ed. (1995). *Trauma: Explorations in Memory.* Baltimore: Johns Hopkins University Press.

Chambers, Iain (1994). *Migrancy, Culture, Identity.* London: Routledge.

Chambers, Iain, and Lidia Curti, eds. (1996). *The Post-Colonial Question: Common Skies, Divided Horizons.* London: Routledge.

Chapman, Dorothy H. (1986). *Index to Poetry by Black American Women.* New York: Greenwood.

Chaudhuri, Una (1997). *Staging Place: The Geography of Modern Drama.* Ann Arbor: University of Michigan Press.

Christian, Barbara (1985). *Black Feminist Criticism: Perspectives on Black Women Writers.* New York: Pergamon. 119–25. (Afro-American Women Poets: A Historical Introduction [1982]).

———— (1987). "The Race for Theory." *Cultural Critique* 6 (Spring): 51–63.

Cixous, Hélène (1992, 1993). "We Who Are Free, Are We Free?" *Critical Inquiry* 19.2: 201–19.

Clark Hine, Darlene, Elsa Barkley Brown, and Rosalyn Terborg-Penn, eds. (1993). *Black Women in America.* 2 vols. Bloomington: Indiana University Press.

Clark, Katerina, and Michael Holquist (1984). *Mikhail Bakhtin.* Cambridge, Mass: The Belknap Press of Harvard University.

Clifford, Michael R. (1987). "Crossing (out) the Boundary: Foucault and Derrida on Transgressing Transgression." *Philosophy Today* 31.3/4: 223–33.

Colomina, Beatriz, ed. (1992). *Sexuality & Space.* Princeton Papers on Architecture. New York: Princeton Architectural Press.

Con Davis, Robert (1992). "Cixous, Spivak, and Oppositional Theory." *LIT* 4: 29–42.

Davidson, Arnold I. (1987). "Sex and the Emergence of Sexuality." *Critical Inquiry* 14.1: 16–48.

Davidson, Cathy N., and Linda Wagner-Martin, eds. (1995). *The Oxford Companion to Women's Writing in the United States.* New York: Oxford University Press.

de Beauvoir, Simone (1953). *The Second Sex.* Harmondsworth, U.K.: Penguin.

de Lauretis, Teresa (1987). *Technologies of Gender: Essays on Theory, Film, and Fiction.* Bloomington: Indiana University Press.

Deleuze, Gilles, and Felix Guattari (1986). *Kafka: Toward a Minor Literature.* 1976. Minneapolis: University of Minnesota Press.

Dent, Gina, ed. (1992). *Black Popular Culture.* Seattle: Bay Press.

Derrida, Jacques (1986). *Schibboleth. Pour Paul Celan.* Paris: Éditions Galilée.

——— (1994). "Living On: Border Lines." *Deconstruction and Criticism.* 1979. Ed. H. Bloom, et al. New York: Continuum.

Donaldson, Laura E. (1992). *Decolonizing Feminism: Race, Gender, and Empire-Building.* London: Routledge.

Dowden, K. (1989). *Death and the Maiden: Girls' Initiation Rites in Greek Mythology.* London, New York: Routledge.

Doyle, Michael W. (1986). *Empires.* Ithaca, N.Y.: Cornell University Press.

Dubey, Madhu (1994). *Black Women Novelists and the Nationalist Aesthetic.* Bloomington: Indiana University Press.

Du Bois, W. E. B. (1986). *Writings.* New York: Literary Classics of the U.S.A.

DuCille, Ann (1995). "African-American Writing: Overview." *The Oxford Companion to Women's Writing in the United States.* Ed. Cathy N. Davidson and Linda Wagner-Martin. New York: Oxford University Press. 22–29.

Ensslen, Klaus (1982). *Einführung in die schwarzamerikanische Literatur.* Stuttgart: Kohlhammer.

Export, Valie (1992). *Das Reale und sein Double: Der Körper.* Bern: Benteli.

Fabre, Geneviève, and Robert O'Meally, eds. (1994). *History and Memory in African-American Culture.* New York: Oxford University Press.

Fabre, Michel (1991). *From Harlem to Paris: Black Americans in France, 1840–1980.* Urbana: University of Illinois Press.

Fanon, Frantz (1968). *The Wretched of the Earth.* Preface by Jean-Paul Sartre. Trans. Constance Farrington. New York: Grove.

Fisher, Dexter, and Robert B. Stepto, ed. (1978). *Afro-American Literature: The Reconstruction of Instruction.* New York: Modern Language Association of America.

Flesch, William (1991). "Quoting Poetry." *Critical Inquiry* 18.1: 42–63.

Foerster, Richard (1874). *Der Raub und die Rückkehr der Persephone in ihrer Bedeutunung für die Mythologie, Literatur- und Kunst-Geschichte* [*The Abduction and the Return of Persephone in their Significance to Mythology, Literature and Art History*]. Stuttgart: Albert Heitz.

Foucault, Michel (1983). *This Is Not a Pipe.* 1982. Ed. and trans. James Harkness. Berkeley: University of California Press.

——— (1986). "Of Other Spaces." *Diacritics* 16: 22–27.

——— (1994; English trans. 1998). *Michel Foucault: Aesthetics, Method, and Epistemology.* Ed. James D. Faubion. Essential Works of Foucault 1954–1984. Paul Rabinow, series ed. Vol. 2. New York: New Press

——— (1994). *The Order of Things: An Archaelogy of the Human Sciences.* 1970. New York: Vintage. [Trans. of *Les Mots et les choses*]

Frank, Ellen Eve (1979). *Literary Architecture: Essays toward a Tradition.* Berkeley: University of California Press.

Frank, Robert, and Henry Sayre, eds. (1988). *The Line in Postmodern Poetry*. Urbana: University of Illinois Press.

Freud, Sigmund (1895–1938; rpt. 1953). *The Standard Edition of the Complete Psychological Works of Sigmund Freud*. Trans. James Strachey. London: Hogarth.

Frischmuth, Barbara (1991). *Traum der Literatur. Literatur des Traumes. Münchner Poetik-Vorlesungen*. Salzburg: Residenz Verlag.

Fuderer, Laura Sue (1990). *The Female Bildungsroman in English: An Annotated Bibliography of Criticism*. New York: Modern Language Association.

Fuss, Diana (1989). *Essentially Speaking: Feminism, Nature, and Difference*. New York: Routledge.

Gates, Henry Louis, Jr. (1981). "Introduction: Criticism in de Jungle." *Black American Literature Forum* 15.4: 123–27.

——— (1984). *Black Literature and Literary Theory*. New York: Methuen.

———, ed. (1985). "'Race,' Writing, and Difference." *Critical Inquiry* 12.1: 1–300.

——— (1985). "Writing 'Race' and the Difference It Makes." *Critical Inquiry* 12.1: 1–20.

———, ed. (1986). "Race," *Writing and Difference*. Chicago: University of Chicago Press.

——— (1987). "Authority, (White) Power and the (Black) Critic; It's All Greek to Me." *Cultural Critique* 7: 19–48.

——— (1987). *Figures in Black: Words, Signs, and the "Racial" Self*. New York: Oxford University Press.

——— (1989). *The Signifying Monkey: A Theory of Afro-American Literary Criticism*. 1988. New York: Oxford University Press.

——— (1990). *Reading Black, Reading Feminist: A Critical Anthology*. New York: Meridian.

——— (1990). "Whose Canon Is It, Anyway?" 1989. *Democracy*. Ed. Brian Wallis. Seattle: Bay Press. 69–75.

——— (1992). *Loose Canons: Notes on the Culture Wars*. New York: Oxford University Press.

——— (1993). "Beyond the Culture Wars: Identities in Dialogue." *Profession: The Modern Language Association*: 6–11.

——— (1993). "Introduction." *Voices in Black and White: Writings on Race in America from "Harper's Magazine."* Ed. K. Whittemore and Gerald Marzorati. New York: Franklin Square. vii–xvi.

——— (1994). *Colored People: A Memoir*. New York: Random.

——— (1997). "The Chitlin Circuit." *New Yorker* 3 Feb.: 44–55.

Gayle, Addison, Jr., ed. (1970). *Black Expression: Essays by and about Black Americans in the Creative Arts*. 1969. New York: Weybright.

Gennep, Arnold van (1960). *The Rites of Passage*. 1908. London: Routledge.

Gilman, Sander L. (1988). *Difference and Pathology: Stereotypes of Sexuality, Race, and Madness*. 1985. Ithaca, N.Y.: Cornell University Press.

Gilroy, Paul (1993). *The Black Atlantic: Modernity and Double Consciousness*. London: Verso.

Glikin, Ronda (1989). *Black American Women in Literature: A Bibliography, 1976 through 1987*. Jefferson, N.C.: McFarland.

Godzich, Wlad (1994). *The Culture of Literacy*. Cambridge: Harvard University Press.

Graham, Jorie (1987). *The End of Beauty*. New York: Ecco Press.

Graves, Robert (1960). *The Greek Myths*. 2 vols. Harmondsworth, U.K.: Penguin.

Grossberg, Lawrence (1996). "The Space of Culture, the Power of Space." *The*

Post-Colonial Question: Common Skies, Divided Horizons. London: Routledge. 169–88.

Gysin, Fritz (1994). "Predicaments of Skin: Boundaries in Recent African American Fiction." *The Black Columbiad.* Ed. Werner Sollors and Maria Diedrich. Cambridge, Mass.: Harvard University Press. 286–97.

Hallberg, Robert von, ed. (1987). "Politics and Poetic Value." *Critical Inquiry* 13.3: 415–672.

Hamer, Mary (1993). *Signs of Cleopatra: History, Politics, Representation.* London: Routledge.

Harper, Michael, and Robert B. Stepto, eds. (1979). *Chant of Saints: A Gathering of Afro-American Literature, Art, and Scholarship.* Urbana: University of Illinois Press.

Harper, Phillip Brian (1993). "Nationalism and Social Division in Black Arts Poetry of the 1960s." *Critical Inquiry* 19.2: 234–55.

Harris, Wilson (1983). *The Womb of Space: The Cross-Cultural Imagination.* Westport, Conn.: Greenwood.

Harrison, Alferdteen, ed. (1991). *Black Exodus: The Great Migration from the American South.* Jackson: University Press of Mississippi.

Hecht, Anthony (1995). *On the Laws of the Poetic Art.* A. W. Mellon Lectures in the Fine Arts. 1992. Princeton: Princeton University Press.

Heidegger, Martin (1954). "Bauen Wohnen Denken." *Vorträge und Aufsätze.* Pfullingen: Neske.

——— (1975). "Building Dwelling Thinking." *Poetry, Language, Thought.* Trans. Albert Hofstadter. New York: Harper and Row.

——— (1977). "Building Dwelling Thinking." *Basic Writings.* New York: Harper & Row.

——— (1983). "Die Kunst und der Raum." *Aus der Erfahrung des Denkens. 1910–1976.* Complete ed. vol. 13. Frankfurt: Vittorio Klostermann. 203–10.

Heller, Thomas C., et al., eds. (1986). *Reconstructing Individualism.* Stanford: Stanford University Press.

Henderson, Mae Gwendolyn (1989). "Speaking in Tongues: Dialogics, Dialectics, and the Black Woman Writer's Literary Tradition." *Changing Our Own Words.* Ed. Cheryl A. Wall. New Brunswick, N.J.: Rutgers University Press. 16–37.

——— (1995). *Borders, Boundaries and Frames: Essays on Cultural Criticism and Cultural Theory.* New York: Routledge.

Henderson, Stephen (1973). *Understanding the New Black Poetry; Black Speech and Black Music as Poetic References.* New York: Morrow.

Hernton, Calvin C. (1984). "The Sexual Mountain and Black Women Writers." *Black American Literature Forum* 18.4: 139–45.

——— (1992). *The Sexual Mountain and Black Women Writers: Adventures in Sex, Literature and Real Life.* 1987. New York: Anchor. 119–55.

Hillman, James (1979). *The Dream and the Underworld.* New York: Harper & Row.

Hirsch, E. D., Jr. (1987). "American Diversity and Public Discourse." *Cultural Literacy: What Every American Needs to Know.* Boston: Houghton. 94–109.

Hobsbawm, Eric, and Terence Ranger, eds. (1983). *The Invention of Tradition.* Cambridge: Cambridge University Press.

Holst Peterson, Kristen, and Anna Rutherford (1995). "Fossil and Psyche." *The Post-Colonial Studies Reader.* Ed. Bill Ashcroft, Gareth Griffiths, and Helen Tiffin. London: Routledge. 185–89.

hooks, bell (1984). *Feminist Theory from Margin to Center*. Boston: South End.
——(1989). *Talking Back: Thinking Feminist, Thinking Black*. Boston: South End.
—— (1992). *Black Looks: Race and Representation*. Boston: South End.
Hull, Gloria T. (1987). *Color, Sex, and Poetry: Three Women Writers of the Harlem Renaissance*. Bloomington: Indiana University Press.
Hull, Gloria T., Patricia B. Scott, and Barbara Smith, eds. (1982). *All the Women Are White, All the Blacks Are Men, but Some of Us Are Brave: Black Women's Studies*. Old Westbury, N.Y.: Feminist Press.
Hurston, Zora Neale (1979). *I Love Myself When I Am Laughing*. New York: Feminist Press.
Hutcheon, Linda (1993). *The Politics of Postmodernism*. 1989. London: Routledge.
Jameson, Fredric (1981). *The Political Unconscious: Narrative as a Socially Symbolic Act*. Ithaca, N.Y.: Cornell University Press.
JanMohamed, Abdul R., and David Lloyd, eds. (1990). *The Nature and Context of Minority Discourse*. New York: Oxford University Press.
Jeanmaire, H. (1939). *Couroi et Courètes. Essai sur l'éducation spartiate et sur les rites d'adolescence dans l'antiquité hellénique*. Lille: Bibliothèque Universitaire.
Jenkins, Ian (1983). "Is There Life after Marriage? A Study of the Abduction Motif in Vase Paintings of the Athenian Wedding Ceremony." *BICS: Bulletin of the Institute of Classical Studies* 30: 137–145.
Johnson, Barbara E. (1987). *A World of Difference*. Baltimore, Md.: The Johns Hopkins University Press.
—— (1989). "Gender Theory and the Yale School." *Speaking of Gender*. Ed. Elaine Showalter. New York: Routledge. 45–55.
—— (1990). "Euphemism, Understatement, and the Passive Voice: A Genealogy of Afro-American Poetry." *Reading Black, Reading Feminist*. Ed. Henry Louis Gates, Jr. Harmondsworth: Penguin. 204–11.
Johnson, Crockett (1955). *Harold and the Purple Crayon*. New York: Harper and Row.
Karrer, Wolfgang, and Barbara Puschmann-Nalenz, eds. (1993). *The African American Short Story: 1970–1990*. Trier: WVT.
Keith, Michael, and Steve Pile (1993). *Place and the Politics of Identity*. London: Routledge.
Keohane, Nannerl O., Michelle Z. Rosaldo, and Barbara C. Gelpi, eds. (1982). *Feminist Theory: A Critique of Ideology*. Chicago: University of Chicago Press.
Kester, Gunilla Theander (1995). *Writing the Subject: "Bildung" and the African American Text*. New York: Peter Lang.
Koethe, John (1991). "Contrary Impulses: The Tension between Poetry and Theory." *Critical Inquiry* 18.1: 64–75.
Kristeva, Julia (1980). *Desire in Language: A Semiotic Approach to Literature and Art*. Ed. Leon S. Roudiez. Trans. Alice Jardin et al. Oxford: Blackwell.
—— (1982). "Women's Time." *Feminist Theory: A Critique of Ideology*. Ed. Nannerl O. Keohane, Michelle Z. Rosaldo, and Barbara C. Gelpi. Chicago: University of Chicago Press.
—— (1988). *Etrangers à nous—mêmes*. Paris: Fayard.
—— (1991). *Strangers to Ourselves*. Trans. L. S. Roudiez. Hertfordshire: Harvester Wheatsheaf.
Lachmann, Renate, ed. (1982). *Dialogizität*. Theorie und Geschichte der Literatur und der schönen Künste. Reihe A, Bd. 1. München: W. Fink.

Laclau, Ernesto (1992). "Universalism, Particularism, and the Question of Identity." *October* 61: 83–90.

Lee, Dennis (1974). "Cadence, Country, Silence: Writing in Colonial Space." *Boundary 2* 3.1: 151–68.

Lee, Don. L. (1987). "Black Poetics / For the Many to Come." *Nommo: A Literary Legacy of Black Chicago (1967-1987)*. Ed. Carole A. Parks. Chicago: OBAhouse.

Lefebvre, Henri (1994). *The Production of Space*. 1974. Trans. Donald Nicholson-Smith. Oxford: Blackwell.

Leisi, Ernst (1987). *Rilkes Sonette an Orpheus. Interpretation, Kommentar, Glossar*. Tübingen: Gunter Narr Verlag.

Leseur, Geta (1995). *Ten Is the Age of Darkness: The Black Bildungsroman*. Columbia: University of Missouri Press.

Levering Lewis, David (1993). *W. E. B. Du Bois. 1868–1919: Biography of a Race*. New York: Holt.

Lincoln, B. (1981). "The Rape of Persephone: A Greek Scenario of Women's Initiation." *Emerging from the Chrysalis: Studies in Rituals of Women's Initiation*. 1979. Cambridge, Mass.: Harvard University Press. 71–90.

Lorde, Audre (1978). *The Black Unicorn: Poems*. New York: Norton.

——— (1984). *Sister Outsider*. Trumansburg, N.Y.: Crossing.

Lotman, Jurij M. (1972). *Die Struktur literarischer Texte*. Trans. Rolf-Dietrich Keil. München: Wilhelm Fink Verlag.

Low, Augustus W., and Virgil A. Clift, eds. (1981). *Encyclopedia of Black America*. New York: Da Capo Press.

MacIver, Robert, ed. (1945). *Civilization and Group Relationships*. New York: Harper. 3–10, 161–69.

Mason, Theodore O., Jr. (1994). "African-American Theory and Criticism." *The Johns Hopkins Guide to Literary Theory and Criticism*. Baltimore, Md.: Johns Hopkins University Press. 9–20.

Mayberry, Katherine J. (1994). "White Feminists Who Study Black Writers." *The Chronicle of Higher Education* 12 Oct.: A48.

McAllester Jones, Mary (1991). *Gaston Bachelard, Subversive Humanist: Texts and Readings*. Madison: University of Wisconsin Press.

McCorkle, James, ed. (1990). *Conversant Essays: Contemporary Poets on Poetry*. Detroit: Wayne State University Press.

McDowell, Deborah E. (1995). *The Changing Same: Black Women's Literature, Criticism, and Theory*. Bloomington: Indiana University Press.

McHenry, Elizabeth (1995). "'Dreaded Eloquence': The Origins and Rise of African American Literary Societies and Libraries." *Harvard Library Bulletin*. n.s., 6.2: 32–56.

Meaney, Gerardine (1993). *(Un)Like Subjects: Women, Theory, Fiction*. London: Routledge.

Merod, Jim (1987). *The Political Responsibility of the Critic*. Ithaca, N.Y.: Cornell University Press.

Miller, Nancy K., ed. (1986). *The Poetics of Gender*. New York: Columbia University Press. 181–207.

Minh-Ha, Trinh T. (1989). *Woman, Native, Other: Writing Postcoloniality and Feminism*. Bloomington: Indiana University Press.

——— (1991). *When the Moon Waxes Red: Representation, Gender and Cultural Politics*. New York: Routledge.

——— (1992). *Framer Framed*. New York: Routledge.

Mitchell, W. J. T. (1989). "Space, Ideology, and Literary Representation." *Poetics Today* 10.1: 91–102

Mitchell, William J. (1995). *City of Bits: Space, Place, and the Infobahn.* Cambridge, Mass.: MIT Press.

Moi, Toril (1986). *The Kristeva Reader.* Oxford: Blackwell.

Morrison, Toni (1989). "Unspeakable Things Unspoken: The Afro-American Presence in American Literature." *Michigan Quarterly Review* 28.1: 9–34.

——— (1992). *Playing in the Dark: Whiteness and the Literary Imagination.* New York: Vintage, 1993.

Mulvey, Laura (1989). *Visual and Other Pleasures.* Bloomington: Indiana University Press.

Nora, Pierre (1984). *Les Lieux de Mémoire.* Vol. 1. Paris: Editions Gallimard.

——— (1994). "Between Memory and History: *Les Lieux de Mémoire.*" *History and Memory in African-American Culture.* Oxford: Oxford University Press. 284–300. [Originally published in *Representations* 26 (1989)]

Ostendorf, Berndt, ed. (1994). *Multikulturelle Gesellschaft: Modell Amerika.* München: Wilhelm Fink Verlag.

Ostriker, Alicia (1982). "The Nerves of a Midwife: Contemporary American Women's Poetry." *Claims for Poetry.* Ed. David Hall. Ann Arbor: University of Michigan Press. 309–27.

——— (1983). *Writing Like a Woman.* Ann Arbor: University of Michigan Press.

——— (1987). "Dancing at the Devil's Party: Some Notes on Politics and Poetry." *Critical Inquiry* 13.3: 579–96.

Perkins, David (1976). *A History of Modern Poetry: From the 1890s to the High Modernist Mode.* Cambridge, Mass.: Belknap Press of Harvard University.

——— (1987). *A History of Modern Poetry: Modernism and After.* Cambridge, Mass.: Belknap Press of Harvard University.

Phelan, Peggy (1993). *Unmarked.* New York: Routledge.

Pinsky, Robert (1987). "Responsibilities of the Poet." *Critical Inquiry* 13.3: 421–33.

Raboteau, Albert J. (1978). *Slave Religion: The "Invisible Institution" in the Antebellum South.* Oxford: Oxford University Press.

Redding, Jay Saunders (1988). *To Make a Poet Black.* 1939. Chapel Hill: University of North Carolina Press. Intro. by Henry Louis Gates, Jr. Ithaca, N.Y.: Cornell University Press.

Redmond, Eugene B. (1976). "Festivals and Funerals: Black Poetry of the 1960s and 1970s." *Drumvoices: The Mission of Afro-American Poetry.* Garden City, N.Y.: Doubleday Anchor.

Renan, Ernest (1882). "Qu'est-ce qu'une nation?" *Oeuvres Complètes.* 1947–1961. Paris: C. Levy.

Riedel, Ingrid (1986). *Demeters Suche.* Mütter und Töchter. Zürich: Kreuz Verlag.

Rilke, Rainer Maria (1955). *Sämtliche Werke.* 1922. Ed. Rilke-Archive and Ruth Sieber-Rilke in collaboration with Ernst Zinn. 6 vols. Frankfurt: Insel Verlag.

——— 1992). *The Notebooks of Malte Laurids Brigge.* Trans. M. D. Herter Norton. New York: Norton.

——— (1993). *The Sonnets to Orpheus.* Trans. and intro. by Stephen Mitchell. Boston: Shambhala.

Roberts, Diane (1995). *The Myth of Aunt Jemima: Representations of Race and Region.* London: Routledge.

Rose, Gillian (1993). *Feminism and Geography: The Limits of Geographical Knowledge.* Minneapolis: University of Minnesota Press.

Roubaud, Jacques (1995). *Poésie, etcetera: ménage.* Paris: Stock. 38–53.

Rowell, Charles H. (1991). "An Interview with Henry Louis Gates, Jr." *Callaloo* 14.2: 444–63.

Said, Edward W. (1978). *Orientalism.* New York: Pantheon.

——— (1983). *The World, the Text and the Critic.* Cambridge: Harvard University Press.

——— (1984). "The Mind of Winter: Reflections on Life in Exile." *Harper's* 269.1612: 49–55.

——— (1993). *Culture and Imperialism.* New York: Knopf/Random House.

Scarry, Elaine (1987). *The Body in Pain: The Making and Unmaking of the World.* 1985. New York: Oxford University Press.

Schweik, Susan (1987). "Writing War Poetry Like a Woman." *Critical Inquiry* 13.3: 532–56.

Sedgwick, Eve Kosofsky (1989). "Tide and Trust." *Critical Inquiry* 15.4: 745–57.

Segal, Charles (1993). *Oedipus Tyrannus: Tragic Heroism and the Limits of Knowledge.* New York: Twayne.

Shaffner, Randolph P. (1984). *The Apprenticeship Novel: A Study of the "Bildungsroman" as a Regulative Type in Western Literature with a Focus on Three Classic Representatives by Goethe, Maugham, and Mann.* New York: Lang.

Sherman, Joan R. (1988). *Collected Black Women's Poetry.* New York: Oxford University Press.

——— (1989). *Invisible Poets: Afro-Americans of the Nineteenth Century.* 1974. Urbana: University of Illinois Press.

Smith, Barbara (1977). "Toward a Black Feminist Criticism." *Conditions II.* Rpt. in *The New Feminist Criticism.* New York: Pantheon, 1985.

Smith, Valerie (1989). "Gender and Afro-Americanist Literary Theory and Criticism." *Speaking of Gender.* Ed. Elaine Showalter. New York: Routledge. 56–70.

Smitherman, Geneva (1986). *Talkin' and Testifyin': The Language of Black America.* Detroit: Wayne State University Press.

Soja, Edward W. (1989). *Postmodern Geographies: The Reassertion of Space in Critical Theory.* London: Verso.

Sollors, Werner (1978). *Amici Baraka/LeRoi Jones: The Guest for a "Populist Modernism."* New York: Columbia University Press.

——— (1990). "Modernization as Adultery: Richard Wright, Zora Neale Hurston, and American Culture of the 1930s and 1940s." Rpt. from *Hebrew University Studies in Literature and the Arts* 18. 109–55.

——— (1994). "'De Pluribus Una/E pluribus Unus,' Matthew Arnold, George Orwell, Holocaust und Assimilation. Bemerkungen zur amerikanischen *Multikulturalismusdebatte.*" *Multikulturelle Gesellschaft. Modell Amerika.* Ed. B. Ostendorf. München: Wilhelm Fink Verlag. 53–74.

Sollors, Werner, ed. (1989). *The Invention of Ethnicity.* New York: Oxford University Press.

———, ed. (1993). *The Return of Thematic Criticism.* Cambridge: Harvard University Press.

Sollors, Werner, and Maria Diedrich, eds. (1994). *The Black Columbiad: Defining Moments in African American Literature and Culture.* Cambridge: Harvard University Press.

Sourvinou-Inwood, Christiane (1988). *Studies in Girls' Transitions. Aspects of the Arkteia and Age Representation in Attic Iconography.* Athens: Kardanitsa.

—— (1991). *"Reading" Greek Culture: Texts and Images, Rituals and Myths*. Oxford: Clarendon Press.

Spillers, Hortense, ed. intro. (1991). *Comparative American Identities: Race, Sex, and Nationality in the Modern Text*. New York: Routledge.

Spillers, Hortense, and Marjorie Pryse, eds. (1985). *Conjuring: Black Women Fiction, and Literary Tradition*. Bloomington: Indiana University Press.

Spivak, Gayatri Chakravorty (1985). "Can the Subaltern Speak? Speculations on Widow Sacrifice." *Marxism and the Interpretation of Culture*. Ed. Cary Nelson and Lawrence Grossberg. London: Verso. 271–313.

—— (1988). "Reading the World: Literary Studies in the Eighties." *In Other Words: Essays in Cultural Politics*. New York: Routledge.

Stewart, Susan (1993). "The State of Cultural Theory and the Future of Literary Form." *Profession: The Modern Language Association*: 12–16.

Suleri, Sara (1993). "Multiculturalism and Its Discontents." *Profession: The Modern Language Association*: 16–17.

Sundquist, Eric J. (1992). *The Hammers of Creation: Folk Culture in Modern African-American Fiction*. Athens: University of Georgia Press.

—— (1993). *To Wake the Nations: Race in the Making of American Literature*. Cambridge, Mass.: Belknap Press of Harvard University.

Todorov, Tzvetan (1982). *The Conquest of America: The Question of the Other*. Trans. Richard Howard. New York: Harper and Row.

—— (1986). "'Race,' Writing, and Culture." *Critical Inquiry* 13.1: 171–81.

Treusch-Dieter, Gerburg (1983). "Das Märchen von Amor und Psyche," Manuskripte. Zeitschrift für Literatur 1983. Graz: Forum Stadtpark.

—— (1984). "Analyse des Demeter-Kore-Mythos." *Mythos Frau. Projektionen und Inszenierungen im Patriarchat*. Ed. B. Schaeffer-Hegel and B. Wartmann. Berlin: Publica. 176–212.

Turner, Victor (1982). *From Ritual to Theater: The Human Seriousness of Play*. New York: PAJ.

Vendler, Helen (1996). *Poetry. Poets. Poetics: An Introduction*. New York: St. Martin's.

Wagner, Jean (1973). *Black Poets of the United States: From Paul Laurence Dunbar to Langston Hughes*. Urbana: University of Illinois Press.

Walker, Alice, ed. (1979). *I Love Myself When I Am Laughing . . . and Then Again When I Am Looking Mean and Impressive*. Zora Neale Hurston Reader. Intro. by Mary Helen Washington. New York: Feminist Press at the City University of New York.

—— (1983). *In Search of Our Mothers' Gardens*. San Diego: Harvest.

Walker, David (1965). *David Walker's Appeal: in Four Articles, Together with a Preamble to the Colored Citizens of the World, but in Particular, and Very Expressly to Those of the United States of America*. 1829. Ed. and intro. by Charles M. Wiltse. New York: Hill and Wang.

Wall, Cheryl A., ed. (1989). *Changing Our Own Words: Essays on Criticism, Theory, and Writing by Black Women*. New Brunswick, N.J.: Rutgers University Press.

Washington, Booker T. (1996). *Up from Slavery*. 1901. Ed. William L. Andrews. New York: Norton.

Washington, Mary Helen (1974). "Black Women Image Makers." *Black World* 23.10: 10–19.

Weigel, Sigrid (1989). *Die Stimme der Medusa. Schreibweisen in der Gegenwartsliteratur von Frauen*. Reinbek bei Hamburg: Rowohlt.

——. (1990). *Topographien der Geschlechter. Kulturgeschichtliche Studien zur Literatur*. Reinbek bei Hamburg: Rowohlt.

Williams, Sherley Anne (1979). "The Blues Roots of Contemporary Afro-American Poetry." *Afro-American Literature: The Reconstruction of Instruction.* Ed. Dexter Fisher and Robert B. Stepto. New York: Modern Language Association. 72–87.

Willie, Charles Vert (1970). *The Family Life of Black People.* Columbus, Ohio: Merrill.

——— (1991). *A New Look at Black Families.* New York: Hall.

Wittgenstein, Ludwig (1993). *Tractatus logico-philosophicus.* 1918. Frankfurt: Suhrkamp.

Yates, Frances A. (1995). *The Art of Memory.* 1966. London: Pimlico.

Yates, Steve, ed. (1995). *Poetics of Space: A Critical Photographic Anthology.* Albuquerque: University of New Mexico Press.

Ziegler, Konrad, and Walther Sontheimer, eds. (1979). *Lexikon der Antike. Der kleine Pauly.* München: dtv.

INDEX

AEC-1917

Printed in the United States
5677

9 780195 134407